D0099618

DESERT WARFARE

By the same author:
A History of Blitzkreig
Knights of the Black Cross — Hitler's Panzerwaffe and its Leaders
Soviet Armour Since 1945
Tank Tracks to Rangoon
The Czar's British Squadron
Weapons of the Falklands Conflict

DESERT WARFARE

From its Roman origins to the Gulf conflict

BRYAN PERRETT

Patrick Stephens Limited

© Bryan Perrett 1988
Foreword © Field Marshal Lord Carver 1988

All rights reserved. No part of this publication may be reproduced, stored in a retrieval system or transmitted, in any form or by any means, electronic, mechanical, photocopying, recording or otherwise, without prior permission in writing from Patrick Stephens Ltd.

First published in 1988

British Library Cataloguing in Publication Data

Perrett, Bryan, 1934-
Desert warfare.
1. Desert warfare
I. Title
355'.02'09154

ISBN 0-85059-917-2

Patrick Stephens Limited is part of the Thorsons Publishing Group, Wellingborough, Northamptonshire, NN8 2RQ, England

Typeset by MJL Limited, Hitchin, Hertfordshire
Printed in Great Britain by The Bath Press, Bath, Avon

3 5 7 9 10 8 6 4 2

CONTENTS

FOREWORD
by
Field Marshal Lord Carver GCB CBE DSO MC

T.E. Lawrence did as much as, perhaps more than, most to create a mystique about desert warfare. To the quotation from Francis Bacon, 'He who commands the sea is at great liberty, and may take as much or as little of the war as he will', Lawrence added, 'He who commands the desert is equally fortunate'. Bryan Perrett's book provides examples, culled from different periods, but concentrating on the twentieth century, which illustrate both the validity and the exceptions to that generalization.

There is no special characteristic of warfare in a desert which makes it possible to limit one's commitment to a degree of one's own choice. Both sides in the conflict must accept the limit. Lawrence's statement was true of all types of guerilla warfare waged against an opponent who has fixed assets to defend, as the Turks had in Lawrence's target, the railway to Medina. That is also true of a naval *guerre de course* waged against a power who is dependent on the sea for his supplies. The other ways in which desert warfare resembles war at sea are that the forces employed cannot draw their supplies from their surroundings — they must return to base or somehow

be supplied from it; that superior mobility confers a great advantage, while the nature of the surface over which the campaign is fought provides few, if any, natural features to aid the defence; and that, resulting from both those factors, one has to be prepared to meet attack from all directions.

Bryan Perrett's accounts of different compaigns, some well-known, some rescued from near oblivion, show that these factors operated in the days when armies consisted of collections of men and animals, but were still valid when the internal-combustion engine revolutionized desert warfare in the form of mechanical vehicles, wheeled or tracked, and aircraft. Essential to their efficient operation was the use of radio for communication. The desert warrior is no longer dependent on the hazards of water supply and on guides to navigate him over the trackless wastes. The limits which the nature of the terrain formerly imposed have almost entirely been removed, and huge mechanized armies can now fight each other in the desert without restraint. If one has to fight wars, there is something to be said for choosing a battleground where there are no, or only very few, inhabitants.

INTRODUCTION
The Nature of Desert Warfare

We are told by geologists that if the earth were the size of an orange the comparative thickness of its crust would be that of a postage stamp. Two-thirds of that crust are covered by water and for millions of years its land mass has been in a state of permanent movement, rising, falling and separating to form the continents as we know them today. In this way ancient sea beds have been forced to the surface and large areas which were once clothed with primeval forest have been drowned by the sea's compensating advance. Volcanic activity and the movement of the polar ice caps have also influenced the basic structure of the earth's crust.

Roughly one-fifth of the earth's land mass consists of deserts, which are defined by the *Encyclopaedia Britannica* as being 'any large, extremely dry area of land with fairly sparse vegetation'. Depending upon where they are situated, such areas are denied rainfall either by the presence of towering mountain ranges, or because equatorial rain forests have already absorbed the available precipitation, or simply because they do not lie in the path of the prevailing rainfall pattern. These conditions have led to the creation of deserts in the western areas of the North and South American continents, in Southern Africa, in Central Asia and Australia, but most notably of all in the so-called Dry Belt stretching across North Africa and into Arabia between 15 and 20° north.

Rainfall in these areas averages about three inches per year. It is possible for several years to pass without any rain falling, yet monsoon conditions can also result in sudden torrential storms, causing flash floods to sweep down the wadis. The rain causes the desert to bloom briefly and replenishes the slender resources of oases, wells and underground cisterns, but water is rarely present in such quantities as to satisfy more than the needs of the few indigenous inhabitants. In wadi beds and known areas of regular rainfall it is possible to locate brackish water sources by digging. The desert contains large areas of hard level going, most consisting of scrub plain, but there are also many topographical features which inhibit movement including soft sand seas, shifting dunes, deep wadis, treacherous salt flats, boulder fields and ancient sea cliffs which have become escarpments.

In high summer, noon temperatures exceeding 130° distort local vision with a shimmering heat haze yet simultaneously induce mirages which project distant scenes with startling clarity. Winds are light but thermal currents raise slender columns known as dust devils which turn slowly in eerie silence before collapsing. In winter the climate is mild during the day but after sunset the temperature plummets and before dawn has reached a point well below zero. Winter, too, is the season of dust storms when howling winds fill the air with sharp flying sand that penetrates the eyes, nose, mouth, garments and every crack and crevice of equipment no matter what precautions are taken. Some of these storms are of such severity that they block the light of the sun for hours at a time. In such an environment, where distances are vast and the means of survival scarce, it was natural that the Bedouin should describe their habitat as 'a fortress to he who knows it and the grave of him who does not'. If the former is today less true than of yore, the latter is unlikely to lose its validity.

The majority of desert wars have been fought in the Dry Belt and in the areas of desert and semi-desert bordering the area defined in ancient history as the Fertile Crescent, that is, the great arc stretching from the Persian Gulf northwards up the valleys of the Tigris and the Euphrates and then southwards through Palestine and into the Nile valley. As neither men nor animals could afford to be separated from their water supply for long, rivers provided the only routes along which armies could march. The possession of major oases and wells were major strategic considerations and their denial to the enemy by means of poisoning was commonplace. Railways and water pipelines eased the situation considerably, but real flexibility in desert warfare was not achieved until vehicles powered by the internal combustion engine conferred the ability to transport water deep into the hinterland. Even so, the logistic burdens of campaigning in the desert remained formidable and the sustained support of river and coastal traffic has always been regarded as essential for success.

As the capacity to deliver water expanded, so did the size of armies serving in the desert. When those armies became mechanized fuel assumed an importance even greater than that of water. Without fuel, the troops could not be supplied with water, food and ammunition, nor was it possible to mount any sort of operation. Together, the lack of fuel and water spelled an army's rapid disintegration.

Again, the psychological aspects of soldiering in the desert require serious considerations. There have always been those who are attracted by the desert, who find peace in its solitude and who welcome its challenge to survival, but they are a minority. Most soldiers are, either consciously or sub-consciously, aware that they are trespassing in areas where man has little business and that nature, while strictly neutral, is capable of exacting a terrible revenge in the event of failure. Acclimatization and familiarization with the techniques of daily living are vital not only to teach troops how to look after themselves and their equipment, but also to bring them to terms with the harsh environment. Demanding exercises enhance self-confidence and diminish the immensity of the landscape. The provision of suitable clothing makes for greater comfort and increases physical efficiency, as the British Army discovered in the nineteenth century when it substituted cool cotton khaki drill uniforms for heavy scarlet woollen serge when fighting in tropical climates. Above all, the morale of troops engaged in a desert campaign is influenced by the quality of their leadership, especially at the lower levels.

Experience has repeatedly confirmed that where the relationship between officers and men is less than satisfactory, and particularly where the shared endurance of danger and hardship is absent, the negative results affect the performance of the troops to a much greater extent than would be the case in a less demanding theatre of war.

Less immediately apparent is the question of hygiene. The desert may possess its own sterility but this vanishes as soon as it is penetrated by armies which daily deposit hundreds of tons of human waste on its surface. Not for nothing was the name Beelzebub, meaning Lord of the Flies, conferred by the Israelites on the Devil, for these loathsome insects feed on excrement and breed by the million, battening on food and open wounds to spread their filthy diseases. Only dust storms provide a degree of temporary relief from their torment. In the days before the connection between hygiene and health was fully understood, armies venturing into the desert tended to sustain higher losses from dysentery and other diseases than they did at the hands of the enemy. Once troops had been taught to localize and bury their waste the problem was brought under control but has never entirely disappeared. In the desert the smallest scratch, let alone a major wound, is quickly infected by grit and flies, the result being the notorious desert sore which refuses to heal and often becomes ulcerated. From time immemorial, Arabs have urinated on their wounds and benefited from the mildly antiseptic element contained in the fluid.

With the exception of purely local tribal conflicts in which the *causus belli* is generally disputed water rights, the types of warfare fought in the desert fall under two main headings. The first is low intensity and involves confrontation between regular troops and irregular dissidents or disaffected tribesmen. The pattern of such wars involves raiding, ambush and attacks on defended posts and oases. In this context the operational radius of regular troops tended to be small unless they could be adequately supplied, but with the advent of mechanization and air support this expanded to the point where their opponents were easily brought within striking distance. Irregular forces, however, are unable to match either the sustained nature of regular operations or the degree of firepower employed against them and take refuge in dispersion, assembling again only when the threat has passed. To counter this, the disputed area is regularly patrolled and the cycle continues until the dissidents' will or capacity to fight has been eroded. The second is high intensity war fought by regular armies which may or may not have irregular support. Such wars follow the conventional pattern in that they are fought at the strategic, operative and tactical levels. Of these the operative strata, concerned with the direction of war at corps and army level, is most relevant to desert warfare, since the size of the forces employed is clearly restricted by the ability to maintain them in the field. While it is true that in 1918 the Turks deployed no less than three armies in Palestine, the strength of these formations was little more than that of weak corps and in total amounted to that of one comparatively small army rather than an army group. It is a phenomenon of desert warfare in the twentieth century that strategic objectives are gained by operative means.

History confirms that mobility holds the key to success and survival in the desert, whether it is exercised by cavalry, camel troops or fully mechanized formations. Marching infantry are terribly vulnerable and, faced with the horrors of dying of thirst, are inclined to give up following a reverse which would be considered acceptable in more temperate zones. Similarly, the holding of open areas of desert for prestige or political purposes has induced more than one major disaster, for however stoutly these might be defended, once they are isolated and denied supplies their fate is sealed, attempts to break out simply placing the exhausted garrison at the mercy of the enemy and the desert itself.

Just as the desert is incapable of compromise, battles fought therein result in total victory or total defeat. Victory in the desert represents a triumph not only over an enemy but also over nature itself. This heady combination can induce hubris in commanders to a greater degree than victories gained elsewhere; Gordon, Townshend, Lawrence Rommel and Sharon all tempted the gods too often with their pride and paid the price in one form or another. Likewise, undue political pressure imposed on able commanders to take premature action generates its own punishment.

The conduct of desert warfare, therefore, is subject to rules which are harsh and inescapable, and the purpose of this study is to examine their nature and application.

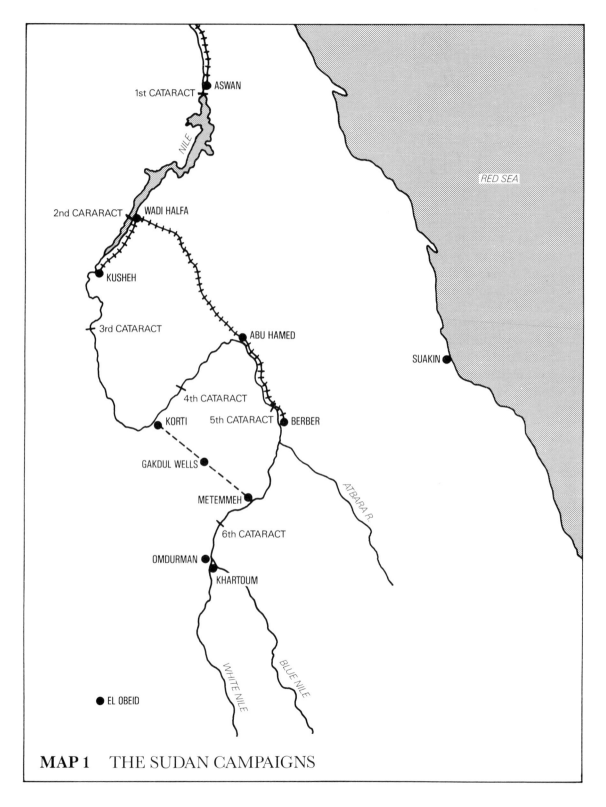

MAP 1   THE SUDAN CAMPAIGNS

CHAPTER 1

'THE GATLING'S JAMMED AND THE COLONEL DEAD'

When Gaius Julius Caesar launched his first invasion of Britain in 55 BC there were living in the forests of North West Germany a people who would one day form a tribal grouping known as the Angles. After the passage of several centuries they would themselves invade Britain, the major part of which would be named England after them. Their guttural speech, utterly unrecognizable today, would evolve into English, the most widely-spoken language in the world. In the year that Caesar launched his second invasion of Britain, 54 BC, there occurred a distant event that would, in due time, add a new and forceful word to the English language. The word is crass, an adjective defined as grossly stupid, and it commemorates in perpetuity the noble Roman whose defeat in the deserts of Parthia was the most complete ever recorded in classical history.

In 60 BC the internal stresses of Roman politics had resulted in the formation of a ruling triumvirate consisting of Julius Caesar, Gnaeus Pompeius (Pompey the Great) and Marcus Licinius Crassus. A patrician to his fingertips, Crassus had defeated the slave army of the former gladiator Spartacus in 71 BC. Vain, inordinately ambitious and jealous of the military reputations possessed by his fellow Triumvirs, he had himself appointed proconsul for Syria and in 54 BC deliberately involved Rome in a dynastic dispute within neighbouring Parthia, hoping to add to his

laurels with another easy victory.

Crassus marched into Parthia at the head of a 39,000-strong army, the bulk of which consisted of marching legionaries, the finest infantry of their time. He crossed the Euphrates and entered a wide area of semi-desert plain near Carrhae, known today as Haran. Here the trudging column was suddenly assailed by swarms of galloping light horsemen armed with bows specially adapted for use from the saddle. Under the incessant arrow storm men began to drop steadily and the column halted to form square. This merely provided the mounted bowmen, circling provocatively just beyond reach, with a more concentrated target. There seemed to be no limit to the Parthians' ammunition, and indeed there was not, for Surenas, their commander, had thought through his tactics thoroughly and had brought up a camel train loaded with arrows. Once a unit had emptied its quivers it retired to replenish them, being instantly replaced by a fresh unit. The Romans' torment continued unabated under a broiling sun and as thirst began to add to the horrors of the day men looked uneasily to Crassus for the leadership the critical situation demanded. Desperate, Crassus decided to counter-attack using a 6,000-strong group commanded by his son Publius, consisting of the legions' small cavalry detachments, the fittest of the legionaries and some auxiliary archers. The Parthians gave way before the group then closed round it and slaughtered it to a man, simultaneously resuming their attack on the main square. Crassus now commenced a slow and difficult retreat, abandoning his 4,000 wounded, to whom no mercy was shown. The following day the pattern of the fighting was the same and when Crassus sought terms he was treacherously killed. The Romans continued their retreat but barely 5,000 of them reached safety; a further 10,000 were captured and sold into slavery but the remainder left their bones in the desert as a memorial to Crassus' vanity.

The clear lesson of Carrhae was that in a desert environment infantry are at the mercy of the enemy who employs combined firepower and mobility unless they possess comparable firepower and have access to water. The lesson was repeated on several occasions throughout history and an interesting variation took place during the Battle of Hattin in 1187, which resulted in the decisive defeat by Saladin of King Guy of Jerusalem's Christian army.

The First Crusade had succeeded in capturing Jerusalem in 1099. Following this, Christian states had been established throughout the Levant, including the Kingdom of Jerusalem, the Principality of Antioch and the Counties of Edessa and Tripoli. These were often at odds with each other and with the two rich and powerful Military Orders which had been established in the Holy Land, the Knights of St John of Jerusalem and the Poor Knights of Christ and the Temple of Solomon, better known by their more familiar respective titles of Knights Hospitaller and Knights Templar. The Hospitallers had been formed to care for the health of pilgrims and the Templars to ensure their safety while they were travelling from the coast to Jerusalem. These noble ideals soon generated wealth in the form of donations, not least in the gift of lands in Europe and Outremer itself, as the Crusader states were collectively known. The feudal influence of the Orders soon equalled that of the

Christian states in which they served and this, coupled with their rivalry, led to continuous intrigue and bickering. This sometimes erupted into violence, and to a shifting series of self-serving alliances, occasionally involving such unlikely partners as the Muslim Sinan Ibn-Salman, the Old Man of the Mountains, and his Brotherhood of Assassins. In passing, it is worth mentioning that although the Military Orders were respected by friend and foe alike for their suicidal courage and ferocity and provided the most significant element of the comparatively few Christian regular troops serving in Outremer, they were poor strategists and their tactical sense was all too often governed by emotional response. The Templars in particular evolved a tradition of never refusing an engagement whatever the odds; furthermore, they made it clear that they neither gave nor expected quarter, the Saracen response being to behead any who were captured. This philosophy, doubtless considered admirable in chivalric terms, led to heavy and needless losses for scant return and could hardly be described as satisfactory in the military sense.

The reason that the quarrelsome rulers of Outremer were able to maintain themselves for so long was that their opponents were frequently in even greater disarray than they were themselves. However, under the strong leadership of Saladin the Muslim factions united and a Holy War was declared. In June 1187 Saladin invaded Palestine and laid siege to Tiberias with a 20,000-strong army. A Christian army assembled at Acre under King Guy of Jerusalem and prepared to march to its relief. As usual, the Crusaders were divided among themselves as to their plan of campaign. Count Raymond of Tripoli, the ablest of the Christian commanders, argued for a waiting strategy, pointing out that in high summer the route between Acre and Tiberias was arid and waterless and that it would be tempting providence to provoke a major engagement in such circumstances. Moreover,

Saladin would be unable to hold Tiberias for long even if he took it, as his troops would soon follow the Saracen practice and disperse to their villages to gather the harvest.

Raymond's plan was sound and would have been adopted had not his bitter enemy Gerard de Ridefort, the Grand Master of the Templars, also been present at the conference. Only weeks previously Gerard had led a tiny force of 130 knights in an incomprehensible attack on 7,000 Saracen horsemen at Nazareth, and since only he and two of his Templars had managed to cut their way out of the ensuing massacre he was hardly a man whose advice should have been heeded! Nonetheless, he proposed an immediate advance on Tiberias, pointing out that on the evidence of past intrigues Raymond could be regarded as a traitor, and that Guy's failure to take the offensive would be viewed as an act of cowardice which would forfeit his further Templar support. Among the prickly, hot-blooded Latin nobility, ever conscious of its honour, such words as treachery and cowardice acted as goads. The purely military considerations were ignored and the decision to engage Saladin in battle was taken.

The Christian army, numbering 1,200 knights and 18,000 men at arms, marched eastwards in intense heat throughout 3 July, subjected to harrassment by Saracen mounted archers. It paused at the spring of Turun and then continued its advance towards the next source of water, which lay beyond the twin peaks of the hill known as the Horns of Hattin. It found the way forward blocked by Saladin's main body and King Guy decided to make camp for the night. Simultaneously, Saladin sent his two wings forward to encircle the Crusaders and deny them access to the water at Turun. Like Surenas twelve centuries earlier he provided his archers with a camel train from which their quivers could be replenished and until nightfall Guy's men suffered the same torment as Crassus's legionaries. The onset of darkness brought relief from the arrow storm but also a new form of torture, for the Saracens set fire to the scrub surrounding the camp, aggravating the Crusaders' already unbearable thirst and that of their unwatered mounts with clouds of choking smoke.

Next morning the dehydrated, exhausted Christian army attempted to break through to the springs at Hattin. It was immediately counter-attacked from the rear and the infantry gave way at once, taking refuge on one of the Horns. For a while the knights held their own against impossible odds, but then they too were compelled to retire up the slope when further scrub fires were started, maddening the horses. With them went the Bishop of Acre, carrying what was said to be the True Cross. The summit was now occupied not by an army but by a thirst-crazed mob of fugitives against whom Saladin launched a final concentrated attack late in the afternoon. Thousands were killed and thousands more captured; 200 Templar and Hospitaller knights were promptly decapitated in the immediate aftermath of the battle. Raymond of Tripoli, accompanied by a small group of mounted followers, managed to cut his way out but died shortly afterwards from the wounds he had received. Saladin spared Guy's life and, at the King's request, that of Gerard de Ridefort, who survived the catastrophe he had precipitated by only two years.

Having destroyed the Christian army, Saladin went on to capture Tiberias, Acre, Ascalon and, on 2 October, Jerusalem itself. His success provoked the launching of the Third Crusade and in June 1191 King Richard the Lion-heart of England arrived in the Holy Land. The fact that Richard was able to impose discipline on an army consisting of contingents from all over Christendom, the Crusader States and the Military Orders was in itself a major achievement, but he was also a remarkably professional soldier in an age when most Western European commanders thought little of war beyond the actual fighting involved. His operations demonstrated not only strategic and tactical abilities of a high order, but also an immediate awareness that the nature of the campaign would be governed by the terrain and climate as well as the enemy's tactics. He recognized, too, that unacclimatized troops were vulnerable to disease, the spread of which he sought to minimize by introducing laundry facilities.

The one thing he was not prepared to do was present Saladin with the sort of opportunity which had resulted in the disaster of Hattin. After he had recaptured Acre in July he set off for Jerusalem, marching south along the coast to Ascalon, supported by his fleet which kept pace offshore. The march was conducted in easy stages to avoid fatigue. Saladin's army hovered the while on his inland flank, its mounted archers making regular attempts to harass the column, being kept at a respectful distance by the strong bodies of crossbowmen which Richard had disposed along its length. Under the strict march discipline imposed the knights were forbidden to institute local counter-attacks. This was interpreted by the Saracens as a sign of weakness and on 7 September, when the column was nearing Arsouf, they closed in. Richard gave the order for a pre-arranged trumpet signal to be sounded and the Christian cavalry wheeled out of line in a co-ordinated response which smashed its way through the startled ranks of the Muslims. Within minutes 7,000 of Saladin's men had been cut down and the rest put to flight. The Crusader army's loss amounted to one-tenth of that figure and its pursuit was carefully controlled. Saladin, recognizing that he now faced an extremely dangerous opponent, never sought to bring Richard to battle again.

After spending the winter at Ascalon, the Crusaders advanced inland on Jerusalem. Saladin retired before them, destroying crops and grazing land over a wide area, and poisoned the wells. It was clear that Richard could not maintain his army if he besieged the city and he withdrew to the coast, concluding a treaty with Saladin which granted special rights and privileges to pilgrims visiting Jerusalem.

Despite these successes and the death of Saladin in 1192 there is no doubt that Hattin represented a major turning point in the fortunes of Outremer. Notwithstanding the mounting of five more Crusades and the negotiated re-possession of Jerusalem from 1229-44, this battle placed the Crusader States on the strategic defensive and for the next century they fought hard but unsuccessfully to retain their possessions. Acre, the last Christian stronghold in the Holy Land, fell after a long and bloody siege in 1291, the event signalling the end of the Crusading era in the Middle East.

The fact that Carrhae on the one hand, and Hattin and Arsouf on the other, were separated in time by more than a millenium, emphasizes how little the essential characteristics of desert warfare had changed in that period. Nor would they change until industrial technology began to make its impact felt during the latter half of the nineteenth century, preparing the ground for desert warfare as we understand it today. The army with which Napoleon fought his campaign in Egypt 1798-9 possessed no greater strategic mobility than Richard's and the muzzle-loading musket's performance did not provide the significant improvement upon that of the crossbow that a distance of five centuries might suggest, although it did equip the bulk of his troops. Only in the field of artillery had there been any real advance and it was this, coupled with the disciplined firepower of his infantry and his own superior tactical skills which enabled him to defeat the Turkish armies which opposed him. Yet within a mere three generations a technological revolution would occur that would begin to alter the face of desert warfare beyond recognition. Together, the invention of satisfactory breech-closing mechanisms and the drawn brass car-

A scene on the projected Suakin-Berber Railway, abandoned in April 1885 after 19 miles of track had been laid. The last truck has been protected with sandbags (Museum of Army Transport).

tridge case led to the development of quick-firing artillery, automatic weapons and the magazine rifle, initiating a period in which the powers of the defence exceeded those of the attack. The harnessing of steam meant that larger armies could be transported and supplied by railways and river steamers. The electric telegraph conferred upon commanders the ability to communicate far beyond the range of the traditional flashing heliograph and before the century closed searchlights would be sweeping the desert to the discomfort of those who relied on darkness to achieve surprise. The day of the desert warrior, who had fought as his fathers had since before recorded history, was drawing to its close with all the dramatic swiftness of one of his own sunsets.

The Victorian era witnessed many desert conflicts as the Great Powers of Europe scrambled for influence and possessions in Africa. The British fought in Egypt and the Sudan, the French in Algeria and Morocco, the Italians in Eritrea and Abyssinia. Simultaneously, the Russians were similarly engaged in Central Asia and the United States Army was involved in more or less continuous operations against an elusive Indian foe in the deserts of the south-west. Their combined experience, and that relating to other forms of irregular warfare around the world, was digested by the future Major-General Sir Charles Callwell in his book *Small Wars: Their Principles and Practice,* which first appeared in 1899 and ran to several revised editions, and was a particular favourite of Field Marshal Montgomery's.

Callwell stressed the importance of the square in desert warfare, emphasizing that while the conventional two-deep fighting line might produce more firepower, its flanks were vulnerable to the inevitably more numerous enemy, whereas the square offered all-round defence against savage armies armed mainly with spears and swords. He favoured placing artillery and machine-guns at the corners of the square, where it was weakest, pointing out that they could fire along two of its faces, so covering a total arc of 270°, but cited several instances where they had been positioned in front or run out from the ranks as required. As a professional artilleryman he felt that guns should be deployed in pairs as a precaution against one of them being out of action; this was especially necessary in the case of machine guns, the early models of which were prone

G.D. Giles's graphic painting of the Battle of Tamai, 13 March 1885, in which the British garrison of Suakin under Major-General Sir Gerald Graham defeated a Dervish force under Osman Digna. During the engagement two Gatling guns were temporarily lost, the limber of one being set on fire by the enemy with a bottle of lubricating oil (National Army Museum).

to stoppages at critical moments. Cavalry should remain at some distance from the square, engaging the flank of the enemy attack with dismounted fire whenever possible and leading the pursuit when it had been repulsed. If the army was large enough two or more mutually supporting squares could be formed, although there was some danger of careless fire from one penetrating another. One major disadvantage of the square was that it provided too large a target if the enemy possessed firearms in any quantity. Another, as Callwell comments, is that 'a square penetrated by an active and deter-mined enemy is liable to be thrown into complete confusion and the whole aim and object of the formation is defeated when it is broken through. Gaps are so dangerous and so difficult to obviate altogether that it seems advisable to provide especially for the case of their occurring'.

The obvious validity of these points is confirmed by the following account of the Battle of Abu Klea, which took place in the Sudan on 17 January 1885.

The force forming the square consisted of 1,200 men, with three guns dragged by hand. Inside the square were the camels for carrying the guns, and others for water, ammunition and wounded. Its advance was covered by skirmishers. The ground was open but undulating. The hostile position in the dry river bed was well marked by banners. It so happened, however, that when about 500 yards from the flags, the rear face became bulged out by the camels, and at that moment the enemy, to the number of about 5,000, suddenly sprang up from the khor where they were concealed to the left front, and charged the square on its left side.

The skirmishers ran for the square and by so doing masked the fire at first. The guns were hurried out on the threatened side. The fire of the front and left faces and of the guns was so severe that the enemy swerved to the right and brought the whole weight of their charge to bear on the left rear corner of the square where—partly due to the bulging out caused by the camels—there was a gap, and where the fire was in consequence not so effective as on the flank. The confusion at this point appears to have been increased by the tendency of the camel corps to push forward and meet the enemy. The result was that the fanatical spearmen broke into the square and that a desperate mêlée ensued in which the British force lost heavily and which only ended when all the Arabs in the square had been killed in a hand-to-hand fight.

Notwithstanding its drawbacks, the square remained an efficient means by which an army could retain the strategic initiative while simultaneously conducting a tactical defence against an enemy who attacked instinctively and who suffered severe casualties as a direct consequence.

Often used in conjunction with the square was the 'zariba', essentially a makeshift obstacle consisting of cut thorn or mimosa bushes piled together to form a cordon around a square or camp, just beyond the range of the throwing spear. The zariba had many uses in the open desert. It formed a physical barrier to the enemy and also prevented surprise attack; it enabled troops to rest and sleep in comparative security; it dispensed with the need for outposts, which were otherwise at serious risk, especially at night; and it enab-

led quickly fortified depots to be established along the line of communications.

With regard to camel corps, Callwell commented that they had much in common with mounted infantry, although their mobility was essentially strategic rather than tactical, enabling them to travel long distances in the theatre of war but not to engage the enemy in any but a dismounted role. The camel's astonishing capacity to survive long periods without water and its ability to live off scrub and bushes which other animals found inedible favoured the former, but its slow pace and the time required to mount and dismount created a number of serious tactical disadvantages. Camel troops, for example, could not evade their pursuers if retreating, nor themselves be used as a pursuit force, and were in grave danger if they were attacked while mounted. In the event of such an engagement being forced upon them, large bodies of camel troops should form square around their mounts, while smaller bodies could use the animals themselves as cover. The correct method of engagement, however, was for the camels to be left in a zariba with the baggage while the troops moved forward to fight on foot. Camel corps provided commanders with a formation capable of operating independently of the main body of the army in the desert, preferably with cavalry attached for reconnaissance purposes.

Of all the desert wars of the latter half of the nineteenth century the largest and best remembered were those fought by the British in Egypt and the Sudan, which caught the public imagination in such a way as to generate more literature, and even films, than any other conflict of comparable size. In part this arose because of the desperate nature of the fighting against an enemy whose dedication to his cause, fanatical bravery and capacity to hate remained unique in the British Army's experience until it fought the Japanese in the Second World War. As Kipling's Tommy Atkins puts it in the poem *Fuzzy-Wuzzy:*

'E rushes at the smoke when we let drive,
An', before we know, 'e's 'ackin' at our 'ead,
'E's all 'ot sand an' ginger when alive,
An' 'e's generally shammin' when 'e's dead.

The 'Fuzzy-Wuzzies', so called because of their wild, frizzed hairstyle, were Beja hillmen from the Eastern Sudan who formed but one part of the army opposing the British. Others were the Jehadia riflemen in their patched jibbahs, the Danagla and the Jaalin, all as anxious as the Beja to close with sword and stabbing spear, and the mounted Baggara Arabs. They feared neither disciplined musketry, nor machine guns, nor artillery, nor cavalry, and against the last would use a heavy, weighted stick which they would throw at a horse's legs, bringing it down, and promptly despatch the stunned rider. If ridden over they would drop to the ground, beyond reach of the curved sabre, and hamstring the horse or stab upwards into the belly; against such opponents the lance was found to be a more efficient cavalry weapon. To these men, fiercely motivated by religious fervour and heirs to all the cruelties of a cruel land, mercy was a sign of weakness and, with the exception of its notables, any army they defeated was ruthlessly butchered. Small wonder, then, that Sir Henry Newbolt, seeking to inspire his young readers with the need for calm, inspired leadership in desperate circumstances, chose the Sudan as the setting for the most graphic verse of his *Vitae Lampada.*

The sand of the desert is sodden red,
Red with the wreck of a square that broke;
The Gatling's jammed and the Colonel dead,
And the Regiment blind with dust and smoke.
The river of death has brimmed its banks
And England's far and honour a name.
But the voice of a schoolboy rallies the ranks:
'Play up! Play up! And play the game!'

That the British became involved at all in so deadly a struggle in this remote corner of the world was, like so many of their wars, a direct result of a series of historical accidents. Egypt

was nominally a province of the Ottoman Empire but had achieved virtual independence under a Khedive (Viceroy) following the Battle of Nisib in 1839. This engagement, all but forgotten today, holds some interest in that it provided the baptism of fire for Helmuth von Moltke, a 39-year-old Prussian staff officer serving with the Sultan's army, whose influence on the German conduct of war at the higher level was to extend well into the next century and, indeed, is still present. Moltke was forced to ride for nine hours to avoid capture in the aftermath of the battle and in later years commented wryly that his period with the Turks had taught him a great deal.

British policy in the Middle East was to shore up the ramshackle Ottoman Empire as a means of checking Russian designs on India. Egypt had always been a vital element in this strategy and her importance increased ten-fold when the Suez Canal was completed in 1869. She was, however, saddled with an immense burden of foreign debt and government finance increasingly came under dual British and French control, particularly after the British government purchased a major shareholding in the Suez Canal Company from Khedive Ismail.

For the next ten years all continued much as before, the Egyptians expanding their control of the Sudan along the Nile and the Red Sea coast. The internal administration of the country nonetheless remained inefficient and corrupt, a situation which did not improve when Ismail was replaced by his son Tewfik in 1879. Simmering discontent erupted into a full-scale rebellion in 1881, led by Achmet Arabi Pasha under the slogan 'Egypt for the Egyptians'. Foreign business interests were so seriously threatened that in May 1882 British and French warships arrived off Alexandria, where some 50 Europeans were massacred by a mob. When the French declined to participate in punitive measures, Admiral Sir Frederick Seymour's squadron commenced a bombardment of the Egyptian forts on the morning of 11 June and by dusk had silenced them.

Arabi, however, remained intransigent and a 25,000-strong force under General Sir Garnet Wolseley entered the Suez Canal, disembarking at Ismailia on 20 August, and prepared to march on Cairo. After his troops had been worsted in preliminary skirmishes at Kassassin, Arabi withdrew his army inside a well-constructed line of entrenchments which had been dug along the summit of a shallow ridge at Tel-el-Kebir. These were about four miles long and their right flank rested on the Cairo-Suez railway and the euphemistically-named Sweet Water Canal, dug to convey Nile river water to the builders of the Suez Canal. The position was held by 22,000 men and contained some 60 guns.

Wolseley decided to storm Arabi's entrenchments with a dawn assault following a night approach-march, knowing that his troops would fight better in the cool of the early morning. The attacking force, numbering 17,000 men and 67 guns, began assembling during the night of 12/13 September, five-and-a-half miles short of the Egyptian position. It was to march in the same order in which it was to go into action, ie with Drury Lowe's Cavalry Brigade on the right or desert flank, then Willis's First Division, the mass of artillery, and Hamley's Second Division on the left, while across the Sweet Water Canal a brigade-sized force would keep pace with the advance. Smoking was forbidden and talking was to be restricted to whispers by those officers responsible for keeping direction. Wolseley wished to arrive within striking distance of the objective only minutes before the sun rose and, calculating that his troops would cover one mile very hour, set them in motion at 01:30.

The opening stages of the march were marked by the inquisitive shouts of a member of the Highland Light Infantry who had somehow obtained drink and wondered where everyone was going. He was quickly chloroformed and left behind, doubtless waking alone in an even greater state of bewilderment and with a severe headache. In other respects the difficult manoeuvre undertaken by Wolseley's army was executed perfectly, although at one stage a brigade's flanks began turning inwards towards each other until the movement was corrected.

The columns were within 150 yards of the Egyptian trenches before the alarm was sounded. The parapets at once blazed with rifle and artillery fire, but it was too late. The British charged home with the bayonet and broke into the position. Arabi's men were routed and fled, leaving 2,000 dead, 500 wounded and losing all their artillery. Wolseley's casualties amounted to 58 killed, 379 wounded and 22 missing, the majority incurred in the opening minutes of the engagement. The cavalry took up the pursuit and reached Cairo the following day, Arabi surrendering his sword personally to Drury Lowe. He was sent to Ceylon to ponder the nature of his defeat.

Tel-el-Kebir was a remarkable achievement by any standard, the more so when one considers that none of Wolseley's troops had been trained for this kind of operation, let alone in a desert environment. Although the battle marked the beginning of 70 years continuous British military presence in Egypt there was at the time no thought of so protracted an involvement. However, even as Wolseley sailed for home and the majority of British troops left Egypt for their peacetime garrisons, events were occurring in the Sudan which would make it inevitable.

On Abba Island, there lived a religious ascetic by the name of Mohammed Ahmed who claimed descent from the Prophet and preached a return to the purest values of Islam, openly despising the corrupt ways of the Turks, as the Egyptians were known. Mohammed Ahmed declared himself to be the Mahdi, the Expected Guide, pointing to the blemish on his right cheek and the gap in his teeth which prophesy said would confirm his identity. Soon he had attracted a large following to whom he proclaimed a Holy War against the Turk, promising Divine favour to those who fell in the sacred cause. There were limits to the degree of subversion which the Egyptians were prepared to tolerate, even from holy men, and in August 1881 they sent a small force to arrest him. Unfortunately, the affair was so badly bungled that they soon had a major rising on their hands. The Mahdi's followers, known collectively as dervishes, grew rapidly in numbers from a mere handful to an army thousands strong, seizing huge areas of the Sudan and confining the Egyptians to a few fortified towns.

In his book *The River War,* Winston Churchill expressed the view that the scum of Arabi's army would have been regarded as the cream of the Egyptian troops serving in the Sudan. This was too much of a generalization to be fair, for although several detachments were wiped out to no purpose, on 2 September 1883 the garrison of El Obeid inflicted a sharp reverse on the dervish host when it attempted to storm the town. El Obeid eventually succumbed not to direct assault but to starvation, and its defiant Governor, Mohammed Said, was vindictively dismembered.

Meanwhile, the Cairo government had mounted a major expedition to restore order. This was commanded by Colonel William Hicks, a retired Indian Army officer who had been appointed Chief of Staff of the Egyptian Army the previous January. Hicks's command numbered 9,000 and was largely recruited from Arabi's defeated troops. Despite this he was successful on a number of occasions but on 3 November his square was forced to a standstill at Sheikan, near El Obeid. The Egyptians began to suffer from thirst although, unknown to them, a source of water lay less than a mile distant. Completely surrounded and outnumbered by three to one, they were subjected to constant attacks alternating with incessant fire from the field artillery, machine guns and 6,000 rifles which

had been captured at El Obeid. On 5 November the Mahdists closed in to massacre the survivors, Hicks being among the last to fall.

The Mahdi's meteoric rise to power brought him a forceful ally in the person of Osman Digna. There is some debate as to Osman's precise origins, and one version has it that he was really a Frenchman called George Vinet, but what is certain is that he was a slave trader whose business had been ruined by the British, for whom he retained an intense hatred. His influence in the Eastern Sudan was great and when the Mahdi appointed him its Governor he set about attacking the Egyptian garrisons on the coast.

A relief expedition was put together under Baker Pasha who, like Osman, had something of an eventful past. Valentine Baker had served in the Crimea and later commanded the 10th Hussars, but his career came to a sudden end when he pressed his unwanted attentions on a lady in a railway carriage. He then entered the service of the Sultan of Turkey and fought against the Russians, becoming a Major-General. In 1882 he was to have been offered the post of Sirdar (Commander-in-Chief) of the Egyptian Army, but rumour had it that no less a person than Queen Victoria herself had intervened to prevent his appointment and instead he became Inspector-General of Gendarmerie. This was merely a device, for his 'policemen' were merely the last scrapings of Arabi's old army who had been transferred to their new service without so much as a change of uniform.

Baker's force, numering 3,656 and six guns, disembarked at Trinkitat at the beginning of February 1884 and at once set out to relieve Tokar. On 4 February it encountered a dervish force one-third its size at El Teb. When the latter attacked the Egyptians panicked, threw down their arms and ran. In the butchery that followed over 2,300 of them were killed and all the artillery was lost, together with some machine guns. To his credit, Baker managed to cut his way out with

A sketch by the war artist Melton Prior showing an incident during the Gordon Relief Expedition. The caption reads: 'The Desert March. Scene at the Wells of Aboo Halfa. Animals no water for three scorching days. Many of the men had only a pint in the morning and a pint at night. Discipline alone prevented a wild confusion setting in' (National Army Museum).

his staff and led the survivors to safety. Shortly after, the garrisons of Trinkitat and Tokar were also overwhelmed and massacred.

The British reaction to this latest series of disasters was that the surviving Egyptian garrisons in the Sudan should be withdrawn, with the exception of Suakin on the Red Sea, which they would assist in holding. With this in mind General Charles Gordon had already been despatched up-river to Khartoum to supervise the evacuation.

Gordon was already a legend in his own lifetime. Commissioned into the Royal Engineers, he had taken part in the siege of Sebastopol during the Crimean War. He had then served in China, where he somehow instilled such discipline and training into a re-

cently raised and most unpromising force that it defeated the Taiping Rebellion and acquired the title of the Ever Victorious Army. Uncompromisingly brave, he was also devoutly religious and when he was stationed at home spent much of his time and most of his money feeding, clothing and finding employment for destitute boys. When he had served in the Sudan during the 1870s his courage and integrity had earned universal respect and it was for this reason that the Egyptian government had requested this further secondment to assist them with their difficulties. It was unfortunate that in addition to his many admirable qualities Gordon was also mercurial, stubborn and wilful and on arriving in Khartoum he decided not to evacuate the city but to hold

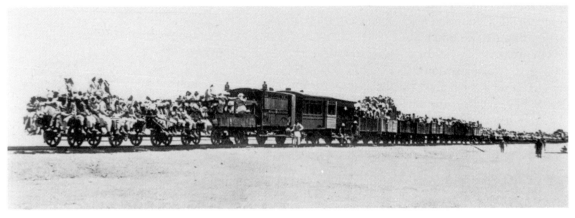

Construction train returning from the railhead during the building of the strategic Wadi Halfa-Abu Hamed Railway (Museum of Army Transport).

it, confident that a British expeditionary force would be sent to his relief.

This was the very situation which the United Kingdom's Liberal Prime Minister, William Gladstone, had sought to avoid. When the Mahdi's army isolated Khartoum at the end of February he came under intense political pressure to extricate Gordon, whom the British public regarded as a high-principled Christian officer who quite rightly refused to abandon those in need. In August Gladstone reluctantly relented, and Wolseley was sent back to Egypt to make preparations for the 1,650-mile march up the Nile.

The river route was not actually the quickest way of reaching Khartoum, but by the time Wolseley reached Egypt it had long been the only option left open. At this period the normal route was from Suakin across the southern edge of the dismal Desert of the Belly of Stones, notable for its strange geological formations, to Berber and thence up-river. Suakin, however, was under constant threat from Osman Digna, and although he was defeated by the newly arrived British garrison under Major-General Sir Gerald Graham at the Second Battle of El Teb (29 February) and again at Tamai (13 March), sustaining heavy casualties and losing most of the arms

captured from Baker Pasha, he was able to sustain these reverses and retained control of the hinterland. Suakin remained under virtual siege and as part of its defences the engineers laid minefields. The local population were greatly attracted to these and would go to any lengths to steal the electric command wires, and even the mines themselves, occasionally being blown to pieces in the process.

Wolseley, with 6,000 men, commenced his advance southwards from Wadi Halfa in October. On 17 November he received a message from Gordon saying that it was doubtful whether he could hold out for more than a month. He therefore decided to send a flying column under Brigadier-General Sir Herbert Stewart straight across the desert from Korti to Metemmeh, lying only 96 miles downstream from Khartoum, while the rest of the army proceeded by river. The 2,000-strong flying column was unable to start before 30 December, but the next day Wolseley's hopes rose when he received another note from Gordon, dated the 14th, confirming that he was still hanging on but that relief had become a matter of real urgency. On 17 January 1885 Stewart's column won the desperate battle of Abu Klea, some details of which have been given above, fighting off further attacks at Abu Kru on the 19th and Gubat, where it reached the Nile, on the 21st. Stewart himself was mortally wounded and command passed to his deputy, Colonel Sir Charles Wilson, who embarked 20 soldiers and a handful of sailors on two of Gordon's tiny steamers which had been sent down river to meet the column. By 28 January the little ships had fought their way to within sight of Khartoum but the red flag of Egypt no longer flew from the walls and the city was only too obviously in the hands of the Mahdi.

Gordon had done what he could to strengthen Khartoum's defences and he had conducted an able and energetic defence, but latterly the fate of the city had rested in the palm of the Mahdi's hand. More than once Mohammed Ahmed had offered Gordon terms and he seemed strangely unwilling to put an end to the matter. The news of Stewart's approach, however, had left him with no alternative and on 26 January his dervishes had overwhelmed the exhausted and starving garrison. Contrary to Mohammed Ahmed's specific instructions, Gordon was killed and beheaded.

Wolseley was ordered to withdraw and with this event the First Sudan War officially ended, although fighting continued for several more years. Someone had decided to build a strategic railway linking Suakin with Berber and work was proceeding round the clock, il-luminated at night by the searchlights of HMS *Dolphin*. Osman Digna naturally objected but was defeated at Hasheen on 20 March and again at Tofrek two days later. After this the railway was abandoned, partly because of the obvious difficulties in building it and partly because of the dervish occupation of Berber. Osman, though regularly worsted, was to re-main a thorn in the side of the Suakin garri-son for some years. His personal courage was no more in doubt than his obvious hold over his men, yet he seldom entered the fray him-self. He preferred to use spiritual weapons against the foe, and occasionally his prayer group could be spotted, just out of range,

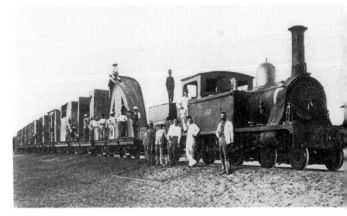

Train loaded with pre-fabricated gunboat sections (Museum of Army Transport).

pestering the Almighty with their unpleasant requests.

On the Nile sector the dervishes' north-ward advance was checked at Ginnis on 30 De-cember 1885, the battle being otherwise remarkable in that it was the last occasion on which British infantry went into action in their traditional scarlet. Skirmishing continued along the frontier, escalating to a seven-hour pitched battle at Toski on 3 August 1889 in which the dervishes were decisively defeated with 1,000 killed, a quarter of their strength, including one of their most notable com-manders, the Emir Wad-el-Nejumi.

The Mahdi had died shortly after the fall of Khartoum, nominating as his successor the Khalifa Abdullahi Ibn Mohammad, who ruled his empire with a blend of puritanical religious fervour and sadistic cruelty. For some years the British were content merely to con-tain the threat, but in 1896 they decided that the Sudan would be reconquered. This deci-sion was taken not for the philanthropic rea-son of rescuing the Khalifa's unfortunate subjects from barbaric oppression, nor entire-ly to ease the pressure on the Italians, who had been seriously defeated by the Abyssinians at Adowa in 1892, but to counter the interest which other great powers, notably France, were showing in establishing control of the upper reaches of the Nile.

Few doubted the difficulties of the undertaking, for in addition to the great distances involved the Khalifa's army numbered not less than 60,000 warriors whose fanatical courage had not diminished with the years. Moreover, the dervishes possessed 40,000 firearms, of which 22,000 were comparatively modern Remingtons captured in earlier engagements, 61 cannon, six Krupp field guns and eight machine guns. Conversely, the dervishes regarded the use of firepower as a mere prelude to the decisive charge with sword and spear, and much of the captured ammunition had been used in the great war which the Khalifa had fought against King John of Abyssinia. In addition, the scientific use of artillery was ignored, while the primitive mechanisms of the machine guns suffered seriously from the attentions of untrained hands.

The main burden of the reconquest would fall on the Egyptian Army. This was now a very different body from that which had existed when the British arrived in Egypt. The remnants of the old army, which cared nothing for its men, had been disbanded by decree and replaced by a smaller force which offered regular pay, promotion, leave, decorations and decent conditions of service. It consisted of eight Egyptian and six Sudanese infantry battalions, a small camel corps, six squadrons of cavalry, four artillery batteries and transport troops. A large contingent of British officers and NCOs had brought it to a high level of discipline and efficiency, and British officers commanded its brigades and all but four of its infantry battalions.

The Sirdar of the Eygptian Army was General Horatio Herbert Kitchener, who had been appointed to the post in 1892. Kitchener, a Royal Engineers officer, had been employed on intelligence duties during Wolseley's abortive attempt to relieve Khartoum and he considered that the British withdrawal from the Sudan had been nothing less than a national humiliation. He had later commanded at Suakin, where he was wounded during the engagement at Handub, and had led the cavalry at Toski. His appointment as Commander-in-Chief had attracted unfavourable comment, for he was far from popular; the glaring eyes and dour expression confirmed such disinterest in the social graces that young Winston Churchill wrote home to the effect that General he might be, but he was 'never a gentleman'. Nor was he a notable tactician. He was, however, expert in the field of supply and transportation, and this was the very quality essential for success in the forthcoming campaign.

Kitchener had two additional, and quite priceless, assets at his disposal. The first was Major (later General) Reginald Wingate, his Chief of Intelligence, a brilliant linguist who had painstakingly constructed a network of spies throughout the Sudan. There was little that happened, even in Omdurman, the Khalifa's capital, that Wingate did not hear about shortly after. The second was the provision of a flotilla of purpose-built river gunboats which were shipped out in sections and assembled in Egypt. These were partially armoured and armed with one 12-pounder, two 6-pounders and four Maxim machine guns. From start to finish the gunboats were to make life extremely unpleasant for the dervishes; one was commanded by a 29-year-old Lieutenant David Beatty, RN, who would later play a critical role in the Battle of Jutland and go on to command the Grand Fleet itself.

When the Second Sudan War commenced in June 1896 both Kitchener and the Khalifa were clear as to their strategic aims. Both were fully aware that in desert warfare a victorious army became progressively weaker the further it advanced from its sources of supply; this was one of the factors which had contributed to the Hicks disaster and it was a factor which was to govern the conduct of operations in the Western Desert between the years 1940 and 1942. The Khalifa's plan,

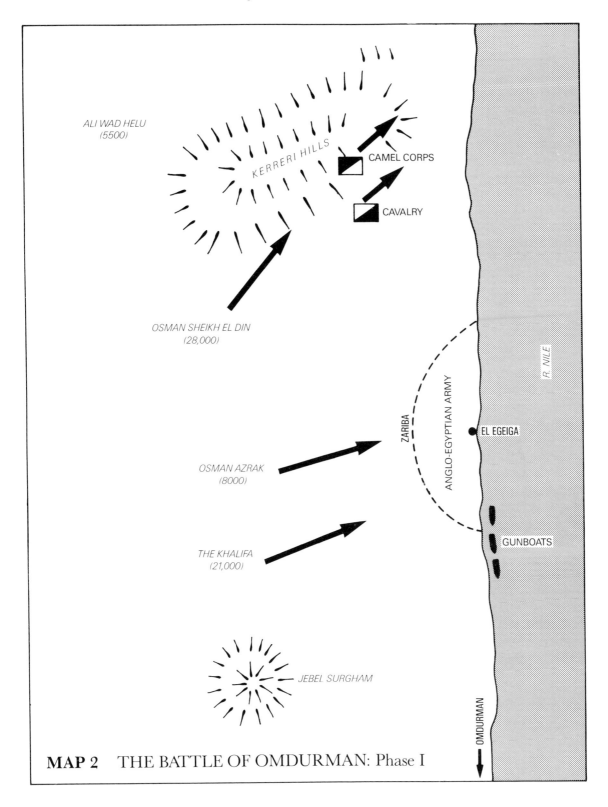

MAP 2 THE BATTLE OF OMDURMAN: Phase I

therefore, was to offer only token resistance to the Anglo-Egyptian advance but to fight the decisive battle near Omdurman, where his own forces were strongest and Kitchener's, he reasoned, would be stretched to their limits. This was acceptable in the terms of nineteenth-century warfare, but Kitchener's thinking already belonged to the twentieth century. The Sirdar accepted that the main issue would be decided near Omdurman, but he intended harnessing the most modern means of transport available, not only to keep his troops supplied but also to reinforce them with fresh British brigades at the critical moment so that when the battle came to be fought his strength would be *twice* that with which he had begun the campaign.

One by one the dervish outposts fell with varying degrees of fighting, these local successes doing much to raise the morale of the Egyptians. When Dongola was captured on 21 September, Kitchener took the bold decision which was to win him the campaign. This was nothing less than to build a railway through the 235 miles of arid and empty desert between Wadi Halfa and Abu Hamed, so forming an arc across the great bend in the Nile's course. Many doubted the feasibility of the project, since without water steam engines were as helpless as men. Fortunately, Royal Engineer survey parties located sources 77 and 126 miles out from Wadi Halfa and the work commenced on 1 January 1897, the average rate of construction being one mile a day. Simultaneously, Kitchener sent a diversionary force into the obverse of the great bend, using the route taken by Stewart's flying column during the Gordon relief expedition, hoping to convince the dervishes that this was his chosen axis of advance.

By July the railhead was within striking distance of Abu Hamed and the following month the town was captured by the advance guard of the army, which had moved up-river with the gunboats. Berber, 135 miles beyond, was abandoned by the enemy and occupied on 13 September. The line reached Abu Hamed on 31 October and was extended southwards.

The importance of Berber as a strategic pivot was soon appreciated by the Khalifa, as were the consequences of failing to defend it. Osman Digna's position in the Eastern Sudan became untenable and he was forced to retire on Omdurman. Soon Kitchener possessed a second line of supply when the route from Suakin was re-opened. With a growing sense of unease the Khalifa realized that he was engaged in a new type of war which he did not fully understand. He had never seen a railway but its workings were explained to him and when his spies told him that each day a mountain of supplies reached the Sirdar's army he knew that it had to be destroyed. However, he still clung to the belief that he would win the final victory under the walls of Omdurman and detailed only 16,000 men under one of his less popular followers, the Emir Mahmud, to execute this extremely important mission.

Wingate had correctly predicted the Khalifa's reaction but guilefully suggested that no less than 100,000 dervishes were marching on Berber. In London Lord Salisbury's government had been temporizing on the question of whether British troops should be employed at all, but accepting Wingate's report at face value it recognized that Kitchener's little army, faced with so great a host, must either risk being overwhelmed or embark on an ignominious retreat. Salisbury agreed that one British brigade should be despatched up the line at once and that a second would follow as quickly as possible. The first of these reinforcements reached Kitchener in January 1898.

Mahmud, accompanied by Osman Digna, seems to have understood that the Khalifa regarded him as expendable, and he resented the fact. He showed a marked reluctance to indulge in anything more than isolated skirmishes and dug himself trenches

An imaginative view of the Battle of Omdurman, 2 September 1898, in which several incidents have been telescoped in time. Kitchener and his staff can be seen in the immediate foreground watching the defeat of the first Dervish attack. Beyond this and on the left of the picture are the 21st Lancers making their charge and gunboats in action on the Nile. Omdurman lies in the distance with the ruins of Khartoum on the peninsular between the Blue and White Niles (National Army Museum).

within a large zariba which had its back to the dry bed of the Atbara river. Kitchener, tired of waiting for his onset, decided to take the initiative himself. At 05:45 on 8 April, his artillery began hammering the trenches and thorn hedge, and at 08:00 the infantry went in with shouts of 'Remember Gordon!' Within half-an-hour the zariba had been cleared. The dervish loss amounted to 3,000 killed and 2,000 captured, the latter including Mahmud, and the survivors, many of whom were wounded, streamed across the Atbara in broken flight. The Anglo-Egyptian army's total casualties amounted to less than 600.

The road to Omdurman now lay open, but Kitchener was not inclined to advance un-

til he could be certain of victory and consolidated his position while the second British brigade moved up to join him. Not until August did he set his troops in motion again. On 1 September the gunboats engaged the defences of the Khalifa's capital, blasting several breaches in its walls and, to the superstitious horror of the dervishes, battering holes in the dome of the Mahdi's tomb. Seven miles to the north the army was constructing a zariba centred on the village of El Egeiga, around which it curved in a half-moon with both flanks resting on the Nile. Beyond the zariba lay a wide, featureless plain bare of cover but intersected here and there by a shallow khor, or depression. Approximately two miles to the

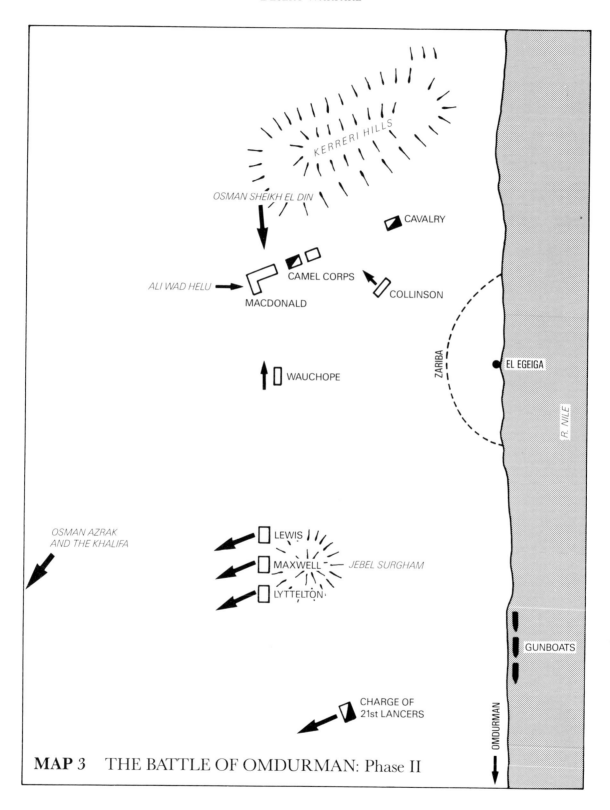

KERRERI HILLS

OSMAN SHEIKH EL DIN

CAVALRY

ALI WAD HELU → CAMEL CORPS

MACDONALD

COLLINSON

ZARIBA

• EL EGEIGA

R. NILE

WAUCHOPE

OSMAN AZRAK
AND THE KHALIFA

LEWIS

MAXWELL — JEBEL SURGHAM

LYTTELTON

GUNBOATS

CHARGE OF
21st LANCERS

OMDURMAN

MAP 3   THE BATTLE OF OMDURMAN: Phase II

south-west lay a rocky feature known as Jebel Surgham, about 250 ft in height, while a
similar distance to the north-west were the
Kerreri Hills. As the sun set, both sides recognized instinctively that this would be the morrow's battlefield and settled down to find what
rest they could. That of the dervishes was disturbed by the eerie probing of the gunboats'
searchlights. 'What is this strange thing?'
asked the Khalifa, pointing to the distant, un-
blinking eyes. 'They are looking at us,' he was
told; and so they were.

At dawn the Khalifa led out his army,
over 60,000 strong, swinging round behind Jebel Surgham for an immediate assault on the
zariba. The British held the left of the line and
the Egyptians the right; both watched in awe
as the horde curved towards them, saw its
many banners and the sun sparkling on thousands of spear-points and sword-blades, and
listened to the rising groundswell of its chant-
ing as the dervishes roused themselves into a
killing frenzy. At 06:25, with the enemy 2,700
yards distant, the artillery opened fire, using
shrapnel and high explosive shells. The gunboats joined in immediately, followed shortly
by the Maxim machine guns. The infantry
fixed bayonets and their front rank dropped
to one knee. Here and there a man pitched
on to the sand as the enemy's scattered return
fire began to penetrate the zariba. At 06:35,
with the range down to 2,000 yards, the
Grenadier Guards began firing precise vol-
leys. Other regiments preferred to wait a little longer but by 06:45 the whole of
Kitchener's line was ablaze. Although their
leading ranks were constantly shot away, the
dervishes continued to press their attack until 07:30, when those who could calmly turned
and walked off. On the British sector only a
few had come within 800 yards of the zariba,
but against the slower-firing Egyptians they
had managed to close the gap to within 400
yards.

To the north of the zariba the Egyptian
cavalry, under Lieutenant-Colonel Broad-

wood, had successfully withdrawn across the
Kerreri Hills and, by alternately combining
fire with movement, had provoked a large part
of the dervish army into following them, so
removing it for the time being from the main
area of the contest. The Camel Corps, however, was at a serious disadvantage in this type
of action and was forced to execute a difficult
withdrawal towards the northern face of the
zariba. Indeed, so hard did the dervishes pursue that the Camel Corps was in real danger
of being cut off and wiped out, until several
gunboats brought their concentrated fire to
bear on the enemy's packed ranks.

If the first phase of the Battle of Omdurman had been won by sheer naked firepower,
the second was to be marked by tactics which
varied between the indifferent and the brilliant. Somewhat prematurely, Kitchener ordered a general advance on Jebel Surgham.
His brigades marched out across the plain,
now littered with thousands of dead and dying dervishes, took the hill without difficulty
and continued to push the defeated enemy
remnants out into the desert. On the extreme
left of the line the 21st Lancers under Colonel
R. M. Martin received an order from the Sirdar at 08:00 to 'worry them on their flank and
head them off from Omdurman'.

The 21st were the most junior cavalry
regiment in the British Army and were very
conscious of the fact that they had never been
in action; one of the crueller wits of the day
had even suggested that the regiment's unwritten motto was 'Thou shalt not kill'. Winston
Churchill, who belonged to the infinitely more
fashionable 4th Hussars, was serving with
them as an attached officer and made no bones
about the fact that he did not like them. Nor,
for that matter, did the Lancer officers care
much for Churchill, whom they regarded as
a prig, wondering how he found his regimental duties compatible with those of *The Morning Post*'s Sudan correspondent.

Be all that as it may, the 21st Lancers were
now committed to action. The regiment had

The gunboat Sultan *in action during the Battle of Omdurman. In the background is the dome of the Mahdi's Tomb, already damaged by shellfire* (National Army Museum).

not gone far when its scouts galloped in to report a body of 700 dervishes drawn up to its right front. This was the flank guard of the Khalifa's army and it had recently been reinforced with a further 2,000 men who were concealed from view in a khor. With the benefit of hindsight it has been suggested that Martin should have avoided becoming seriously involved and executed his designated mission within the overall context of the battle, but as the regiment drew level with those of the enemy who were visible it came under fire and the challenge was irresistible. He ordered his trumpeter to sound 'Right wheel into line' and without the necessity of further command, the entire regiment broke into a thundering charge. It had 300 yards to cover and was closing rapidly when the khor suddenly came into view, jammed 12-deep with dervish-

es. The 21st Lancers had fallen for one of the oldest tricks in the desert warrior's book, but there was nothing for it but to generate the momentum which would drive the horses through the mass.

When it came, the impact shook both sides, but after two minutes of hacking, stabbing and shooting the regiment was scrambling up the far bank of the khor; Churchill had sheathed his sword during the charge and very sensibly shot his way through with a privately purchased Mauser automatic pistol. Rallying his men, Martin brought them on to the khor's flank and opened dismounted fire with carbines. The dervishes also changed front and attacked, but were beaten back and retired sullenly from the field.

The Lancers sustained 21 killed and 46 wounded during the mêlée and the dervish loss was comparable. However, 119 horses had also been killed or injured, seriously reducing the regiment's mounted strength. It was 09:30 before it was ready to move off again and it played little further part in the day's events. Kitchener was less than pleased by the incident, which had hurt the dervishes little and deprived him of the services of a cavalry regiment when he needed them most. Perversely, the British public regarded the 21st Lancers as the heroes of the entire battle, for in the midst of the hideous close-quarter fighting three of its members had earned the award of the Victoria Cross. When Queen Victoria herself heard of the charge she promptly awarded the regiment the title of 'The Empress of India's'.

Meanwhile, events had taken an even more dramatic turn on the opposite side of the battlefield. Having led their pursuers a merry chase across the Kerreri Hills, Broadwood's Egyptian cavalry had returned to the zariba along the river. Rather more slowly the dervishes themselves, to the number of some 20,000, streamed back to the plain to discover that a situation had developed which might enable them to turn the tables on the Anglo-Egyptian army. On the extreme right of Kitchener's line, and detached from it by the better part of a mile, was Colonel Hector Macdonald's 1st Egyptian Brigade, still engaged with the enemy to the west. Now it was to be simultaneously assailed from the north, and if it was overwhelmed the entire Allied right flank would be placed in serious jeopardy.

Macdonald, a Highland crofter's son who had risen from the ranks, was a tough, no-nonsense soldier who had served throughout the campaign and he was not the man to panic in a tight spot. He coolly changed front so that his brigade resembled an 'L', shifting battalions from the left flank to the right across the inner angle. He then opened a tremendous fire, supported by his Maxims and attached artillery batteries, the latter being compelled

to resort to case shot, which even by 1898 was regarded as distinctly old-fashioned. The dervishes managed to close in to within 30 yards and the infantry were down to six rounds per man when the first reinforcements arrived. The Camel Corps came up and extended his firing line to the right, followed by the Lincolnshire Regiment. The 4th Egyptian Brigade, which had been left guarding the zariba, marched towards the action, around the eastern edges of which Broadwood's troopers were now hovering. Finally the 1st British Brigade, hurrying across the battlefield, fell on the enemy flank and the attack crumbled away.

By 11:30 the battle was over and the Sirdar re-deployed his army for the last stage of its march on Omdurman, which fell that afternoon. So ended the first major desert conflict of the modern era. A total of 9,700 dervishes died in the battle and perhaps twice that number sustained wounds of one sort or another. The Khalifa was hunted down and fought to the death, but Osman Digna survived a comfortable captivity and lived on until 1926. The Anglo-Egyptian army had five officers and 43 other ranks killed, plus 428 men wounded.

Many of the British officers who were present at Omdurman would leave their mark on history. Kitchener, of course, was to win further laurels in the Boer War and First World War before he lost his life at sea aboard HMS *Hampshire*. Lieutenant David Beatty, the future Admiral of the Fleet, had a grandstand view of the 21st Lancers' charge, which he described to Churchill, then First Lord of the Admiralty, as being 'like plum duff—brown currants scattered about in a great deal of suet'. Captain Douglas Haig, who led a squadron of Broadwood's cavalry, was to become a Field Marshal and, during the First World War, command British armies whose size would once have seemed impossible. Major Charles Townshend, the commander of the 12th Sudanese Battalion, was to win desert victories of his own, yet was also to be responsible for the British Army's most humiliating desert defeat. Colonel Hector Macdonald's part in the victory was readily acknowledged and he became a public hero; 'Fighting Mac' commanded the crack Highland Brigade during the Boer War but his career was to end in tragedy. In 1903 he was accused of sodomy during his tour as Commander-in-Chief Ceylon. Snubbed publicly by the King, he wished to spare his family and the Army further shame and shot himself in a Paris hotel.

Only 13 years after Omdurman armoured cars and aircraft, manned by Italians, made their first hesitant contributions to desert warfare. Seven years later it had become unthinkable that operations could be conducted in the desert without adequate mechanization and air support.

CHAPTER 2

FIRST WORLD WAR (1)

The Senussi War and the defence of Egypt

In 1855 a devout Algerian named Mohammed es Senussi who, like the Mahdi, claimed descent from the Prophet, settled in the oasis of Jarabub, deep in the Libyan desert, and there founded the religious order which bears his name. The aims of the Senussi Brotherhood were the return of Islam to its original simple ideals and the restoration of fertility to the land, these long term objectives being achieved peacefully by careful planning and hard work. The Senussi were not a tribal grouping and were Pan-Islamic in their appeal, attracting a large following of Sudanese, Tuaregs, Berbers and Bedouin. By 1902 they had established lodges and caravanserais across an area stretching from the green plains of northern Nigeria to the coast of Cyrenaica, controlling most of the trans-Saharan trade routes in the process; most of the inhabitants of the Western Desert were Senussi, and a large proportion of the population of Egypt itself was, if not actually Senussi, in sympathy with the movement. The Mahdi had sought to bring the Brotherhood within his orbit and had even offered the Grand Senussi the position of Khalifa, but the Senussi envoy had been so sickened by the barbarities which he had witnessed during the sacking of Khartoum that its members were forbidden to have further dealings with the Omdurman regime. Needless to say, this removed any anxieties the British may have had concerning their western flank during the reconquest of the Sudan and

an excellent relationship existed between themselves and the Senussi for many years.

Unfortunately, the same was not true of the relationship between the Senussi and the other colonial powers. There was friction with the French in Tunisia and with Italian colonists in Libya. Over the years the original pacific ideals gave way to a more war-like zeal and the formation of a formidable body of semi-regular troops known as the Muhafizia whose potential was soon to be revealed.

Italy had long nurtured a wish for a North African possession and in 1911 declared war on the Ottoman Empire, claiming that her colonists in Libya, then a Turkish province, were being ill-treated. Tripoli was bombarded and a 50,000-strong army was landed to secure the principal towns. The Turks were caught totally unprepared and the result was a foregone conclusion, but the war is of some interest in that it witnessed the first use of aircraft and armoured cars. Altogether, the Italians deployed nine aircraft (two Blériots, three Nieuports, two Farmans and two Etrich Taubes), which were used mainly for reconnaissance, and two airships, which occasionally dropped a few 4½ lb grenades, provoking Turkish expressions of outrage at the inhumanity of aerial attack. The armoured car detachment consisted of a pair of 4 ton Bianchis armed with a single machine gun each, but these seem to have been employed purely in support of local operations. When a peace treaty was concluded in 1912 the Italians had succeeded in establishing themselves in a few coastal garrisons but further progress into the hinterland was barred by the Turks' Senussi allies and, although Libya was ceded to Italy, this situation remained unchanged for several years.

While the war was in progress Egypt, though still nominally subject to the Sultan of Turkey, had declared herself neutral at British insistence and refused to permit the passage of Turkish troops to Libya. This was naturally resented by Constantinople and marked a further decline in the amicable relations which had existed between the United Kingdom and Turkey throughout the nineteenth century. Furthermore, the recently established Balkan nations, sensing Turkey's inherent weakness, attacked her and by the autumn of 1913 had stripped her of virtually all her remaining territory in Europe.

The waning of British influence within Turkey was matched by the growth of that of Imperial Germany. Berlin saw the Ottoman Empire not only as a potentially valuable ally in the event of war with Russia, but also as a major threat to Great Britain's communications with her possessions in the Far East and the oil supplies of the Persian Gulf upon which the Royal Navy now relied. Such a threat would undoubtedly absorb a major part of the British Empire's resources and prevent them being deployed elsewhere, and with this in mind a major effort was made to woo Turkey into the German camp. German officers supervised the reorganization and re-equipment of the Turkish Army, and German financiers and industrialists embarked upon such projects as the Berlin-Baghdad railway. Anti-British intrigue reached new heights throughout the Middle East, led by no less a person than Kaiser Wilhelm II, who, since his visit to Mecca, preferred to be known in the region as Hadji Mohammed Guilliano. Pro-

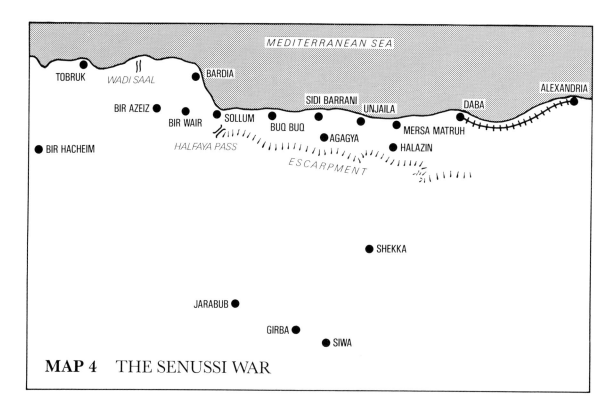

MAP 4   THE SENUSSI WAR

jected by his image-makers as the Champion of Islam—a curious stance for a Christian monarch—he hastened to lay a gilt wreath at the tomb of the great Saladin, emphasizing the need for a Holy War to restore the faith. Few entertained doubts as to the enemy's identity in such a war.

By the end of October 1914 German diplomacy had triumphed and Turkey was at war with Great Britain. British strategy in the Middle East required the re-opening of warm-water communications with Russia by forcing the Dardanelles; the occupation of Basra to secure the Mesopotamian and Persian oil supplies; and a defensive stance in Egypt along the Suez Canal and in the Western Desert, where it was becoming increasingly clear that the Senussi regarded the Libyan question as being far from settled.

Although the defenders of the Canal were provided with some protection by the Sinai Desert, this could be crossed by an army provided adequate logistic preparations had been made. In this respect, however, the Turks were at something of a disadvantage, for coastal traffic along the Syrian and Palestine coasts had been brought to a standstill by British and French naval activity. Furthermore, their rail supply route was awkwardly constructed, and since this had a bearing on subsequent operations it is worth describing in some detail. In theory, a standard gauge single-track line ran all the way from the Bosphorus through Asia Minor and into Syria as far as Riyaq; in practice, the line was broken by two long un-completed sections in the Taurus and Amanus Mountains, which troops and supplies had to detour by road. At Riyaq these difficulties were compounded by the fact that the line became narrow-gauge, necessitating trans-shipment for the next stage of the journey. This could be along a branch which crossed the mountains to Beirut or down the main line, which continued south to Damascus and thence to Dera'a. There it forked again, one branch running to El Auja near Beersheba

with connections to Haifa, Jaffa and Jerusalem, and the other, the famous Pilgrim Railway, going straight down through Arabia to Medina. The operation of the system was laborious at the best of times, and since the war denied Turkey much of her locomotive coal the meagre supply available had to be supplemented by felling sparse local timber. Again, a narrow-gauge single-track system could not hope to keep pace with the voracious demands of a modern army in the field, and even with the generous assistance of animal transport there was obviously a ceiling on the number of troops that could be supported beyond the railheads.

If, for the moment, the narrow-gauge system seemed secure from British interference, the same could not be said of the standard-gauge, which passed within a few miles of the coast as it rounded the Gulf of Alexandretta (Iskenderun), sending a branch line down into Alexandretta itself. If the main line could be cut this would effectively sever the Palestine Front's major supply artery and simultaneously compromise the logistics of the Turkish armies serving in Mesopotamia as well. In December 1914 an Allied naval squadron did considerable damage to the branch line and even occupied Alexandretta for a short period. This success led to plans being drafted for the permanent occupation of Alexandretta and the destruction of the main line. Unfortunately, these were shelved, initially because the Dardanelles operation held a higher priority and latterly because, after the traumatic failure at Gallipoli, the risks involved in further landings on the Turkish coast were not politically acceptable. Had the effort been made the entire course of the war in the Middle East could well have been very different, for during the winter of 1914/15 the Turks sustained a disastrous series of reverses in the Caucasus, culminating in a Russian invasion of Asia Minor from the north-east. The fact remains that it was not and this in itself made some kind of initiative by the Turks against the Suez Canal inevitable.

Obviously the scope and duration of the operation could only be limited and what was contemplated amounted to little more than a large-scale raid which would cause damage to installations and possibly block the Canal with sunken ships. Even so, the objectives set were vague and the possibility of Allied warships being integrated into the Canal defence scheme seems to have been largely discounted.

The troops detailed for the operation were Djemal Bey's VIII Corps, accompanied by a team of German advisers under Colonel Freiherr Kress von Kressenstein. By the middle of January 1915 the corps was ready to leave Beersheba and embark on its crossing of the Sinai, from which the British had withdrawn the previous autumn. The coastal route was avoided, as this would have brought the marching columns within range of naval gunfire. The inland route, though hot and arid in summer, was now quite passable, as heavy winter rains had filled pools and cisterns along the way. Even so, 5,000 water-carrying camels were still required to prevent thirst from becoming an acute problem.

The advance had been expected by the British and its progress was reported by Nieuport seaplanes flying off the Canal. The defenders, therefore, had plenty of time in which to set their house in order. On 3 February the Turks launched a series of unco-ordinated attacks along a wide front and were defeated in detail by a storm of fire from Allied warships and British positions on the west bank. The majority of assault boats launched were riddled and sunk; only three managed to cross the Canal and their occupants were all quickly killed or captured. Djemal retired slowly to Beersheba, having sustained 2,000 casualties, approximately 10 per cent of his strength. British casualties amounted to only 163.

Lieutenant-General Sir John Maxwell, the Commander-in-Chief Egypt, was natural-ly satisfied with the outcome of the engagement but made no attempt to pursue Djemal and remained sensitive regarding the prospect of a further Turkish offensive. His anxieties were aggravated by the incessant demands of the Dardanelles, which had reduced the garrison of Egypt to a dangerously low level, by the wave of anti-British feeling which was sweeping the country, and by the growing belligerence of the Senussi across the frontier in Libya. There was little doubt that the Senussi were preparing to extend their activities beyond the guerrilla war they were waging against the Italians, for along the largely deserted coastline of Italy's newest colony German U-boats came and went more or less as they pleased, landing small arms, machine guns, mountain artillery, ammunition and Turkish instructors. By the autumn of 1915 the merest spark was required to explode Senussi antipathy into outright hostilities against the British.

That spark was provided, unwittingly if not unwillingly, by Lieutenant-Commander Waldemar Kophamel, the commander of *U-35*, on 5 November 1915. Kophamel, who was to survive the war as Germany's sixth highest-scoring submarine ace with 190,000 tons of Allied shipping to his credit, was an officer who somehow managed to preserve his sense of chivalry despite the growing brutalism of total war, and the previous day he had arrived in the little harbour of Bardia brazenly towing two schooners loaded with munitions for the Senussi. Next morning he set off on his return journey to Turkey but five miles out in the Gulf of Sollum he sighted the smoke of a twin-funnelled vessel and dived.

The ship was HMS *Tara*, under the command of Captain R. S. Gwatkin-Williams, RN. In peacetime her owners had been the London and North Western Railway Company and she had operated as SS *Hibernia* on the run between Holyhead and Dublin. On the outbreak of war she had been requisitioned by the Admiralty, armed with three six-pounder guns, and became an armed boarding vessel. Now, she was engaged on a routine visit to the frontier post of Sollum.

Kophamel quickly brought *U-35* into an attacking position and fired a single torpedo, which struck *Tara* amidships. The British ship began settling at once and launched her boats. Kophamel surfaced among these and towed them back into Bardia, taking some of the survivors on to his own deck. Having handed over his prisoners to the senior Turkish officer present, he resumed his journey the following day, sinking one Egyptian gunboat and severely damaging another at Sollum, then adding a horse transport to his score on the way home.

The British authorities in Egypt at once sent an envoy to the Senussi to negotiate the release of *Tara*'s survivors. At first the Grand Senussi, Said Ahmed, denied all knowledge of the affair. Under pressure, he admitted that the prisoners were being held at an undisclosed location, but declined to hand them over as they had been left in his care as hostages by the Turks. He was, in fact, under the influence of two Turkish senior officers by now,

One of the Duke of Westminster's Rolls-Royce armoured cars at Sollum, April 1916 (Imperial War Museum).

Nuri Bey, the brother of Enver Pasha, and Ja'far Pasha, who had received his training from the German Army. These two had arrived with gifts of gold and a flattering letter from the Sultan himself. They pointed out that the Turkish army had not only defeated the Gallipoli landing but was also doing extremely well in Mesopotamia, and that in view of recent events in the Gulf of Sollum the claim of the Royal Navy to rule the waves was obviously no longer valid. An invasion of Egypt, they argued, would bring about the collapse of the weakened British, particularly if the large number of Senussi supporters in Egypt rose against them. Said Ahmed was convinced and gave orders for his troops to march.

During the night of 17 November the Sollum garrison beat off an attack, and was then brought out by steamer. Sidi Barrani was attacked on the 18th and held, although many of the Egyptian coastguards deserted to the enemy. The remainder marched along the coast to Mersa Matruh spreading alarm and despondency.

In Cairo, Maxwell was seriously alarmed by the invasion and the Egyptian desertions, knowing that the despatch of troops to fight the Senussi would leave very little in reserve with which to mount counter-insurgency operations, should the need arise. Nonetheless, a number of Territorial infantry battalions and Yeomanry cavalry regiments were assembled under Major-General A. Wallace and designated Western Frontier Force. Wallace fought a number of costly holding actions west of Mersa Matruh, and these succeeded in containing the Senussi advance. As the position stabilized, his strength was augmented by South African and New Zealand infantry, as well as troops recently returned from Gallipoli.

Wallace's command also included the first British armoured unit to serve in the Western Desert, the Emergency Squadron Royal Naval Air Service Armoured Car Division. As its name implies, this was formed hastily in November from Nos 3 and 4 Armoured Car Squadrons, elements of which had taken part in the Gallipoli fighting. It was equipped with Rolls-Royce armoured cars based on the Alpine chassis, with a four-speed gearbox and a strengthened back axle. The body was sheathed in armour plate, leaving a small carrying platform at the rear, and an Admiralty pattern turret mounting a Vickers-Maxim machine gun was fitted over the main body of the vehicle. Comfort there was none, the driver sitting on a pile of small square mats, his back supported by an adjustable sling. Only the smallest men could operate efficiently in the cramped turret, which one contemporary account refers to as 'the cylinder'.

The Emergency Squadron saw little fighting, largely because the winter rains had turned the going into a quagmire, much as they did in the same area after the Second Battle of Alamein, 27 years later. However, by January 1916 the squadron had acquired considerable desert experience and, having been relieved by the Duke of Westminster's armoured car brigade (formerly No 2 Squadron RNAS Armoured Car Division), was sent up the Nile to Upper Egypt where Senussi bands were threatening the security of the west bank of the river, having occupied the oases of El Kharga, Dakhala, Farafra and Baharia. In due course its cars, and those of its personnel who wished, were transferred to the Army, as was the case with every naval armoured car unit, with the notable exception of one which continued to pursue an adventurous career in Russia.

The Duke of Westminster's unit, having seen active service in Flanders, had already made the change and consisted of three batteries of four Rolls-Royce armoured cars and a small headquarters, supported by an echelon of Model T Ford tenders. Its morale was high, the Duke having selected his officers and men with care, the majority, including Second-Lieutenant Griggs, his own jockey, coming from cavalry and yeomanry regiments, with

a leavening of professional motor drivers and mechanics.

In January, air reconnaissance revealed that the Senussi were occupying an entrenched camp at Halazin, 22 miles south of Mersa Matruh, and Wallace decided to eject them. A move by the cavalry to isolate the camp was foiled by a counter-attack led by Ja'far, but the Senussi fled when their trenches were stormed by the infantry. The battle was fought in atrocious conditions, the wounded having to be carried by hand across several miles of sodden ground, while the troops were compelled to spend the night without blankets or shelter of any kind, exposed to the wind and rain.

Wallace's health had begun to deteriorate, and on 10 January he was relieved by Major-General W. E. Peyton. The Western Frontier Force was now in a much stronger position and Maxwell ordered it to take the offensive and recapture Sollum, allocating 2,000 transport camels for its support. A forward base was established at Unjaila and when aircraft reported that the main Senussi camp was located at a place called Agagya some way to the south-east of Sidi Barrani Peyton led out a column to deal with it, consisting of two battalions from Brigadier-General Lukin's South African infantry brigade, the Dorset Yeomanry, one squadron of the Buckinghamshire Yeomanry, a Royal Horse Artillery battery and four of the Duke's armoured cars.

By the evening of the 24th the column was within eight miles of Agagya. Peyton decided to rest his men throughout the following day and attack on the 26th. The Senussi, 1,500 strong and supported by artillery and machine guns, were holding a ridge five miles north of their camp and brought the infantry under fire as soon as they were within range. Ja'far again attempted a counter-attack but this was defeated by a reserve which Peyton had retained for the purpose. The South Africans then fought their way forward on to the ridge and through the enemy position. After several hours of hard fighting the Senussi began to pull out, watched closely by Lieutenant-Colonel Souter, commanding the Dorset Yeomanry, from the British right flank. Once he was certain that the enemy were clear of their trenches he set his regiment in motion. At once machine-gun fire from the rearguard began to cut swathes through the ranks of his troopers, but the gap closed steadily and the lines of galloping horsemen swept into the mass of the enemy, cutting down 300 of them and pursuing the rest across the desert. At the critical moment Souter's horse was shot dead beneath him and he almost landed on top of Ja'far, who was promptly taken prisoner. Ja'far, himself wounded, acknowledged that the yeomanry's charge had been devastating, but commented that it had been made contrary to the normal usages of war. The Dorsets' casualties amounted to 58 out of 184 men taking part, but the loss of 85 horses effectively reduced the regiment's strength by half. For the armoured cars, Agagya had been a disappointing battle, their part being confined to providing machine gun support from ground mountings when they became bogged in soft sand.

Sidi Barrani was occupied on 28 February and on 9 March Peyton resumed his advance on Sollum. Lukin's brigade and the cavalry were to advance along the coast to Buq Buq and then swing inland to climb the coastal escarpment near Augarin Wells. The Duke's armoured cars would head south from Sidi Barrani and climb the escarpment by way of a pass which, it was thought, might just be passable for motor vehicles, although the last wheels to make the journey had probably been Roman. It was a struggle, but all the cars made it, some having to be man-handled over the difficult stretches as they flogged their way upwards with boiling radiators.

Next day they picked their difficult passage along the edge of the escarpment, trying to keep in visual touch with the troops on the coastal plain below. After they had covered 14 miles the Duke ordered a halt and opened heliograph communication with Lukin. The news conveyed by the distant winking light was far from good.

LEFT BUQ BUQ EARLY THIS MORNING ... WELLS HERE ALMOST DRY. SEARCHING FOR WATER. POSITION SERIOUS.

The cars continued on their way and some miles further on the first South Africans came scrambling up the escarpment, desperate for water, many with their tongues hanging out; one, a former bank manager, willingly offered £50 for a drink. There was little that the crews could do for them. Their spare water tanks had already been drained by the greedy radiators, and apart from what little remained in the men's water bottles, the only other sources lay within the radiators themselves or the machine guns' cooling jackets, and to touch either of these had been declared a court martial offence.

Early next morning the cars discovered a source of water which enabled the advance to continue. On 14 March Peyton's force reached Halfaya Pass, and from there marched the remaining three miles to Sollum, which the enemy had abandoned. Once again the Union Flag was hoisted over the little white fort, but Peyton was not satisfied with having evened the score; he wished if possible to complete the destruction of the Senussi field army and when aircraft reported a large enemy camp at Bir Wair he instructed the Duke to take his armoured cars and act with such aggression as the situation demanded.

Bir Wair technically lay in Italian territory, but since the Italians themselves were unwilling or unable to do anything about the Senussi, little embarrassment was felt, especially since Italy had become the United Kingdom's ally the previous year. Across the frontier the going was found to be excellent and the cars were able to maintain a high average speed. At Bir Wair the Senussi camp fires were still burning but the enemy had pulled off to the west and the armoured cars caught up with them at a well called Bir Azeiz.

The Senussi had established themselves in a rocky position fronted by some rough going and opened up on the cars with mountain artillery and machine guns. The cars fanned out and went straight for them, machine guns chattering. Inside, conditions quickly began to deteriorate as the heat of the racing engines added to that of the sun, while choking fumes from the machine gun turned the atmosphere blue. The noise level within the vehicles was almost intolerable, being a compound of their own machine gun fire, rounds striking the armour plate, the roar of the engine and the shouts of commanders as they ordered the drivers to change direction. One driver at least suffered the added torment of hot cartridge cases falling on to his bare neck and into his shirt, where they burned his back. The cars concentrated their fire on the enemy gunners, whose own rounds were badly ranged and exploded beyond their moving targets. When the gun crews, mostly Turks, began going down around their weapons the whole Senussi army suddenly broke and ran. Hundreds were killed or wounded during the ensuing pursuit; among the fugitives was Nuri Bey, who narrowly escaped capture.

The Duke's men spent the night near the battlefield and returned to Sollum the following morning with their prisoners and booty—three 4-inch guns, nine machine-guns, an assortment of small arms and 250,000 rounds of ammunition. Their own casualties amounted to one or two very slightly wounded, almost certainly as a result of bullet-splash penetrating the visors and interior flaking of the armour under impact, and some vehicle tyres punctured. The engagement at Bir Wair, though small in scale, marked a major turning point in the history of desert warfare, for a mere 34 men, protected by armour plate and possessing the superior mobility

conferred by the internal combustion engine, had routed an entire army. In recognition of the fact, Peyton had the unit paraded in front of the fort and thanked it personally for its invaluable services.

Meanwhile, there was still no news of *Tara*'s survivors. No one knew whether they were alive or dead and none of the prisoners could give any information. Quite possibly they would never have been heard of again had not a letter written by Captain Gwatkin-Williams, the ship's commander, been discovered in a house in Sollum. The letter had been addressed to the commander of the British garrison, but it had been delivered during the period of Senussi occupation; it gave the prisoners' location as El Hakkim Abbyat, or Bir Hacheim.

In Arabic Bir means well, or more specifically an underground cistern. The desert is dotted with Birs, but at that period no maps existed of the interior and none of the inhabitants of Sollum had any idea where Bir Hacheim might be located. The prisoners taken at Bir Azeiz were questioned and at length an elderly man named Ali confessed that in his youth he had tended stock there. Bir Hacheim, he said, was five days' journey by camel from Sollum, and he would be prepared to act as guide.

The Duke of Westminster at once volunteered his armoured cars to lead a rescue attempt. A column was quickly assembled, including Ford tenders and motor ambulances, a total of 45 vehicles including the armoured cars. It left Sollum at 01:00 on 17 March and proceeded through the darkness along the track leading through Bir Wair to Tobruk. Leaving two of their number to act as rearguard to the column, the armoured cars led the advance, with the tenders, loaded with spare petrol, water and provisions, following behind. A short halt was made at first light for breakfast and then the march resumed.

After 50 miles had been covered Ali spotted a camel caravan moving along a parallel course to the south. A diversion was made and the caravan intercepted by the armoured cars. It was found to be carrying supplies for the Senussi and these were confiscated, the drivers captured and the camels shot. This took more time than had been bargained for and it was almost noon when the column started off again. The route took them ever westward with no further instructions from Ali save to continue in the same direction. The interpreter pointed out testily to the old man that motor vehicles were unlike camels and had to be fed regularly, but Ali steadfastly maintained that this was the way to Bir Hacheim.

After about 100 miles had been covered Ali indicated that the column should swing left and head south over the desert. This generated serious doubt as to whether the guide knew his business. Halts were made frequently to verify the position. By 15:00 the vehicles had travelled over 120 miles since leaving Sollum and the Duke, who had by now completely lost faith in Ali, decided that they had gone far enough. The fuel state indicated that the point of no return had been reached and to venture further would simply result in the temporary immobilization of the Western Frontier Force's armoured element, and most of its motor transport as well. Suddenly the guide shouted that he could see Bir Hacheim. Through his binoculars the Duke observed two small hummocks on the horizon and Ali assured him that the wells lay beneath.

The cars spread out and charged the mounds. Armed men could be seen scurrying about and running off into the desert, evidently taking their families with them. Soon other, horribly emaciated, figures tottered into view, waving and cheering in cracked voices.

'The scene when we got there was one I shall never forget,' wrote an officer serving with the brigade's supply tenders. 'Numbers of prisoners were crying without any effort to hide their tears while a number of our men found great difficulty in not following suit; I personally had a very big lump in my throat if nothing more! The majority were so weak from dysentery and starvation that they could only just stand, and most were half naked and ravenous.'

Gwatkin-Williams was in slightly better shape than the rest of his crew, although he had escaped once and been recaptured. He had lost six stone in weight and four of his men had died as a result of their privations; for another, the rescue had come just too late. The Senussi had not been deliberately cruel and had, in fact, lived on the same rations as their prisoners, but food was in terribly short supply and the latter had been forced to eke out their meagre diet with desert snails and roots.

Seized by blind rage, the armoured car crews roared off in pursuit of the guards. Gwatkin-Williams' pleas for mercy were ignored and neither age nor sex was spared. The only survivors of the massacre were two babies who were brought back with the column. It was a stain on an otherwise perfect operation, deeply and sincerely regretted when calmer thoughts had returned.

The column set off on its return journey to Sollum as soon as the released captives had been clothed and fed, reaching Bir Wair, now held by a unit of the Australian Camel Corps, at 23:00. The drivers were exhausted and most collapsed over their wheels the minute they arrived. The Duke had gone ahead to make arrangements for the survivors, who were placed aboard a hospital ship for passage to Alexandria as soon as they reached Sollum. The armoured cars remained at Bir Wair for two days until a sand storm blew itself out, but drove up to the fort to the cheers of the infantry and a salute fired by the artillery. Once again, General Peyton congratulated the unit on its remarkable achievement.

Shortly after, the three batteries of the armoured car brigade were split, one remaining at Sollum, a second returning to Mersa Matruh, while the third, by rotation, patrolled the 150 mile stretch between. By now the

Italians had begun to take an interest in the proceedings and had established a post of their own at Bardia. They brought news that Nuri Bey had managed to rally a number of Senussi and had established a camp in the Wadi Saal, which ran down to the sea somewhere between Bardia and Tobruk.

A combined Anglo-Italian operation was planned to flush the enemy from the position with the support of a Royal Naval monitor firing into the wadi from the sea. The attack took place on 26 July. The Rolls-Royce armoured cars lined both banks of the wadi while the Australian Camel Corps and the Italians, who were equipped with some light Fiat cars mounting a machine-gun, fought their way down it from the top. The operation went entirely as planned and, after a brisk fight, the Senussi escaped down the wadi to the shore, led by Nuri Bey on his fine piebald horse. The wadi itself proved to be a treasure trove of munitions which were stored in caves closed by stout wooden doors. Obviously the Wadi Saal was the principal route through which the Turks supplied their Senussi allies and its loss was a serious blow to the enemy.

The Italians did not venture outside their perimeter at Bardia very often, but they regularly provided liaison officers to accompany the armoured car patrols which were now operating regularly on their territory. However, by the autumn of 1916 it was clear that the Senussi's power on the coast had been broken, although from time to time caravans with supplies destined for their southern strongholds were intercepted, many of the sacks containing, as one officer put it, 'a nourishing mixture of grain and cartridges'.

Plans were now made to recapture the oases which the Senussi were occupying in Upper Egypt. Said Ahmed, located at Dakhala with the remains of his army, was informed of these and withdrew to Siwa early in October. A motorized column took Dakhala on the 17th and by the end of November all the oases were once more in British hands.

At Siwa, however, Said Ahmed must have felt secure. The oasis lay 200 miles south of Mersa Matruh, much further than any army had ever dared penetrate into the desert. Moreover Siwa and its neighbouring oases of Girba and Jarabub lay in a valley some 1,000 ft below sea level and could only be approached by descending a difficult escarpment. While fertile, the valley was extremely hot and humid during the summer months and was a breeding ground for the malaria mosquito. Very few Europeans had visited the place, the most notable being the German explorer Ehrenberg.

Notwithstanding the difficulties involved, the British had decided to bring the Senussi War to an end with a motorized raid on the area. The troops detailed for the task included the Duke of Westminster's armoured car brigade and three light car patrols, the latter equipped with Model T Fords mounting a Lewis gun. The force, commanded by Brigadier-General Hodgson, assembled at Shekka, 185 miles south of Mersa Matruh, on 2 February 1917 and the next day attempted to force the difficult pass down to Girba while a flanking patrol was sent off in the direction of Jarabub.

The route wound its way between barren hills with numerous side gullies. No sign of the Senussi could be observed, but suddenly the leading cars came under intense small arms fire and the advance was halted.

Next morning the cars probed forward again, passing the site of the previous day's ambush. Progress was difficult and continued at a snail's pace, men having to continually move ahead of the cars and remove obstacles from the camel track with picks, shovels and crowbars. After some hours of this, the leading car was halfway round a bend when a shell exploded on the cliff above. The vehicle was half buried in the resulting rockfall and the crew wasted no time in racing for safety.

For some reason the Senussi gunners did not pursue their advantage, for two more cars arrived on the scene and, having attached their tow ropes, managed to extricate the vehicle with manual assistance from their crews. Too late the Senussi awoke to what was happening, for the car was safely back round the bend when their next shell landed precisely on the spot from which it had been recovered.

With difficulty two men climbed the cliff and hauled up a machine-gun after them. A Ford light car was sent round the bend and successfully drew the enemy's fire. The flash of the gun was spotted immediately and the machine-gun opened fire at once. The Senussi promptly abandoned their weapon and the cars continued their advance.

The cars came under fire from every direction when they emerged from the pass at the bottom of the escarpment. As control in an action of this sort was virtually impossible, each car fought its own battle against the almost invisible Senussi riflemen until its ammunition was expended. Some damage was sustained by tyres and in one instance a bullet penetrated the water jacket of a machine gun, the holes being quickly plugged with a cake of soap. The noise level was even greater than had been experienced at Bir Azeiz, rendering the majority of the men half deaf for several days afterwards.

At dusk the armoured cars retired and, after carrying out repairs and replenishment during the night, returned to the attack the following morning. By now the heart had gone out of the Senussi and no difficulty was experienced in dispersing the thin screen of riflemen, which melted away in the direction of Jarabub, covering the flight of Said Ahmed.

Rallying, the brigade drove on to Siwa. To the desert-weary crews of the armoured cars it seemed as though they had stumbled into the Garden of Eden and not even the squalor of the mud-built town could dispel this feeling; mile upon mile of palms stretched away to the east while avenues of fruit trees provided welcome shade and lakes of clear water sparkled in the sun. For their part, the

Model T Fords photographed near El Alamein, May 1916. Model Ts were used by the Light Car Patrols which operated in the Western Desert and, later, in Palestine (Imperial War Museum).

inhabitants of the oasis were equally startled by the appearance of the cars; few had even heard of, let alone seen, a motor vehicle, and while some stood rooted to the spot, others ran in horror to hide. The Siwa operation was the last to be carried out by the Duke's unit, and before returning to the high desert and the greater war against Turkey, its men were entertained to a lavish banquet by the Sheik. The operation finally broke the power of Said Ahmed who bowed to the will of his disgruntled followers and abdicated in favour of his more acceptable neutralist cousin Said Idris.

Lieutenant G. W. Richards of the Royal Welsh Fusiliers had joined the armoured car brigade shortly after its rescue of *Tara*'s survivors and took part in several of its subsequent operations. Occasionally he was required to visit the Italian garrison at Bardia and was astonished to discover how well it lived—to the point, in fact, where ladies were available to provide post-prandial entertainment of the more basic sort! He later transferred to a light car patrol with which he travelled as far south as Siwa and as far west as Bir Hacheim, little imagining that 25 years later he would command an armoured brigade

Traction engines were used to haul heavy artillery over suitably hard going (Imperial War Museum).

in a hard-fought action near the latter.

The Light Car Patrols established a set of desert-wise principles which hold good to this day. Good navigation was essential and once a route had been chosen no variation was permitted. A team of fitters and recovery experts accompanied each patrol in the manner of modern Light Aid Detachments; for emergency use air recognition panels were carried, as were at least two spare wheels per vehicle, and an adequate margin of petrol and water was always allowed for. In those days cooling systems were not pressurized and boiling was the rule rather than the exception. In such circumstances, the vehicles had the prior claim on the available water and if necessary the men were expected to go thirsty. As well as monitoring the activities of the now-quiescent Senussi, the work of the Light Car Patrols provided the Army with detailed maps which were used in the Second World War and a thorough knowledge of how men and machines could be made to operate efficiently in such harsh, demanding conditions.

CHAPTER 3

FIRST WORLD WAR (2)

Mesopotamia

As mentioned previously, the third element of British strategy in the Middle East had been the seizure of Basra and the Shatt-al-Arab waterway to protect the local oil supplies. These limited objectives had been secured without difficulty in November 1914 and subsequent counter-attacks were defeated with such comparative ease that the Government of India, responsible for this theatre of war, mistakenly assumed that the poor quality troops thus far encountered were representative of the Turkish Army as a whole and decided to extend the venture into an advance on Baghdad, the loss of which would seriously damage the enemy's prestige throughout the Muslim world. The nature of the terrain

A battalion of the Buffs on the march during the Mesopotamian Campaign. If many of the men seem scrawny by today's standards, this was balanced by lower expectations and extreme mental toughness (Imperial War Museum).

over which the advance would be made was recalled by the historian of the 14th Hussars:

> This great delta of the Tigris and Euphrates is peculiarly lacking in natural features. The great marshes encountered were generally too saline and brackish for the use of man and horse and as there was scarcely any other water away from the big rivers, military operations were considerably limited in consequence, and elaborate and prolonged outflanking movements were to a great extent unfeasible. In the great area between Basra and Daur, apart from Baghdad and a few riverine villages, there was not a tree. This lack of landmarks necessitated all moves being made by compass and affected tactics to the extent that there were no features to make the objective or bound, and there was no cover to provide shelter from view. Minor tactics were in consequence particularly simple. There was little opportunity of making use of ground and units advanced from one point to another in direct line. Lack of cover increased vulnerability and minimized the chance of effecting surprise; consequently, approach marches by night increased both in length and frequency.

In summer this wilderness became an anvil on which the sun beat down with such merciless intensity that temperatures in the shade—if any could be found—regularly soared above 120°. In winter torrential rain swelled the marshland and created ubiquitous mud in which sleep and rest were difficult to find. To the ever-present desert plague of flies the swamps added clouds of mosquitos which rose at dusk to torment and infect. Cholera and dysentery scythed their way through the ranks, while around the armies hovered vicious bands of Arab scavengers, in sight but invariably out of range, ready to murder stragglers, slit the throats of the wounded and vanish into the desert with their pickings. Mesopotamia may once have been the site of the Garden of Eden, but to those forced to soldier there there were times when it came close to their private imaginings of Hell.

In the spring of 1915, the British army in Mesopotamia was commanded by Lieutenant General Sir John Nixon and consisted of two Indian infantry divisions, the 6th and the 12th, and one cavalry brigade. Nixon had enjoyed a long and honourable career in the Indian Army, but many regarded him as impetuous, lacking in strategic sense and ambitious to the point at which his decisions were based on optimism rather than a cool analysis and thorough appreciation of the facts. Today it seems incredible that serious consideration was ever given to the despatch of so small a force hundreds of miles into the heart of a hostile empire, against an objective which was bound to be heavily defended, especially as the 12th Division as yet lacked its artillery, and river transport, supply and medical services were woefully deficient. Nonetheless, Nixon and his immediate superior, Sir Beauchamp Duff, the Commander-in-Chief India, were so influenced by events as to sanction the enterprise, the catalyst being provided by Major General Sir Charles Townshend, the commander of the 6th Indian Division.

Townshend, whom we last met at Omdurman, had first attracted public attention by his successful defence of Chitral Fort in 1895. He was courageous, professional, a good tactician and a sound strategist. Unfortunately, he was also narcissistic, driven by ungovernable ambition, and habitually sought place and preferment wherever they might be found. A master of the personality cult, he unhesitatingly subordinated his otherwise sound military judgement to the furtherance of his own interest, and for this his men would pay a terrible price.

In May, Nixon detailed Townshend's division to break through the enemy position at Qurna and advance up the Tigris to Amara, possession of which would, he felt, consolidate his hold on the Delta. The sudden collapse of Turkish resistance on the 31st was followed by the incident known as Townshend's Regatta. With a handful of troops hastily embarked, Townshend set off upstream in a strange assortment of craft, including the sloops HMS *Espiègle, Odin* and *Clio,* four armed launches

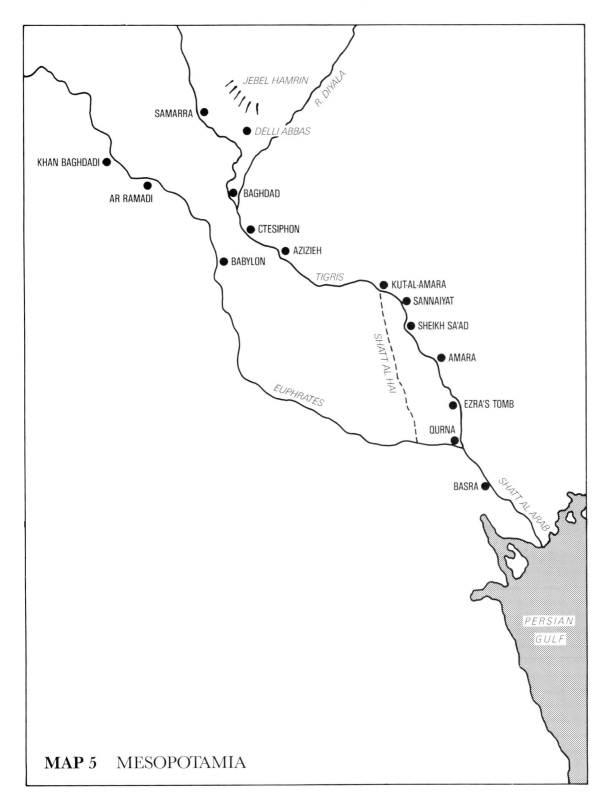

MAP 5 MESOPOTAMIA

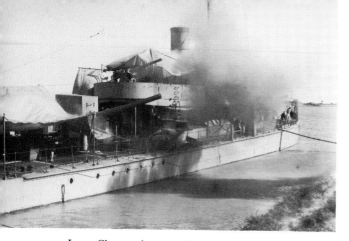

Insect Class gunboat providing fire support from the Tigris (Imperial War Museum).

Indian cavalry near Jebel Hamrin, Mesopotamia, December 1917 (Imperial War Museum).

and several smaller vessels. Ezra's Tomb was passed on 1 June and two days later the panic-stricken garrison of Amara, over 1,000 strong, surrendered. During the 80 mile advance a Turkish gunboat, *Marmariss,* had been disabled and the steamer *Mosul* captured.

Shortly after this remarkable success Townshend fell a victim to the climate and was sent to India to recover. By the time he returned Nasiriyah on the Euphrates had been captured and Nixon had decided that it would be necessary to press on up the Tigris and take Kut-al-Amara if the Basra enclave was to be really secure.

The Turks had constructed a formidable fortified zone on both banks some way below Kut and this was held by over 6,000 men with 30 guns under the command of Nur-ed-Din Bey. Townshend's eviction of them from a position which he described as resembling Torres Vedras was little short of brilliant. On 27 September he made a feint attack against the

Draw Swords! An entry in the sketchbook of Private Baggot, 14th King's Hussars, showing a counter-attack by the regiment during Townshend's retreat to Kut-al-Amara (Courtesy Regimental Association 14th/20th King's Hussars).

entrenchments on the right bank, causing Nur-ed-Din to transfer his reserves to meet it. Then, after sunset, two brigades crossed a bridge of boats six miles downstream and carried out a night march to fall on the flank of the Turkish positions on the left bank at dawn. After a hard fight the trenches there were taken and held against repeated counter-attacks. During the night the Turks pulled out and air reconnaissance the following morning revealed that they were retreating through Kut.

Having taken Kut, a ramshackle, dirty town situated on a peninsula, Nixon believed that the road to Baghdad lay open and obtained qualified permission to attempt its capture. To his credit, Townshend had serious reservations, commenting in his diary:

> We are now some 380 miles from the sea and have only two weak divisions, including my own, in the country. There is my division to do the fighting and Gorringe's to hold the line of communications from Kut to the sea. There is no possible support to give me if I receive a check and the consequences of a retreat are

not to be imagined. Thus, I feel it my duty to give my opinion plainly to the Army Commander, whether he likes it or not!

His signal to Nixon emphasized the difficulties, adding that the falling water level was making river transport extremely difficult. He further suggested that 'on all military grounds' the consolidation of the position at Kut offered a more sensible alternative and stated his considered opinion that an advance on Baghdad in anything less than corps strength would be attended by 'great risk'. Nixon would have none of it; the 6th Indian Division and the cavalry brigade were going to Baghdad, and that was that.

After spending five weeks preparing for the advance at Aziziyeh, Townshend set off. Even as his columns were trudging north Nixon received intelligence that 30,000 good-quality troops under the command of Khalil Pasha, one of the best generals in the Turkish service, were converging on Baghdad, and that the German Field Marshal von der Goltz had been appointed overall commander in Mesopotamia. Townshend was marching in-

Another of Baggot's sketches showing cavalry leaving the doomed fortress of Kut (Courtesy Regimental Association 14th/20th King's Hussars).

to a hornets' nest, but Nixon declined to reverse his decision.

At Ctesiphon, 30 miles from Baghdad, Nur-ed-Din had again constructed entrenchments on both banks of the Tigris. As the ground on the right bank was impassable in places, Townshend was compelled to mount a frontal assault on the two lines of trenches which had been dug opposite, concentrating the weight of his attack against the Turkish left flank. The battle which began on 22 November and continued for two days, was marginally a British victory, if a Pyrrhic one. The Turks sustained 6,200 casualties and were finally ejected, but Townshend's losses amounted to 4,600 of the 11,000 men engaged and his ammunition stock had dwindled alarmingly. On the morning of the 25th air reconnaissance reported fresh Turkish formations streaming out of Baghdad and he wisely decided to withdraw.

The wounded had gone ahead and the complete inadequacy of the medical services makes their story one of the most horrible in the annals of warfare. After hours of agonizing jolting in unsprung carts they were crammed so tightly aboard the steamer *Mejidieh* and two steel barges she was to tow that there was no room to move; nor was there any protection for them against sun and rain. When, days later, *Mejidieh* reached Basra under a cloud of battening flies, her deck and sides were covered with excrement, while to the stench of human waste was added the sickly smell of gangrene from untreated wounds. Those who began their ghastly journey without dysentery or cholera soon acquired one or the other from the infected water they were given. The affair generated a national scandal which guaranteed a dramatic improvement in the medical service, but for many who travelled aboard *Mejidieh* it was too late.

Meanwhile, Townshend's retreat continued, covered by river gunboats and the cavalry brigade. However, by 1 December the enemy had caught up and he turned to give battle at Umm-al-Tubal. The Turks launched a holding frontal attack while they attempted to turn his open desert flank, but this movement was thwarted by the cavalry and they drew back having sustained 1,500 casualties to the British 500.

Next day Kut was reached and the retreat ended. At this point Townshend's own ambition and burning desire for self-advertisement clouded his judgement, with tragic consequences. He had done extremely well so far but, having failed to capture Baghdad, he sought to compensate by re-creating the very conditions which had brought him honour and reward in his youth. No sooner had he entered the town than he signalled Nixon: 'I mean to defend Kut as I did Chitral.' In short, he was deliberately allowing himself to be trapped; Chitral Charlie had become Townshend of Kut. It has been suggested that the exhaustion of the infantry made a protracted halt, and therefore a siege, inevitable. Yet a few hours' sleep can work wonders and in a remarkably short space of time those same 'exhausted' infantrymen had dug six miles of trenches across the neck of the peninsula. Given that the majority of soldiers, offered the choice between digging or marching, will unhesitatingly opt for the latter, Townshend could easily have continued his withdrawal down river, had he chosen to do so. Here, as the Turks themselves were to demonstrate, excellent defensive positions existed and his troops could have been supplied, reinforced and relieved. Nixon, infallibly optimistic, nevertheless endorsed his decision and promised relief within two months at the most; needless to say, he lacked the means to make good his promise. In fact, Kut was not isolated until 7 December and when the cavalry brigade left the previous day it encountered no serious difficulties.

On the 24th the Turks attempted to storm the town but were so seriously rebuffed that von der Goltz decided that he would starve

"OUTPOST DUTY
(AT ALI-EL-GARBI) Dec 1915

Baggot's sketches captured the almost featureless nature of much of the Mesopotamian battlefield (Courtesy Regimental Association 14th/20th King's Hussars).

Townshend into surrender and concentrate on blocking attempts to relieve the beleaguered fortress. In this the terrain favoured him, for on the left bank of the Tigris the only approach lay along a narrow neck of land known as the Hanna Defile situated between the river and an extensive salt marsh in which movement was impossible, while on the right bank the ground was cut up by canals which in this, the wet season, proved to be a serious obstacle. Furthermore, after heavy rain the river, marshes and canals all expanded their bounds to further constrict the area of front which the British could attack.

Townshend deliberately dramatized the situation by stating that he had only one month's rations in hand. This prompted Nixon into ordering Lieutenant General Sir Fenton Aylmer, commanding the relief force, to make a premature attempt to break through. It failed, as did every subsequent attempt, Aylmer's requests that his attacks should coincide with a sortie by the Kut garrison going

unheeded. Soon names like Hanna, the Dujailah Redoubt, Sheikh Saad and Sannaiyat became as familiar as the most bitterly contested sectors of the Western Front as reinforcements reaching Mesopotamia were sucked into a killing match. In fact, Townshend's ration state did not become really critical until early April 1916. It was estimated that the garrison's daily requirement was 5,000 lb, and from 15 April onwards an attempt was made to deliver this by air drop. The actual lift capacity amounted to only 3,350 lb but as the heat severely affected the performance of the flimsy aircraft available there was always a shortfall. In the event, only 16,800 lb were delivered, and some of this consisted of such items of secondary importance as rifle pull-throughs.

While men were fighting and dying to relieve him, Townshend repeatedly requested his own promotion. It is an interesting comment of his psychology that when his rival, Major General Sir George Gorringe, was promoted on his appointment to succeed Aylmer, Townshend burst into tears in front of a startled subaltern.

In London the government was far from pleased that a comparatively minor operation, undertaken at the Admiralty's request, had been allowed to escalate to the point that it had become a new war front. Nixon was dismissed, his place being taken by General Sir Percy Lake, and the War Office assumed control of operations in Mesopotamia from the India Office.

On 24 April the steamer *Julnur* failed to break through to Kut with fresh supplies and was driven aground. By now 23,000 casualties had been incurred in abortive attempts to relieve a garrison numbering only 13,000 and it would have amounted to nothing less than criminal lunacy to have continued. That night Kitchener signalled Lake that further effort would not be justified and that unless he and his senior officers held contrary views he was authorized to open negotiations.

Townshend was advised during the early hours of the 26th and, unreservedly blaming the relief force, arranged a meeting with Khalil aboard the latter's launch, von der Goltz having died of cholera some days previously. Hoping to appeal to traditional Turkish susceptibilities, he offered £1 million in gold in exchange for the garrison's parole and the surrender of its guns. Khalil was interested but Enver Pasha wanted the prestigious General Townshend and his men as trophies and refused to sanction the arrangement, although the offer was doubled. The most the Turks would agree to was the exchange of 345 hospital cases for an equal number of fit prisoners and a promise that the garrison would be treated as 'honoured guests'. In all other respects the surrender was unconditional and the formalities were concluded on the 29th.

During their captivity, 7,000 of the 'honoured guests' died of starvation, disease, lack of medical attention or brutal indifference on the part of their guards. 'I must go into captivity with my troops, even though the heat will kill me,' Townshend had said. But he did not; instead, he allowed himself to be treated like visiting royalty during his journey to Constantinople and spent the remainder of the war in a luxurious villa on a pleasant island in the Sea of Marmara. For this he was never forgiven and when he returned home the War Office pointedly refused his requests for a fresh appointment. He died in 1924, his quest for fresh laurels having resulted in the very obscurity he so dreaded.

After the Kut débâcle the Mesopotamian Front remained quiet for several months. In August, Lake was replaced by Lieutenant General Frederick Maude, an officer whose temperament was the precise antithesis of those of Nixon and Townshend. Many found him cold and uncommunicative save for an unfortunate tendency to meddle in the internal workings of subordinate formations, but he was also a sound strategist and an able administrator whose plans left little to chance. He enjoyed the confidence of the War Office and therefore received most of what he asked for to avenge the recent defeat. Like Kitchener in the Sudan, he appreciated that the possession of a sound logistic infrastructure was essential if lasting successes were to be gained. This led to the completion of a narrow-gauge railway between Qurna and Amara and the arrival on the Tigris of a fleet of specially-designed shallow-draught P Class river steamers with which the army could be supplied. A flotilla of modern gunboats also arrived, as did an adequate artillery train and several Light Armoured Motor Batteries (LAMBs) equipped with Rolls-Royce armoured cars. By December, Maude's army consisted of two corps and a cavalry division of two brigades.

Meanwhile, Russian advances in Asia Minor and northern Persia had compelled Khalil to withdraw many of his troops from the Tigris, leaving only three divisions under

Kiazim Karabekir to hold the line. Kiazim, seriously alarmed by Maude's growing strength and anticipating that sooner or later he was to be attacked, requested reinforcements. Khalil, whose attention was concentrated on events in Persia, had formed a poor opinion of British troops and bluntly refused, commenting that the positions below Kut had proved impregnable and were likely to remain so.

Maude knew that Kiazim had deployed the whole of his command well forward, leaving nothing in reserve. The core of the Turkish defences still lay on the narrow neck of land on the left bank of the river, but their positions on the right bank were not so formidable and Maude decided to eliminate these one at a time, steadily working his way upstream past Kut, and then to cross. The effect of this indirect approach would trap his opponent

unless he had the foresight to withdraw in good time.

The British offensive began on 13 December with a feint attack on the left bank, causing Kiazim to concentrate his troops there. On the right bank Maude maintained a steady, step-by-step progress until by the third week of February 1917 the advance had reached a point several miles north of Kut. On 23 February the demoralized defenders of the left bank, having endured weeks of shelling from across the river, were finally driven from their trenches. Kiazim's decision to abandon Kut came too late for on that same day Maude's 14th Division crossed the river at Shumran Bend and put in a pontoon bridge. On the 24th the Cavalry Division crossed and passed through the infantry to find Kiazim's troops streaming across the neck of the peninsula, covered by a strong flank guard. This

Army Service Corps convoy of Model T Ford tenders, Mesopotamia, 1917 (Imperial War Museum).

Rolls-Royce armoured car of a Light Armoured Motor Battery attracts shellfire as it reconnoitres a Turkish wire entanglement. Mesopotamia 1917 (Imperial War Museum).

withdrew during the night and next day the cavalry became the spearhead of Maude's pursuit; unfortunately, thanks to conflicting orders from Maude himself, both brigades became bogged down in dismounted attacks against the enemy rearguard, which again pulled out after dark.

The 26th belonged to the gunboats HMS *Tarantula, Mantis* and *Moth* which sank two of their three opponents, *Pioneer* and *Basra,* and drove the third, *Firefly,* on to the bank. *Firefly* was one of the vessels which had been abandoned during Townshend's retreat from Ctesiphon and, having been towed off, she resumed her career under the White Ensign—by coincidence, under her original captain. At the Nahr Kellek Bend *Tarantula, Mantis* and *Moth* caught up with the marching enemy column and engaged it with the sustained fire of their main armament and automatic weapons, dispersing it and turning the retreat into a rout.

Since crossing the Tigris, 4,000 prisoners had been taken and it was obvious that Kiazim's army had reached the point of disintegration. An officer of the 14th Hussars wrote:

The Turkish dead littered the road. There was every sign of panic and rout—guns and carts abounded, bullocks still alive and unyoked, broken wheels, cast-off equipment, overturned limbers, hundreds of live shells of various calibres scattered over the country for miles. Every bend of the road told of confusion and flight. Here a wrecked field post office with Turkish money and notes circling in the wind; there office furniture, piles of books and documents; cartloads of small-arms ammunition, grenades, hats, boots, oil drums, things destroyed or half-destroyed and dead animals. A brand new Mercedes motor-car abandoned for lack of petrol was an item of interest to the

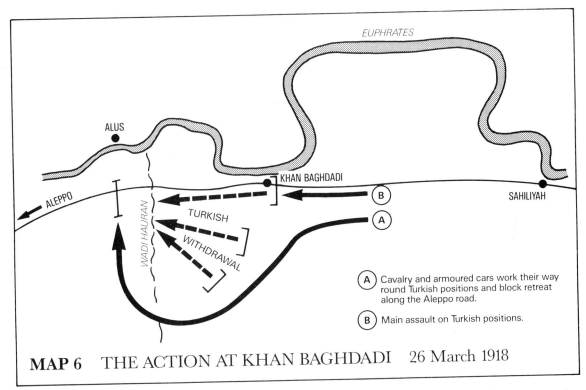

EUPHRATES

ALUS

ALEPPO

KHAN BAGHDADI

SAHILIYAH

WADI HAURAN

TURKISH

WITHDRAWAL

A Cavalry and armoured cars work their way round Turkish positions and block retreat along the Aleppo road.

B Main assault on Turkish positions.

MAP 6   THE ACTION AT KHAN BAGHDADI   26 March 1918

weary pursuers. White columns of smoke ahead, telling of further destruction, and enough litter by the road to keep an army in fuel for weeks. A whole battery of 12 cm field-guns was found half-buried, their breech-blocks removed.

After pausing for several days at Aziziyeh to consolidate his supplies Maude continued his advance on 5 March. At Lujj the Turks had attempted to form a new front but after a determined attack by the Cavalry Division they abandoned their trenches overnight in the belief that their flank was about to be turned. Next day the cavalry crossed the now-silent battlefield of Ctesiphon and by the evening of the 7th had reached the Diyala, a tributary of the Tigris which flowed in from the north-east. On the horizon were the domes and minarets of Baghdad itself.

Maude decided to employ the same tactics against Baghdad that he had used at Kut. While the 13th Division crossed the Diyala to mount a holding attack, the Cavalry Division

and two infantry brigades re-crossed the Tigris and began advancing up its right bank to by-pass the city. Khalil was conducting the defence in person and although his troops were offering determined resistance he was thoroughly unsettled by the cavalry's threat to his rear and managed to squeeze out of the trap which was closing round him. Maude entered the city of the Caliphs on 11 March to find it somewhat grubbier than legend or its distant prospect might suggest.

The British strategy now became one of offensive defence, designed to push the beaten Turks away from Baghdad to the north and east. A major threat was posed by Ali Ishan Pasha's XIII Corps advancing down the Diyala from Persia but this was contained by the Cavalry and 13th Divisions in a series of brisk actions at Delli Abbas and by the end of April Ali Ishan had begun to withdraw through the Jebel Hamrin. Elsewhere the advance upstream from Baghdad had continued, and Samarra was captured on 24 April. After this the onset of the hot season put an end to campaigning for several months.

On 18 November, Maude died of cholera. His death was deeply regretted throughout the army, especially in the 13th Division which he had led at Gallipoli. The troops had respected and trusted him and, despite his reserve, they had liked him too, for he was always concerned about their food, health and conditions and was notably quick to reward acts of bravery. He was succeeded in command by Lieutenant General Sir William Marshall.

During the last year of the war Mesopotamia assumed a lower priority for both sides. This resulted in part from British successes in Palestine which absorbed Turkish reinforcements originally destined for the Mesopotamian front, and in part from the sudden collapse of Russia, which required Marshall to detach troops for the defence of the Baku oilfields, an undertaking involving the establishment of a long and difficult line of communication across northern Persia and the Caspian. In spite of this additional heavy demand Marshall retained the initiative and throughout 1918 steadily extended his hold on the upper reaches of the Tigris and Euphrates.

These operations were marked by efficient co-operation between the cavalry and the armoured cars of the LAMBs, and by the regular use of motor transport for the infantry. For example, that directed against the Turkish position at Khan al Baghdadi on the Euphrates involved the 11th Cavalry Brigade, three LAMBs, two-and-a-half infantry brigades riding in 300 Ford vans, and supporting artillery, the whole commanded by Major General Brooking of the 15th Division. Prior to the main attack the cavalry and LAMBs worked their way round the enemy flank under cover of darkness and established themselves across the Aleppo road. When Brooking's infantry stormed Khan al Baghdadi on 26 March 1918 the Turks attempted to withdraw but found their retreat cut and

surrendered *en masse*. The cavalry and armoured cars then set off on a ruthless exploitation down the Aleppo road. The cars were soon out ahead and shortly after dawn on the 28th the 8th LAMB under the command of Captain D. Tod passed through 'Anah and were told that two British officer prisoners and their escort had left two hours previously. The two were Colonel J. E. Tennant, commander of the Royal Flying Corps in Mesopotamia, and Major P. C. S. Hobart of the Bengal Sappers and Miners, whose aircraft had been shot down while flying over Khan-al-Baghdadi on the 25th. Tod was ordered to pursue to a distance of 100 miles and told that aircraft would re-supply him with fuel if the need arose. He caught up with the party 32 miles from 'Anah and rescued the prisoners just as their escort was turning ugly and threatening to murder them. He then availed himself of the long-distance ticket he had been given and continued for a further 40 miles, returning with an assortment of German and Turkish notables and their papers. There can be little doubt that the episode influenced Hobart's post-war decision to transfer to the Royal Tank Corps and 20 years later it would be he who so thoroughly prepared what was to become the legendary 7th Armoured Division for desert warfare.

The war in Mesopotamia ended quietly when the armistice with Turkey came into effect on 31 October. In turn it had witnessed triumph and tragedy and from it many bitter lessons were learned. It had succeeded in its primary object of securing the Gulf oil supplies, albeit at far greater cost than had been anticipated, and it had absorbed a considerable proportion of the enemy's strength which could have been usefully deployed on other fronts; but for the events which led to the destruction of the Turkish army and caused Constantinople to sue for peace it is necessary to study the parallel campaign in Palestine.

CHAPTER 4

FIRST WORLD WAR (3)
The Arab revolt, Sinai and Palestine

If the Turkish attempt to create a running sore for the British in the Western Desert had failed, the reverse was true of the British attempt to do likewise for their opponents in Arabia. Here the Arab tribes, led by Sherif Abdullah and Emir Feisal, had broken out in full-scale revolt in June 1916, capturing Mecca and a number of ports on the Red Sea. British military aid to the rebels began to flow at once,

accompanied by a team of advisers, of whom the best remembered is the then Captain T. E. Lawrence.

The Arabs had failed to capture Medina, which was held by a tough, uncompromising old scoundrel named Fakhri Pasha, who had at least one massacre to his name. Military common sense dictated that holding the city was not an economic proposition, but as na-

Rolls-Royce tender of the Hedjaz Motor Battery at base camp. Lawrence was to comment that 'a Rolls in the desert was above rubies' (Imperial War Museum).

tional prestige was involved the Turks had no alternative other than to give Fakhri their full support. This involved the movement of supplies and reinforcements along the Pilgrim Railway, where they were clearly vulnerable. Lawrence, who gained in rank and stature following the capture of the port of Aqaba in June 1917, saw the Turkish weakness and decided to exploit it. His policy was to allow the railway to function, but only just. His raids, resulting in wrecked trains, captured stations, blown bridges and unusable track, suited the Arab temperament and ultimately resulted in no less than 25,000 men being pinned down in garrisons and blockhouses for little or no return.

There have been many attempts to analyse the complex, tortured personality of Lawrence, some unstinting in their praise, others resorting to simple denigration. Here it is only necessary to state that he believed profoundly in the Arab cause which he was supporting, enjoyed irregular warfare and excelled in its practice. Many, like S. C. Rolls, who had served under the Duke of Westminster in the Western Desert and often drove Lawrence in his Rolls-Royce tender, saw in him not the image of the desert mystic which the press would create in the years to come, but a rather more straightforward individual than isolated yet oft-recorded episodes within the legend might suggest to us, dedicated to the pursuit of his objectives and frequently spurning the stupidities of the military establishment in the process.

Francis Bacon had once written that 'He who commands the sea is at great liberty and may take as much or as little of the war as he will', and to this Lawrence added his own rider: 'He who commands the desert is equally fortunate.' He likened the operations of his desert army to those of a fleet at sea 'in their mobility, ubiquity, their independence of bases and communications, in their ignoring of ground features, of strategic areas, of fixed directions, of fixed points'. Lawrence, the 'Supreme Irregular', was speaking of irregular operations, and in this context his comments were entirely valid. Unfortunately, he came to be regarded as the fount of all desert wisdom between the wars and this qualification tended to be forgotten, the result being that for part of the Second World War his concept was applied to regular troops engaged in conventional operations, with extremely serious consequences for the British Army.

Despite their dislike of the Turks and a sincere wish to be rid of their rule, the majority of Arab troops serving with Lawrence fought only for gold and loot and were prone to disappear over the horizon in droves on the conclusion of a successful raid, the effect of a victory sometimes being as bad as that of a serious defeat. Without in any way wishing to diminish the Arabs' role in these events, it would shatter but few illusions to suggest that the only troops upon whom Lawrence could rely at all times were his small British motorized contingent. This consisted of the Hedjaz Armoured Car Battery with four Rolls-Royce armoured cars and five Rolls-Royce tenders, some of the vehicles and crews having seen previous service with the Duke of Westminster; a Light Car Patrol with six Model T Fords; and a Heavy Section which included two Talbot lorries each mounting a 10-pounder mountain gun, one Talbot mounting a Maxim Pom-Pom, and three Talbot tenders. In cost-effective terms, these vehicles achieved better results than the entire Arab army, but it must also be remembered that without the Arabs to fall back on they could not have been used at all.

Important diversions though they were, neither the Senussi War nor the Arab Revolt could in themselves hope to resolve the central contest between the British and Turkish armies. However, following the successful evacuation of Gallipoli and the arrival of Imperial troops, the year 1916 began with the now considerable British military presence in Egypt being formed into an Egyptian Expeditionary Force under the command of Lieutenant-General Sir Archibald Murray, who had recently held the post of Chief of the Imperial General Staff. Officially, British strategic policy was still to remain on the defensive but, stung by Kitchener's taunt 'Are you defending the Canal or is it defending you?', Murray was forced to think along more aggressive lines. Calculating that a renewed Turkish advance would have to enter Sinai through El Arish or El Kusseima, he decided to establish a 50 mile front between these two points. In more recent years, these dispositions have repeatedly been shown to be faulty, but in an era of only very limited mechanization the concept was perfectly tenable.

Nevertheless, before even this modest objective could be achieved much logistic groundwork had to be carried out and in this Murray was nothing if not thorough. Thousands of local labourers were engaged in constructing a standard-gauge railway from El Kantara on the Canal, and this advanced across the Sinai at the rate of 50 miles per month. In parallel, a fresh-water pipeline was laid, complete with storage tanks, a portable reservoir holding 500,000 gallons and batteries of standpipes. Beyond the railhead an efficient Camel Transport Corps supplied the forward troops; in addition, a logical casualty evacuation system was established to avoid the disgraceful and demoralizing episodes which had characterized the opening stages of the campaign in Mesopotamia.

Murray's slow, methodical movement across Sinai was made with his infantry close to the coast and railhead and his cavalry and camel troops covering the open desert flank. The cavalry was commanded by an Australian regular officer, Major-General Harry Chauvel, who has been described as the greatest leader of horsed cavalry in modern times. Most of his men were Australian Light Horse or New Zealand Mounted Rifles, trained to fight a fast-moving mounted infantry battle. By and large, they were taller, tougher and generally healthier than their British counterparts, many of whom had grown up in the deprived conditions of industrial slums. Naturally hard riders, they were mounted on large hardy horses known as Walers, a breed which stood up to the testing climate better than any other. A large proportion of the men were veterans of the Boer War or Gallipoli, or both. Their discipline, while effective, was informal and visiting British officers had, perforce, to become used to being hailed cheerfully as equals by troopers. The New Zealanders tended to be less extrovert than the Australians but were just as tough and formidable and their Mounted Rifles Brigade was considered by many Australians to be the finest cavalry formation in the Middle East. Both often took tremendous risks to maintain their unwritten law that no man, wounded or not, should be allowed to fall alive into Turkish hands.

Also present were British Yeomanry regiments who were more flexible in their approach than their regular cavalry counterparts, joined later by Indian cavalry regiments used to soldiering in hard climates. Chauvel was soon promoted to Lieutenant-General and his divisions were formed into a Desert

Horse artillery of the Yeomanry Division in Sinai, during the First World War (Imperial War Musuem).

Major-General H.G. Chauvel and the staff of the Anzac Mounted Division. Chauvel later commanded the Desert Mounted Corps and is regarded as the greatest cavalry leader of modern times (Imperial War Museum).

Mounted Corps, consisting of the Australian Mounted Division, the Australian and New Zealand Army Corps (ANZAC) Mounted Division, and the 4th and 5th Cavalry Divisions. The Australian Mounted Division was, at its own request, additionally trained with the sword, but the ANZAC Division was not, retaining its purely mounted infantry role. A regiment of French Chasseurs d'Afrique arrived to show the flag and performed well in action, although its North African Arab and Barb mounts found difficulty in keeping up with the big Walers of the Australian brigade to which it was attached.

Each division contained three mounted brigades, each consisting of three regiments, a mounted machine-gun squadron with 12 Vickers-Maxims, and a Royal Horse Artillery battery of three troops each equipped with four 13-pounder guns. Because of the divisions' unique character, the attachment of infantry was neither necessary nor desirable. Some divisions possessed an organic Light Car Patrol which could be used for forward reconnaissance, flank protection and other duties, and one or more Light Armoured

Motor Batteries (LAMBs), each equipped with four Rolls-Royce armoured cars, could be attached for specific missions.

Another formation which operated under Chauvel's command was the Camel Corps. This had a strength of 60 officers and 1,600 other ranks and was recruited mainly from the Australian Light Horse. It consisted of ten rifle companies, each equipped with five Lewis guns, a machine gun company with eight Vickers-Maxims, and an artillery battery armed with six 9-pounder pack mountain guns. During the advance across Sinai the Camel Corps, part of which had already seen action in the Western Desert, generally filled the gap between the marching infantry divisions on the coast and the mounted troops on the desert flank.

By way of contrast the army of Kress von Kressenstein, now effectively commanding the Turks' Sinai sector, consisted almost entirely of infantry. It was not, however, to be underestimated, for the tough, stoical Turkish soldier was notably stubborn in defence and a hard, vindictive fighter when he attacked. Kressenstein was fully aware of what was happening in Sinai and to him the British advance eastwards from the Canal looked very much like the start of an offensive rather than the extension of a strategic defence. At the end of July he decided to mount a spoiling attack against Murray's railhead, which had reached Romani. The progress of his 18,000 men, mainly good quality Anatolian troops and Gallipoli veterans, was, of course, regularly reported and when he launched his attack on 3 August he found the British waiting for him. After the Turks' opening assault had been blunted by the 52nd (Lowland) Division, Chauvel's brigades moved in to counter-attack from the south-west. Even so, the battle was so fiercely contested that for a while it was far from clear just who was attacking whom. An enthusiastic Australian brigade commander, riding along the firing line, encouraged his men with shouts of 'Stick to it, lads! They're retreating in hundreds!' At least one trooper, peering over the lip of his sand-scrape, had a very different perspective: 'The bastards were advancing in thousands!' Ultimately, it was the combination of ANZAC firepower and mobility which won the day. After the Turks had been forced off a vital ridge their will broke and large numbers threw down their arms. Kressenstein succeeded in effecting a difficult disengagement, but there could be no disguising the fact that for him the Romani venture had been an unqualified disaster involving the loss of 5,000 men killed and wounded and a further 4,000 captured. Total British casualties amounted to little more than 1,000.

The slow, measured British advance continued. On 21 December the Turks, worried by the possibility of a joint land and naval assault on El Arish, abandoned the town; it was promptly occupied and steps were immediately taken to incorporate it in the logistic pattern by constructing a pier on which supplies could be landed. Two days later, when Chauvel's cavalry and the Camel Corps stormed a strong position at Maghdaba, 20

miles up the Wadi El Arish, Murray had secured the base line for his strategic defence of Egypt.

One Turkish post remained on Egyptian soil, situated at Magruntein, some 25 miles beyond El Arish and just south of Rafah. The main feature of the position was a fortified hill known as The Redoubt, with its summit 200 ft higher than the surrounding country offering a good field of fire in every direction. On 9 January 1917 this was subjected to concentric attacks by the ANZAC Mounted Division, the Camel Corps and the British 5th Mounted Brigade (Warwickshire Yeomanry, Worcestershire Yeomanry and Gloucestershire Hussars). Attached to the Yeomanry brigade was the 7th (Australian) Light Car Patrol, which raced along the Rafah road, by-passing the main defences and then opened up with its Lewis guns on the Turkish machine gun posts. Despite this and the fact that they were virtually surrounded, the Turks held on and the usual bitter fire-fight was maintained for several hours. However, at 17:00 hours, with the Imperial troops actually making plans to disengage, the 1,600-strong garrison surrendered. British casualties were high for a comparatively minor engagement, amounting to 487.

David Lloyd George, the British Prime Minister, believed that the elimination of Turkey would have a domino effect upon the Central Powers and be followed in turn by the collapse of Bulgaria, Austria-Hungary and Germany. General Sir William Robertson, the Chief of the Imperial General Staff, did not altogether agree, but as he was violently opposed to the opening of a fresh offensive on the Western Front and Murray seemed to be doing rather well, he sanctioned further operations which, it was hoped, would result in the capture of Gaza.

Murray waited until his railhead had caught up with him and planned his attack to start on 26 March. His objective sprawled across a low hill about two miles from the sea and was dominated from the east by a ridge, topped by the shrine of Ali el Muntar, once a Templar church. To the south of the town lay three further ridges, from east to west the Sheikh Abbas, the Burjabye and the Es Sire. Everywhere the ground was broken up by numerous fig and olive orchards separated by huge and almost impenetrable cactus hedges. Relying on the natural protection afforded by these, the Turks had done little to fortify the town, which was held by only 3,500 men with 20 guns, the garrison being commanded by a German officer, Major Tiller.

The method adopted by Murray called for a conventional infantry advance on the left by the 53rd (Welsh) and 54th (East Anglian) Divisions, while the ANZAC Mounted Division swung round the eastern end of Sheikh Abbas ridge and advanced north in a wide flanking movement to enter Gaza from the north and north-east, taking the Ali el Muntar ridge in the process. Simultaneously, the Camel Corps and other mounted elements would screen the operation against Turkish intervention from the east.

The day began well, British movements being screened for several hours by a dense sea mist. An Australian serving with the 5th Light Horse, Ion L. Idriess, has left a graphic account of the ANZAC Division's attack:

We galloped straight towards massive walls of cactus hedges ten feet high and I wondered what calamity might happen when we struck those giant walls of prickly pear. The Colonel threw up his hand; we reined up our horses with their noses rearing from the pear; we jumped off; all along the hedge from tiny holes were squirting rifle puffs. The horse-holders grabbed the horses while each man slashed with his bayonet to cut a hole through those cactus walls. The New Zealanders had galloped by to the left of us, the 7th Light Horse were fighting on our right. Then came the fiercest excitement—man after man tore through the cactus to be met by the bayonets of the Turks, six to one. It was just berserk slaughter. The Turkish

Vehicles of No 12 Light Armoured Motor Battery and No 7 Light Car Patrol halted at the roadside near Aleppo during the closing stages of the Palestine campaign (Imperial War Museum).

battalion simply melted away; it was all over in minutes. Men lay horribly bloody and dead; others writhed on the stained grass, while all through the cactus lanes our men were chasing the demented Turks. Amateur soldiers we are supposed to be but, by heavens, I saw the finest soldiers of Turkey go down that day in bayonet fighting in which only shock troops of regular armies are supposed to have any chance. Bayonet fighting is indescribable—a man's emotions race at feverish speed and afterwards words are incapable of describing feelings.

Everything was jolly lively here. We fired down the streets of the suburbs, the great mosque was quite close, the bulk of Ali el Muntar was reverberating on our left above us, bullets were ricocheting off the trees, machine guns stuttering—our fellows were laughing and shouting what they would buy in the city shops.

Turks swarmed to counter-attack—confident, big chaps they were. I thought how fine they looked as in massed formation they came roaring out of a street—'Allah! Allah! Finish Australia!' Things looked desperate for us little crowd when way to the right we saw the felt hats of the 7th Light Horse—one man knelt down in the open, an officer levelled a Hotchkiss over the shoulder of the kneeling man and blazed away taking the massed Turks in the flank; they fell in writhing masses sprayed by the Hotchkiss bullets and melted away under the crossfire of the New Zealanders.

By dusk the 53rd Division had linked up with the ANZACs on Ali el Muntar ridge and both were looking down into the defenceless streets of Gaza. Incredibly, within minutes orders to withdraw were received. Furious officers demanded verification or written confirmation, but the orders were quite definite and had to be obeyed. To the Turks, their deliverance seemed little short of miraculous. Their morale soared and, having been reinforced, they counter-attacked the following day, driving the British back to the line of the Wadi Ghazze. In confused, muddled fighting the 7th Light Car Patrol again distinguished itself by engaging hull-down as it covered the withdrawal of the 3rd Light Horse Brigade from crest to crest. There were few other

bright spots for the bewildered and angry British and ANZAC troops. The First Battle of Gaza had cost them 523 killed, 2,932 wounded and 412 missing. Turkish losses amounted to 301 killed, 1,085 wounded and 1,061 missing.

The débâcle was the result of one of the worst command and communications failures of the war. The two senior officers responsible for the operation, Lieutenant-General Sir Charles Dobell in overall command and Lieutenant-General Sir Philip Chetwode in charge of the flanking attack, had established a joint headquarters at In Seiret, and as this was *15 miles* distant from Ali el Muntar, they naturally knew little of what was taking place; nor did their staffs take the trouble to find out. During the afternoon the two generals decided that if Gaza had not been physically captured by sunset the troops should disengage rather than risk being caught during the night between the garrison and the reinforcements which Kressenstein was already rushing up to the front. Also troubling them were quite groundless anxieties regarding the availability of water for the horses. Yet at 18:00 hours, approximately the same time that the withdrawal orders were issued, Tiller was in radio contact with Kressenstein, telling him that the position was desperate and that if further pressure was applied he would have to negotiate a surrender. The transmission was monitored in Cairo but, in spite of its critical importance, was not relayed to Dobell until midnight; by then the damage had been done.

Although Murray was not personally to blame, the responsibility was his. Used to reporting success, he was loath to admit failure, one of his despatches tripling the Turkish casualties and claiming that 'the operation was most successful and owing to the fog and waterless nature of the country round Gaza just fell short of a complete disaster to the enemy'. This was bending the truth with a vengeance. The King sent him a personal telegram of congratulation and Lloyd George, greatly heartened, pressed him to resume the attack. This he was most reluctant to do, but he was now well and truly caught in his own trap.

Kressenstein's first act following the conclusion of the March battle was to turn Gaza into a fortress by constructing an elaborate trench system to the south of the town among the orchards and cactus hedges. A series of redoubts with interlocking fields of fire was built along the Beersheba road, so preventing the sort of mounted flank attack which had so nearly succeeded on 26 March. Finally, Beersheba itself was also fortified.

Murray's options were thus apparently confined to a frontal assault, and this, perhaps unwisely, he entrusted to Dobell. Three infantry divisions would attack the Gaza trench system in line, the 54th on the right, the 52nd in the centre and the 53rd on the left. Their attack would have the support of eight tanks, the first ever to fight in a desert environment.

The tanks, obsolete Mark Is and IIs, were crewed by members of the original E Company Heavy Branch Machine-Gun Corps (later successively the 5th Battalion Tank Corps and 5th Royal Tank Regiment) and commanded by Major N. Nutt. As the specialist Nutt would have pressed the Tank Corps doctrine that the best results would be obtained by using his detachment *en masse*. Dobell, however, was not inclined to take advice and parcelled out the vehicles in penny packets to his divisional commanders, each of whom was clamouring for them.

The Second Battle of Gaza began on 17 April, the infantry suffering severely in conditions which now resembled those of the Western Front. Only two tanks were in action

HMLS Pincher *of the Gaza Tank Detachment attracts the curious. Less than 20 years separated the Battle of Omdurman from the tank's appearance in the desert* (RAC Tank Museum).

on this occasion, under the command of 54th Division; one was disabled by a direct hit, but the second penetrated the Turkish trenches north-west of Sheikh Abbas ridge and inflicted heavy casualties. Two days later the attack was resumed. On 54th Division's sector one tank attacked the Kirbet Sihan redoubt and the Turkish garrison surrendered, but just as the infantry arrived to take over the position the explosion of a shell severed a track and the vehicle had to be abandoned when a counter-attack recaptured the redoubt. Of the three tanks working with 52nd Division one ditched in a nullah, a second was knocked out clearing the last defenders from Outpost Hill, and the third covered the infantry's withdrawal when another counter-attack recovered the position. On the left, the attack of the 53rd Division was supported by two tanks, one of which broke a track before getting into action.

The other assisted in the capture of Samson ridge and went on to penetrate the formidable El Arish redoubt, where it remained for six hours, firing off no less than 27,000 rounds of machine gun ammunition. At the end of this period, with the infantry pinned down and unable to consolidate the gains which it had made, the vehicle came out of action with every member of its crew bearing some sort of wound.

The battle ended in a bloody reverse. British casualties came to 509 killed, 4,539 wounded and 1,576 missing; in addition, the Tank Detachment's losses amounted to 50 per cent. The Turks lost 402 killed, 1,364 wounded and 245 missing. Murray dismissed Dobell but on 11 June was himself told that he was to be relieved. This capable, intelligent officer who had brought his army across Sinai in good order, was neither the first nor the last desert

Anzac Light Horse inspect the wreckage of a Turkish column destroyed by air attack on the Nablus-Beisan road, September 1918 (Imperial War Museum).

general to become the victim of his own vanity.

His successor was General Sir Edmund Allenby, a former Inspector General of Cavalry who had commanded the Cavalry Corps during the vital First Battle of Ypres and had only recently commanded the Third Army at the Battle of Arras. Big and bluff, he was given to bellowing with rage when angry and, not surprisingly, was known as The Bull. He was also vigorous and energetic and he saw his first task as being the restoration of his new command's badly dented morale. To this end, he moved his General Headquarters from among the flesh-pots of Cairo to a more spartan site just behind the lines at Rafah, where he could exercise an efficient forward control and at the same time become a familiar figure to the troops. It was one of the hallmarks of his style of command that, just before an operation, he would personally visit and brief even the most junior formation so that its officers would understand exactly what was required of them.

Shortly after he had arrived, Allenby was told by Lloyd George that he wanted Jerusalem as a Christmas present. With reinforcements drawn from the Salonika front and the Aden garrison, the Palestine army rose in strength to three corps: the Desert Mounted Corps, XX Corps with four infantry divisions, and XXI Corps with three infantry divisions. The first problem was how to break the stalemate along the Gaza–Beersheba line. Always an apostle of mobility, Allenby willingly accepted a suggestion put to him by Chetwode, now commanding XX Corps, that the line should be turned by the capture of Beersheba. However, as the country to the south of the town was almost totally arid, the entire plan turned on water supply. The future Field Marshal Earl Wavell, who was to write a history of the campaign and later win one of the most remarkable series of desert victories ever, was serving as a staff officer in Palestine at the time, and he summed up the difficulties as follows:

When the question of transport and supply had been closely examined, it was found that the ruling factors were these: by the employment of all the transport available, including the trains (ie supply columns) of the three divisions opposite Gaza, the striking force could be supplied with food and ammunition up to Beersheba and for one march beyond; but it could only be supplied with water up to Beersheba; its further advance would be dependent on the water supplies at that place. The *rapid* capture of Beersheba therefore became the corner-stone of the whole plan.

Both Allenby and Chetwode have been sharply criticized for assuming that the Turks would permit them to capture the Beersheba wells intact. Nevertheless, in war it is rarely possible to eliminate the risk factor completely and the only alternative was the unattractive prospect of yet another frontal assault on the defences of Gaza.

Only Chauvel's Desert Mounted Corps possessed the speed and punch necessary to seize Beersheba by *coup de main* before the Turks could destroy the wells. The corps would carry out a long approach march through the desert and then launch an immediate attack on the town from the south east and east while XX Corps mounted holding attacks on the Turkish line to the west. To divert the Turks' attention a feint attack, supported by a heavy preparatory bombardment, was to be launched on Gaza itself by XXI Corps.

Allenby waited until his preparations were complete and did not strike until 31 October. Appearing out of the desert, the ANZAC and Australian Mounted Divisions were forced to overcome stiff resistance from the outposts of the 5,000-strong garrison, but in a dashing charge made in open order the 4th Light Horse Brigade swept over two lines of trenches and on into Beersheba itself. So shaken were the Turks by the onset of this torrent of thundering horsemen that many of them were subsequently found to have forgotten to lower the sights on their rifles. Resistance suddenly collapsed and most of the

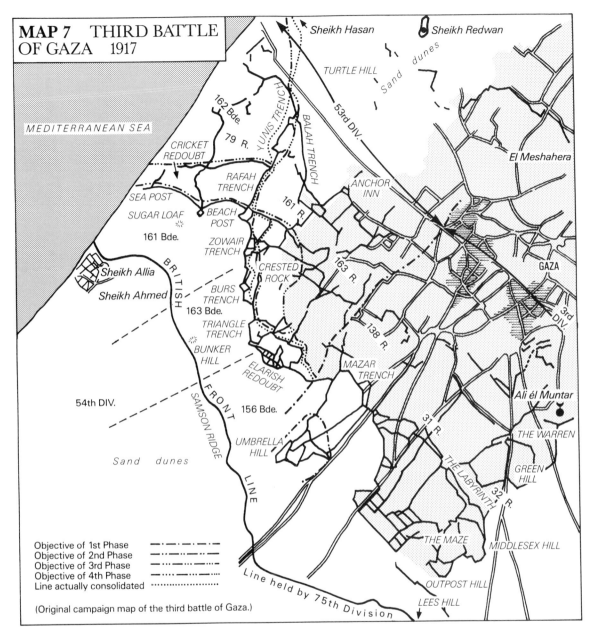

MAP 7 THIRD BATTLE OF GAZA 1917

MEDITERRANEAN SEA

162 Bde.

YUNIS TRENCH

79 R.

CRICKET REDOUBT

RAFAH TRENCH

SEA POST

SUGAR LOAF

161 Bde.

BEACH POST

161 R.

BALAH TRENCH

53rd DIV.

TURTLE HILL

Sand dunes

Sheikh Hasan

Sheikh Redwan

El Meshahera

ANCHOR INN

ZOWAIR TRENCH

CRESTED ROCK

163 R.

GAZA

Sheikh Allia

Sheikh Ahmed

BURS TRENCH

163 Bde.

TRIANGLE TRENCH

BUNKER HILL

ELARISH REDOUBT

MAZAR TRENCH

138 R.

3rd DIV.

BRITISH

54th DIV.

156 Bde.

UMBRELLA HILL

Ali él Muntar

THE WARREN

GREEN HILL

Sand dunes

SAMSON RIDGE

FRONT

LINE

31 R.

THE LABYRINTH

32 R.

THE MAZE

MIDDLESEX HILL

OUTPOST HILL

LEES HILL

Line held by 75th Division

Objective of 1st Phase — — — — —
Objective of 2nd Phase — ·· — ·· — ··
Objective of 3rd Phase — · — · — ·
Objective of 4th Phase — ··· — ··· —
Line actually consolidated ············

(Original campaign map of the third battle of Gaza.)

wells were captured intact.

The hinge had been knocked out of Kressenstein's line and XX Corps began pushing away the Turks to the north east. The Desert Mounted Corps was only able to carry out a limited exploitation to the north of Beersheba because the wells, although capable of maintaining a static garrison, proved to be in-

capable of supporting the demands of a continued advance. Even then, regiments in the line had to be relieved regularly so that they could return and water their mounts.

It was a completely unexpected success elsewhere which turned the enemy's defeat into a rout. The feint attack on Gaza, made by the 54th Division on a front of 5,000 yards between Umbrella Hill and the sea, had gone in during the night of 1/2 November and had broken clean through the defences. This was largely due to the fact that Allenby had placed the entire Tank Detachment, recently brought up to strength by the arrival of some Mark IVs, under the command of this single division, which planned to use them six up with two in reserve. The tanks crossed their start lines at 03:00 on 2 November, having to be guided forward on compass bearings because the moonlight was unable to penetrate the haze of dust and smoke thrown up by the bombardment and the Turkish reply. Two broke into the El Arish redoubt but became ditched in the maze of trenches. Two more broke into the Rafah redoubt; of these, one lost direction in the dawn mist and wisely rallied, to be joined by the other after it had tackled the Rafah, Balah and Yunis trench systems. A fifth tank had something of an epic run, capturing in succession Sea Post, Cricket Redoubt, Beach Post, Turtle Hill and Sheikh Hassan, where it dropped consolidation stores for the infantry, having broken through into open country. The Tank Detachment's casualties for the entire operation amounted to one killed and two wounded. Its influence had been decisive and although its achievements were eclipsed by the great tank attack at Cambrai later in the month, the results were more permanent. Allenby reinforced XXI Corps's success on the coast and, threatened by this and indirect pressure from the Beersheba flank, the Turks began retreating to the north. On 7 November the Ali el Muntar ridge fell with hardly a fight and the Third Battle of Gaza was over.

The pursuit lasted until 16 November, ending with the capture of Jaffa by the ANZAC Mounted Division. Twice the Turks attempted a holding action, first at Huj on 8 November and again at El Maghar five days later; on both occasions vigorous attacks by Yeomanry regiments pitched them out of their positions. On 14 November two armoured cars of the 12th LAMB charged into Junction Station, where the Jerusalem branch met the main line, and caught a Turkish battalion carrying out demolition tasks. Opening fire, the cars chased them out of the station and for two miles beyond, less than half the fugitives escaping.

Most of the British infantry divisions now became involved in heavy fighting in the Judean Hills. The Turks managed to slow the pace of the advance but were unable to halt it and on the morning of 9 December the last Turkish garrison of Jerusalem left the city; later that day the first British troops entered by the Jaffa Gate. On the 11th Allenby used the same gate to make his ceremonial but simple entry on foot to read a proclamation guaranteeing the safety of all religious institutions in the city. Lloyd George had received his Christmas present.

In military terms, the loss of Jerusalem meant little, but following the loss of the other Holy Cities of Mecca and Baghdad the moral damage to the Turkish cause was immense. The price of Allenby's 1917 offensive had been 18,000 casualties; it had, however, cost the Turks 25,000 men and it had severely shaken their morale. Kressenstein had been dismissed but his place was taken by General Erich von Falkenhayn, a former Chief of General Staff who had been responsible for the defeat of Romania the previous year. When the Gaza front had collapsed Falkenhayn was commanding a force of 14 divisions and the 6,000-strong German Asia Korps, which had been detailed for the recovery of Baghdad. This force was known as the Yilderim or Lightning Army Group, a title which provoked a wry humour among its German advisers, who were frequently driven to distraction by the leisurely pace at which their allies liked to conduct their affairs. Falkenhayn had always regarded Palestine as being potentially more dangerous than Mesopotamia, in which he doubted that the Yilderim could be adequately maintained anyway, and when the storm broke he had redirected his army group against Allenby. The rickety railway system had prevented it reaching the front before Jerusalem fell, but in the fighting to the north of the city he was able to establish something like a coherent defence. Further operations were brought to a standstill by the heaviest rains in living memory, the opposing lines eventually stretching from the sea to the Jordan Valley.

Whatever Allenby's intentions might have been for the spring of 1918, they had to be abandoned when a series of major German offensives almost succeeded in breaking through the Western Front, and he was forced to send reinforcements to help hold the line. When the situation in France and Flanders improved, two Indian cavalry divisions were despatched to Palestine, though without their statutory British regular regiment per brigade which were replaced by Yeomanry regiments on arrival. This increment brought Chauvel's corps up to its maximum strength and enabled Allenby to plan an autumn offensive, which he hoped would destroy the Turkish army at a stroke. The essence of the plan was to use the same indirect approach that had levered the Turks out of the Gaza–Beersheba line. An infantry breakthrough on the coastal sector would be exploited by the Desert Mounted Corps with a huge wheel to the right, severing the Turks' communications as it took the Upper Jordan fords as its objective.

To some extent, Allenby's plan was assisted by his opponent's dispositions. Falkenhayn had wished to execute a voluntary strategic withdrawal to the more easily defended watercourse of the Nahr Iskenderun, running through Tul Karm to the sea. However, he had fallen from favour and been replaced by General Liman von Sanders, head of the German Military Mission and successful defender of the Gallipoli Peninsula. Although he was himself a former cavalryman, Sanders's experience at Gallipoli had convin-

ced him that ground should be held at any price, despite the fact that in Palestine ground was of infinitely less value than in the Dardanelles. He therefore refused to sanction his predecessor's planned withdrawal, the result being that his right flank, the destruction of which was Allenby's first objective, still rested on the sea in a not especially favourable position some ten miles north of Jaffa.

Sanders had under his command three armies, none of which was stronger than a weak corps. Djevad Pasha's Eighth Army of 10,000 men and 157 guns included most of the Asia Korps and held a 20 mile front from the sea to Furqa. From Furqa to the Jordan Valley the front became the responsibility of Mustapha Kemal's Seventh Army, with 7,000 men and 111 guns. The trans-Jordan and desert flank was held by Djemal Kuçuk's Fourth Army, the strength of which was 8,000 men and 74 guns, including the German 146th Regiment. In immediate reserve were 3,000 men and 30 guns. General Headquarters was situated rather too far behind the front at Nazareth, connected to Eighth Army Headquarters at Tul Karm and Seventh Army Headquarters at Nablus by telephone lines which ran through a main switchboard at Afula.

Sanders' deployment had been made with static defence in mind and assumed that the British offensive would be mounted on the Jordan Valley sector. This was exactly what Allenby hoped he would think, and he had gone to considerable trouble to convince him of the fact. Dummy camps had been constructed from old, worn tents; dummy gun parks and battery positions were made from old wheels, pipes and logs; dummy horses were assembled from wood and canvas and arranged in formal horse lines; and, to give the whole the appearance of life-like bustle the ANZAC Mounted Division had moved into the area to simulate the presence of the entire Desert Mounted Corps. Simultaneously, Lawrence's Arab army, advancing north through the desert on Allenby's right flank, had intensified its efforts against the railway, particularly against the vital junction at Der'a, through which all rail traffic into Palestine had to pass.

The success of Allenby's deception enabled him to effect the secret concentration of Lieutenant-General Sir Edward Bulfin's XXI Corps (54th, 60th, 75th, 3rd Indian and 7th Indian Divisions), the Desert Mounted Corps (4th and 5th Cavalry Divisions and the Australian Mounted Division) and a small French contingent on a 15 mile sector close to the coast. Along the remaining 45 miles of front he had only the two divisions of Chetwode's XX Corps (10th and 53rd) and the troops in the Jordan Valley.

The railhead from Egypt had now reached Lod and the problem of water supply was no longer as grave as it had been. On the other hand, with cavalry horses consuming an average of 20 lb of feed a day, animal transport would be too slow to meet divisional requirements for long in the sort of sweeping, fast moving operation that was envisaged and a fleet of lorries had been assembled and organized to cope with the demand.

In addition, Allenby intended using the air component of his army, consisting of seven squadrons equipped with Bristol Fighters, SE5As, DH9s, some Nieuports and a single Handley Page bomber capable of carrying 16 112 lb bombs, to decisive effect, first by destroying Sanders' command telephone links and then by continuous strafing of Turkish columns behind the front, so paralysing the enemy's communications when they were at their most vulnerable.

The battle, which was to take its name from the historic battlefield of Megiddo some miles to the north, began on 19 September. At 04:30 the combined artillery of the XXI and Desert Mounted Corps erupted in a whirlwind bombardment at the peak of which 1,000 shells per minute were exploding on the Turkish positions. Then, as the guns shifted their fire to targets in the rear, Bulfin's infan-

try swamped the stunned defenders of Djevad's trenches. Immediately these had been secured Chauvel's mounted columns picked their way through and galloped out into the open country beyond. The infantry divisions themselves then effected a wheel to the right, rolling up the shattered fragments of the Eighth Army.

At first light the RAF eliminated the central telephone exchange at Afula, leaving Sanders groping in a fog of war in his distant headquarters at Nazareth. Not until noon was he able to talk to Kemal over the restored line to Nablus, but Kemal was only able to tell him that Djevad had been routed and that since the right flank of his own Seventh Army had been irrevocably turned he too would have to withdraw; the one definite piece of intelligence he could provide was that the mass of Allenby's cavalry was advancing rapidly towards the Plain of Esdraelon.

If Sanders had known this earlier he could have denied Chauvel entry to the Plain by directing his reserves to hold the Musmus Pass through the Mount Carmel range. As it was, the lost hours enabled the British to seize the Pass before its defences could be organized, thereby eliminating any chance the remnants of the Eighth Army might have had of retreating to the north. All that was left of Djevad's command, a hopeless jumble of men, animals, guns and vehicles, streamed across the rear of Seventh Army, complicating the latter's own withdrawal, to be caught by the RAF strung out along the Tul Karm-Mus'udye road and bombed and strafed to destruction.

For neither victors nor vanquished was there to be any rest that night. At 05:30 on 20 September the 5th Cavalry Division's 13th Brigade galloped into Nazareth itself, overcoming fierce but hopeless resistance from the German and Turkish GHQ Staff. Sanders narrowly avoided capture and managed to reach Tiberias by car; in later years he was to deny strenuously the persistent legend that he had made good his escape clad only in his pyjamas! Elsewhere during the day the 4th Cavalry Division took Bet Shean and the Australian Mounted Division Jenin, both lying on Seventh Army's line of retreat. Kemal fought a skilful rearguard action against the British infantry but he was now in danger of being completely surrounded and after dusk he began to withdraw towards the Jordan along the Wadi Far'a. The RAF discovered his columns at dawn on the 21st and Lawrence describes the result:

The modern motor road, the only way of escape for the Turkish divisions, was scalloped between cliff and precipice in a murderous defile. For four hours our aeroplanes replaced one another in series above the doomed column; nine tons of bombs and 50,000 rounds of small arms ammunition were rained upon them. When the smoke had cleared it was seen that their organization had melted away. They were a dispersed horde of trembling individuals, hiding for their lives in every fold of the vast hills. Nor did their commanders ever rally them again. When our cavalry entered the silent valley next day they would count 90 guns,

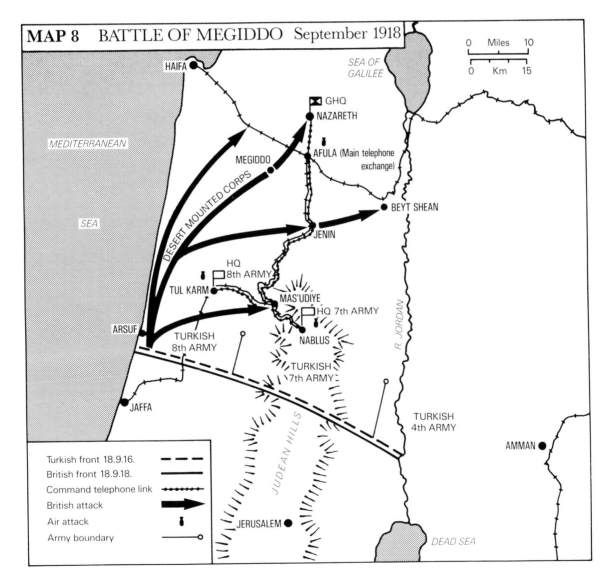

MAP 8   BATTLE OF MEGIDDO September 1918

Turkish front 18.9.16.	-----
British front 18.9.18.	———
Command telephone link	••••••
British attack	➡
Air attack	↟
Army boundary	——○

El Kantara marshalling yard, the start of the Trans-Sinai Railway (Museum of Army Transport).

50 lorries and nearly 1,000 carts abandoned with all their belongings. The RAF lost four killed; the Turks lost a corps.

This was the first occasion in history when unaided air power completed the destruction of an army.

It had taken Allenby a mere two days to smash two of his opponent's three armies, taking 25,000 prisoners in the process. The fugitives from the battle streamed across the Jordan fords and up the road to Damascus. Sanders strove to construct a new line based on the confluence of the Yarmuk and Jordan Rivers but this was soon broken when the 4th Light Horse Brigade captured Samakh after a hard fight on 25 September.

Djemal Kuçuk's Fourth Army, now isolated, survived only a little longer. Major General E. W. C. Chaytor had already led the ANZAC Mounted Division, an Indian and a Jewish brigade across the lower reaches of the Jordan and received the surrender of the en-

tire Turkish corps defending Amman without a shot having to be fired. Lawrence's Arabs, driven to blind fury by Turkish atrocities in one of their villages, captured Der'a on the 27th and indulged in an orgy of slaughter and mutilation which even extended to the patients and crew of a hospital train. When the 4th Cavalry Division reached Der'a the following day its commander, Major General Sir George Barrow, was revolted by the Arabs and took an instant dislike to Lawrence, although to be fair, he met both in circumstances which were quite unrepresentative. Whatever his feelings, Barrow was stuck with his new allies for Allenby ordered his division to swing north with them and go hard for Damascus along the railway and parallel road.

The 5th Cavalry and Australian Mounted Divisions were also converging on Damascus along the axis Kuneitra–Sa'sa–Kau Kab, having passed between the Sea of Galilee and Lake Hula. The only troops upon whom Sanders could now rely to provide an effective rearguard were the survivors of the Asia Korps, of whom Lawrence wrote,

> For the first time I grew proud of the enemy who had killed my brothers. They were 2,000 miles from home, without hope and without guides, in conditions mad enough to break the strongest nerves. Yet their sections held together in firm rank, sheering through the wreck of Turk and Arab like armoured ships, high-faced and silent. When attacked they halted, took position, fired to order. There was no haste, no crying, no hesitation.

Damascus was not defended and was entered on 1 October. A few miles north-west of the city the Australian Mounted Division trapped the remnants of the Turkish army in the Barada Gorge and pounded it until the road was blocked with wreckage and bodies.

Despite the capture in rapid succession of the ports of Haifa, Acre and Beirut, lengthening lines of communication were beginning to affect the British logistic situation and Allenby decided to limit the size of his pursuit force to Major General H. J. MacAndrew's 5th Cavalry Division and the Arabs. MacAndrew's advance was led by a spearhead force, known as Column A, consisting of the 15th Cavalry Brigade plus three attached LAMBs and three Light Car Patrols, giving the necessary speed, punch and firepower, while the rest of the division followed as quickly as possible and deployed for action as and when needed. Only scattered, local opposition was encountered and on 26 October the armoured cars entered Aleppo to find that it was already in Arab hands. Three days later Muslimie Junction, through which passed the rail lifeline to the Mesopotamian front, was also captured. On 31 October Turkey requested, and was granted, an armistice.

In the 38 days which had elapsed since the start of the Battle of Megiddo, Allenby's troops had destroyed three Turkish armies, advanced 350 miles, and captured 76,000 prisoners, 360 guns and 89 locomotives; no accurate figures are available for the numbers of enemy killed and wounded. This victory, as complete as any in history, had been won at a cost of 782 killed, 4,179 wounded and 382 missing. Lawrence added a characteristic footnote to the campaign by removing the Kaiser's gilt wreath from Saladin's tomb and sending it home with a note to the effect that the deceased had no further use for it; it reposes today within the Imperial War Museum.

It is sometimes forgotten that together the desert campaigns of the First World War involved an approximate cumulative total of 98 months' fighting, while the North African campaign of 1940-43 lasted for only 35 months. Because, with the notable exceptions of Kut and Gaza, the density of barbed wire and number of machine guns and artillery weapons per mile of front had never approached comparison with the Western Front, the key elements had proved to be mobility and logistics. Armoured cars had proved their worth throughout and tanks had made a brief but important appearance in 1917. During the final phases the motor lorry had ceased to be simply a supply vehicle and was being used regularly for the operational transport of infantry in mechanized columns. In the air, reconnaissance aircraft had forced the desert to give up its secrets and although the first attempt to supply a besieged garrison by air had not succeeded, the destruction of the Turkish Seventh Army by ground strafing provided a notable landmark in the history of air warfare. By October 1918 the picture was almost complete and battles such as Third Gaza, Khan-al-Baghdadi and Megiddo clearly projected the form desert warfare would take in an era of total mechanization.

CHAPTER 5

'FOX KILLED IN THE OPEN'

Under the terms of the peace treaty imposed by the Allies, large areas of the former Turkish Empire passed under British and French control, the British being responsible for Palestine, Transjordan and Mesopotamia (renamed Iraq), and the French for Syria. The transfer was far from welcome to many of the inhabitants of these territories and sporadic fighting continued until 1920, but the combination of aircraft and armoured cars proved effective in suppressing local revolts. During March 1922 a Colonel Lindsay, commanding No 1 Armoured Car Group in Iraq, carried out an interesting joint exercise with the Royal Air Force in which 17 of his vehicles remained in the desert for three weeks, relying entirely upon aircraft for re-supply, daily requirements being transmitted by a Rolls-Royce fitted with radio to RAF ground stations up to 200 miles distant.

The cost of maintaining large garrisons in these volatile territories was a matter which caused the British Government considerable concern until Air Marshal Sir Hugh Trenchard, the Chief of Air Staff, suggested that they could be more economically controlled by 'air policing', backed up by armoured cars and locally controlled levies. The idea was accepted, and in October 1922 Iraq became the first of several territories to become the RAF's responsibility. The attitude of the Army was less than helpful to the new service and the RAF was forced to form its own armoured car

companies, although a number of veterans who had served in LAMBs and LCPs during the war, and subsequently with the Tank Corps, elected to transfer because they enjoyed their work. The next decade was indeed full of interest, for in addition to the continuous task of keeping the peace between rival tribes and their rulers, the RAF armoured car companies also set up emergency landing ground, supply dumps and navigation markers for the trans-desert flights of Imperial Airways as well as organizing overland mail routes.

The policy of air policing was also followed to a lesser degree by the French and Spanish in Morocco against Abd el Krim's Riffs. In Libya, where a state of almost continuous friction existed with the Senussi, the Italians introduced a vicious refinement to the method by flinging their more important captives out of aircraft high above the desert, in full view of their own people. As might be expected, such means, far from acting as a deterrent, were counter-productive in their effect.

In Egypt the British garrison resumed its peacetime routine and, as men left the colours with the passing of the years, much of the desert lore and experience accumulated during the First World War went with them. There were, however, new arrivals who were drawn to the desert and welcomed its challenge, and prominent among these was Major Ralph Bagnold, who had been commissioned into the Royal Engineers in 1915, served on the Western Front and transferred to the Royal Corps of Signals in 1920. Bagnold assembled a group of like-minded individuals, soldiers and civilians, men and women, and with them set out on a series of trips from Cairo into the Sinai or to Siwa Oasis, gradually extending the range of his travels until by the mid-1930s his group was embarking on journeys of 6,000 miles. Operating as it was on a niggardly budget, the Army provided no support for such ventures, which were undertaken in the participants' spare time and at their own expense. On average, these trips cost £100 per head, a not inconsiderable figure at a time when £500 was regarded as being a very reasonable annual salary, but some assistance was provided by occasional contributions from the Royal Geographical Society. Bagnold's group improved the sun compass, developed the condenser so that water from boiling radiators would not be lost, evolved various means of extracting vehicles stuck in dunes, soft sand and salt flats, including the lightweight sand channel, and learned how to calculate the probable fuel consumption on any type of going and how to fix their position by the stars. Probably no man alive knew more about the topography of the Western Desert than Bagnold and when the moment came he was to form the most famous of all desert elites, the Long Range Desert Group.

The Abyssinian Crisis of 1935 left no room for doubt that the Fascist dictator Benito Mussolini had extravagant territorial ambitions in Africa and led directly to the formation of a mechanized group known as the Matruh Mobile Force. In fact, the only mobile elements of this were the 11th Hussars with armoured cars, the 7th Hussars with light tanks and the 8th Hussars riding in lorries, the whole concept being dubbed the 'Immobile Farce'. By degrees, however, more armour became available, as did a motorized infantry battalion, an artillery regiment and organic support units and the force was re-

designated the Mobile Division Egypt. In August 1939 it consisted of an armoured car regiment (11th Hussars), a Light Armoured Brigade (7th and 8th Hussars with light tanks), a Heavy Armoured Brigade (1st and 6th Royal Tank Regiments, the former with cruiser tanks and the latter with light tanks and cruisers), a Pivot or Support Group consisting of the 1st Battalion King's Royal Rifle Corps and the 3rd Royal Horse Artillery with field and anti-tank guns, a supply company and a field ambulance. It had also become a thoroughly trained organization which had been brought to a high pitch of efficiency by its commander, Major-General P. C. S. Hobart, the same officer who had been rescued by the 8th LAMB in the aftermath of the action at Khan al Baghdadi in Mesopotamia.

After the First World War, Hobart had transferred to the then Tank Corps and had been involved in the Army's early experiments with armoured formations, which had convinced him that the tank had become the weapon of decision. When he assumed command of the Mobile Division Egypt in 1938 he immediately began to prepare it for war with a series of demanding exercises which tested men and machines to the limit, his primary purpose being to produce a formation capable of executing the sort of operations he envisaged in a desert environment. He was a hard taskmaster who did not suffer fools *at all;* those who actually served under him describe the experience as being 'absolute hell', although they also comment that he was capable of many acts of individual kindness. He was, too, a difficult subordinate who could be blunt to the point of insult. Added to this, his ideas were as yet untested and neither General Sir Archibald Wavell, the Commander-in-Chief Middle East, nor Lieutenant-General Maitland Wilson, commanding the British troops in Egypt, felt that it was in the general interest to continue to employ a senior formation commander whose thoughts apparently revolved around the tank

Gloster Gladiators overfly their desert airfield, 1940. When Italy declared war the Royal Air Force could muster only a handful of these fighters, some Blenheim light bombers, plus a few Wellington and Bombay medium bombers (Imperial War Museum).

to the exclusion of all other arms. In September 1939 this irascible genius was dismissed and returned home to leave the Army. He was serving as a Lance-Corporal in the Home Guard when Churchill decided to recall him and he later raised and trained the 11th and 79th Armoured Divisions, commanding the latter in Europe.

Hobart's successor as commander of the Mobile Division Egypt was Major-General Michael O'Moore Creagh, a cavalryman. Creagh recognized the value of his inheritance and wisely continued with the training programme. In February 1940 his command was re-designated 7th Armoured Division and about the same time he introduced the jerboa or desert rat as the divisional sign, so emphasizing that the desert was its natural element.

On 10 June 1940, with France all but

beaten to her knees and the neglected resources of the United Kingdom stretched to their limit, Mussolini declared war on the Allies, remarking cynically to his Army Chief of Staff, Marshal Pietro Badoglio, that he 'needed a few thousand dead so that he could sit at the conference table as a man who has fought'. The implications for British interests in the Middle East were grave, for Wavell had only 50,000 under-equipped troops to cover a vast area stretching from the Syrian border to Somaliland, of which only 36,000 were available for the defence of Egypt and the Suez Canal. Against this was arrayed a 250,000-strong Italian army in Libya, while in East Africa a further 200,000 men were poised to strike into the Sudan, Kenya and British Somaliland. At sea, the Royal Navy had the advantage of being able to deploy two aircraft carriers and could oppose seven battleships to the enemy's six, but in every other class of warship the Italian strength was apparently as disproportionately overwhelming as it was on land, 21 cruisers being matched against eight, 50 destroyers against 37 and 100 submarines against eight. In the air the Regia Aeronautica could put up some 2,000 aircraft against the handful of more or less obsolete types possessed by the RAF and the Fleet Air Arm. Furthermore, following the surrender of France on 22 June, most of the Mediterranean coastline was either in enemy hands, or belonged to neutral powers who were unsympathetic to Britain or potentially hostile towards her. The French, for example, were extremely bitter about the Royal Navy's neutralization by force of their battle squadron at Mers-el-Kebir, near Oran, on 3 July, involving as it did the destruction of ships and heavy loss of life. In Spain, Franco owed debts to Hitler and Mussolini for their assistance during the Spanish Civil War and would, at the very least, close the Straits of Gibraltar if he felt that an Axis victory could be guaranteed, and, as a preliminary step towards this he occupied the International Zone of Tangier two days after Italy's declaration of war, carefully defining his status as that of a 'non-belligerent'. Both politically and militarily, therefore, the situation demanded an early Axis offensive in the Middle East, the prizes being the acquisition of its oil supplies and the severing of Britain's shortest trade route to the Far East. Inevitably, the success or failure of such an offensive would depend on the outcome of fighting in the Western Desert.

In Egypt, the highly-trained but still incomplete 7th Armoured Division was immediately available, along with the 4th Indian Division and two infantry brigades, one of which was permanently engaged on internal security duties among the anti-British population, while in Palestine the 6th Australian Division was assembling. The troops Wavell was actually able to deploy in the Western Desert amounted to a single weak corps and never rose above this level during the ensuing campaign, although their professionalism and use of mobility went far to offset the discrepancy in numbers between themselves and their opponents. The quality of the Italian army group in Libya, commanded by Marshal Italo Balbo, was less satisfactory, for in essence it was an infantry army which was chronically short of mechanical transport and still relied to some extent on pack animals for its supplies. Each infantry division did possess its own organic tank battalion, but this was

By the end of September 1940 an air-ferry route had been established across Africa from the Gold Coast (Ghana) to Egypt and the first modern Hurricane fighters were beginning to arrive in the Middle East. This photograph, taken only days before the start of Operation Compass shows how the almost universal 'vic' of three aircraft had given way to the more flexible 'finger-four' developed during the Battle of Britain (Imperial War Museum).

equipped with L3 tankettes which had no place in the tank battle and, being armed solely with machine-guns, were barely capable of destroying their own kind. Early in July the I and II Battalions of the 4th Tank Regiment, equipped with 70 badly designed M11/39 medium tanks, also arrived in Libya. The Italian artillery was obsolete, many of its guns dating from the First World War, and its lack of a modern anti-tank gun was to prove a fatal handicap, although morale among the gunners themselves was high and they invariably fought to the muzzle. In general, however, the relationship between officers and men in the Italian service was poor, the former receiving privileges which were not matched by responsibilities to their troops and tactlessly included better rations in the field. The Italians, too, had lost none of the defensive mentality they had shown during the Senussi War a generation earlier, and had heavily fortified Tobruk and Bardia as well as building a string of frontier forts at Capuzzo, Sidi Omar and Maddalena.

The troops detailed to defend Egypt against Italian attack were designated Western Desert Force and placed under the command of Lieutenant-General Richard O'Connor. A light infantryman, O'Connor had served with great distinction on the Italian Front during the First World War and was a recipient of the Italian Silver Medal for Valour. He understood how his former allies thought and how much they disliked surprise in every form, especially if operations were directed against their flanks or rear. He was determined to dominate the frontier zone by aggressive patrolling and, on the day of Italy's declaration of war, elements of the 7th Armoured Division were ordered to push through the barbed wire entanglement marking the border, generally referred to as The Wire, and raise hell in the broadest possible sense beyond. Simultaneously, RAF Blenheims raided the Regia Aeronautica's base at El Adem, south of Tobruk, causing heavy

Lieutenant-General R.N. O'Connor, commander of Western Desert Force during Operation Compass and its sequel. On 1 January 1941 Western Desert Force became XIII Corps (Imperial War Museum).

damage.

The regiment most continuously involved in the opening phase of the war was the 11th Hussars, commanded by Lieutenant-Colonel John Combe. The Eleventh, otherwise known as the Cherry Pickers, were instantly recognizable by their badgeless brown berets, and were equipped with 1924-pattern Rolls-Royce armoured cars mounting a Boys anti-tank rifle and Bren light machine-gun, plus similarly armed but roomier Morris armoured cars in squadron and regimental headquarters. They had been one of the first regular cavalry regiments to be mechanized, although as events were to show this in no way inhibited their traditional sense of style and dash.

During the evening of 11 June, a patrol under Lieutenant Miller ambushed a convoy of four lorries heading for Sidi Omar. After a short exchange of fire two Italian officers and 50 Libyan soldiers surrendered, the former protesting vehemently against the use of 'neutral' Egyptian territory as a base for such aggressive acts. The following day the two small forts at Sidi Omar were found abandoned and gutted, but when a troop attempted to shoot its way into Fort Maddalena it was driven off by concentrated machine gun fire then subjected to an hour's bombing and strafing by Italian aircraft, from which it emerged unscathed. It was decided that the whole of the Eleventh's A Squadron would attack Maddalena on the 14th in the wake of a raid by Blenheims, but when the bombers arrived to pulverize the defences most of the garrison had already pulled out and the remainder surrendered to the cars after a token resistance. Simultaneously Fort Capuzzo, covering the approach to the fortress of Bardia from the British frontier position at Sollum, capitulated following a brief exchange of gunfire with a force consisting of the 7th Hussars, whose light tanks had been supplemented by some cruisers, and a motorized KRRC company. However, at the fortified

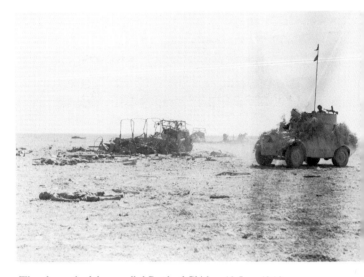

The aftermath of the so-called Battle of Ghirba, 16 June 1940, in which an Italian column was wiped out by elements of the 7th Armoured Division. In the background is the wreckage of an L3 tankette, blown apart by an internal explosion. The armoured car is a Morris, used by 11th Hussars as regimental and squadron command vehicles (Imperial War Museum).

post of Sidi Azeiz some way to the north, the Italians held their own against the 7th's light tanks and the armoured cars of the Eleventh's C Squadron. An L3 tankette company mounted a counter-attack on the latter as they withdrew but broke contact after one of their number had fallen victim to an anti-tank rifle. Next day an 11th Hussar patrol ran down a staff car containing a portly engineer general and his two lady companions, out for a spin; in the general's possession was a detailed set of plans of the Bardia defences, which were gratefully received.

To restore some sort of order on the frontier the Italians despatched a flying column consisting of two companies of lorried infantry, four guns and a company of L3 tankettes, commanded by a Colonel D'Avanzo. The column was intercepted by the armoured cars near Ghirba on the 16th and after two L3s had been knocked out D'Avanzo gave the barely credible order to form square with the lorried infantry in the centre, the tankettes on the flanks and a gun at each corner. These were the correct tactics for establishing a night leaguer in hostile tribal territory, but against regular mechanized troops with plenty of firepower at their disposal they amounted to little more than a death-wish. When Brigadier J. A. L. Caunter, commanding the British troops on the frontier, was advised of the situation he promptly despatched a troop of anti-tank guns and a squadron of 7th Hussars to assist the Eleventh, but by the time the tanks had arrived breakdowns had reduced their numbers to two cruisers and three lights. The officer commanding the tankette company was himself a cavalryman and, appreciating the absurdity of the situation, gallantly launched a counter-attack. One of the Seventh's cruisers found an L3 hanging grimly on to its tail, hammering away with its machine guns until the larger vehicle increased speed sufficiently for its 2-pounder to be depressed over the engine deck, sending a round through it. One by one the remaining L3s were destroyed, one at least being blown into its component parts by a huge internal explosion. The tanks and armoured cars then circled the square, raking it through and through with their fire. The Italian gun crews fought on until they were shot down around their weapons but the infantry broke, attempting to escape across the desert in their lorries with the 11th Hussars in hot pursuit; those that did not surrender were harried until their vehicles were burning wrecks. D'Avanzo was shot dead in his car and the survivors of his column, seven officers and 94 men, about one-third of the original force, were herded back across the frontier along with the captured guns and a solitary L3 under tow. The so-called Battle of Ghirba had cost the British not a single casualty.

During the remainder of June and throughout July the armoured cars and each of 7th Armoured Division's four armoured regiments continued their operations across the frontier. By the end of July, however, there were few easy pickings to be had for now the

Italians only moved in strength and with air cover on call. On 25 July an 11th Hussar patrol engaged in raiding the Bardia–Tobruk road was shot up by aircraft and its survivors were rounded up; chivalrously, the Italians dropped a list of the prisoners they had taken and an account of the engagement during an air attack. On 5 August the Italian medium tanks at last entered the fray, fighting an inconclusive action with the 8th Hussars between Sidi Azeiz and Fort Capuzzo. By now Wavell was worried that continuous wear and tear on the frontier would reduce the efficiency of his armoured regiments when the time came for real fighting and he withdrew them to refit out of the line. The 11th Hussars and other units of 7th Armoured Division remained to harass the enemy whenever possible, the result being that in the first three months of the war the Italians sustained 3,500 casualties and the British only 150.

More important still was the tremendous moral ascendancy which the British had obtained over their opponents. The Italians had attempted to deal with small, regular mechanized forces using the methods of colonial warfare and air policing, and they had failed dismally. Colonel Heinz Hegenreimer, the German Liaison Officer at General Headquarters in Libya, found his allies nervous, depressed and given to reassuring each other of their determination to resist, a situation which he found surprising in view of their great numerical superiority.

It was, perhaps, typical of the malaise afflicting the Italian armed services generally that, on 28 June, Marshal Italo Balbo, the Commander-in-Chief Libya, was shot down and killed by his own anti-aircraft gunners at Tobruk. He was succeeded by Marshal Rodolfo Graziani, Marchese di Nogheli, who had earned something of a reputation during earlier colonial campaigns. Balbo had planned to take the offensive in July but when Mussolini urged Graziani to do likewise the new Commander-in-Chief was far from keen on the idea. With a realism that was totally lacking in Rome he recognized that his logistic infra-structure was unequal to supporting a protracted offensive and, that being the case, the sheer numbers required for such an operation would themselves place it at risk. 'The water supply is entirely inadequate,' he told Count Ciano, the Duce's son-in-law. 'We move towards a defeat which, in the desert, must inevitably develop into a total disaster.' Mussolini was not impressed and by the beginning of September his patience had run out. Graziani, offered the alternatives of mounting an immediate offensive or being dismissed, chose the former.

The offensive was to be undertaken by the Tenth Army under the command of General Berti who, like many Italian senior officers, enjoyed a colourful nickname—in this case Sly Murderer. Tenth Army consisted of two corps, XXI and XXIII, a Libyan Group and the motorized Group Maletti which was intended to cover the desert flank during the march into Egypt, air cover being provided by the 300 aircraft of General Porro's 5th Squadra of the Regia Aeronautica.

On the evening of 11 September, Berti told Hegenreimer officially that an offensive was in the offing.

He also asked me to take charge of front reconnaissance as I had done in Spain, and to intervene directly in his name whenever I found bottlenecks or snarls in the convoy traffic; twice a day I was also to report to him the exact frontline situation. These certainly were not the customary duties of a foreign liaison officer, but they offered me the desired opportunity for personal participation and observation. I was also pleased that at last I had escaped the scheming atmosphere of Headquarters in Cyrene. At dawn on 13 September we drove to Capuzzo. Everywhere the troops had already been deployed along the line of departure. The attack began about 10:00, after the British advance positions and Fort Sollum had been subjected to a short artillery preparation. Then the first waves of infantry, composed of Italian and Arab troops, attacked without meeting serious opposition. We went along with them because here we could best judge the morale of the Italian troops. The Italians were calm and confident, the morale of the Arab troops even excellent, although the proclamations of the Grand Senussi, an ally of the British, had caused the Italian High Command some misgivings on account of the Askaris. The troops swiftly crossed the English trenches and obstacles which were under zone fire. Some mines exploded but losses were negligible, and the partly destroyed Fort Sollum was found evacuated. Only the demolition of a wide curve in the road leading to the bay momentarily stopped the motorized column which had been detailed for a quick advance along the coastal road. The column was quickly re-routed through several empty wadis and the Italian engineers set out to repair the road, which was still under British fire. From the eastern parapet on top of the fort we observed the British motorized field batteries and machine gun squads retreat in leapfrog fashion along the crest of the ridge that follows the bay. From time to time harassing fire of medium and heavy calibre struck the fort, presumably from the guns of the British cruisers which were visible far away on the horizon. The motorized Italian advance guard quickly pushed along the coast while the main body moved on foot along the crest of the escarpment towards the east.

The British had received ample warning of Italian intentions and their rearguard withdrew in good order, inflicting 500 casualties as it did so. O'Connor hoped that Berti's troops would close up to the fortified position which had been prepared at Mersa Matruh as this would enable 7th Armoured Division to fall on their exposed desert flank while they were engaged with the defences. This was not to be, for on 18 September the Italians halted at Sidi Barrani, some 60 miles distant, having exhausted their supplies and with their vehicles in poor mechanical shape. Berti then began to consolidate his position while he prepared for the next phase of the offensive, establishing an advance post at Maktila and a chain of fortified camps which stretched away from Sidi Barrani to the southwest. These presented the illusion rather than the reality of security for they were too far apart to provide mutual support for each other if attacked, while in the centre of the chain was a 20-mile stretch of open desert which became known as the Enba Gap.

Once the Italians had lapsed into their defensive mentality the British again began to dominate the open spaces between the armies, including the Enba Gap, just as they had dominated the frontier zone. Wavell was still anxious to spare his tanks needless running and this was achieved by using small columns consisting of armoured cars, lorried infantry, anti-tank and field guns, these being named Jock Columns after their originator, Lieutenant-Colonel Jock Campbell of the 4th Royal Horse Artillery. The anti-tank guns, which at this period included the British 2-pounder and the Bofors 37 mm, were carried *portée* on the back of a cut-down lorry to eliminate the constant battering they receiv-

ed when towed across bad going, an idea put forward by a Rhodesian subaltern named Gillson. The original intention was that the gun should be dismounted before going into action but this seldom happened, partly because time did not permit and partly because the ammunition was stowed on the vehicle.

Days passed into weeks during which Graziani temporized about continuing his advance. In October Major-General Wilhelm Ritter von Thoma, one of Germany's most experienced armoured commanders, was sent to North Africa, ostensibly on a fact-finding mission, but in reality to ascertain as tactfully as possible whether German assistance was required to inject some ginger into the Italian offensive. Thoma's opinion was that it would be impossible to support a large German contingent as well as a major portion of the Italian Army, given the Royal Navy's command of

December 1940: Matildas attacking Sidi Barrani (Imperial War Museum).

A10 Cruiser Tank in blue-grey and sand desert camouflage scheme (Imperial War Museum).

the sea. The appropriate German contribution, he felt, should be four armoured or mechanized divisions since this was the minimum required for success and the maximum which could be maintained in the field. The Italians, however, were less than enthusiastic at the prospect. 'Everyone is scared of the British,' commented the General in his report. 'What the Italians are afraid of is that the arrival of German troops might cause the British, who have meanwhile been considerably reinforced, to become more active.'

The reinforcements which von Thoma referred to included three armoured regiments which Churchill had despatched round the Cape from the United Kingdom, reaching Egypt in early October. They were the 3rd Hussars with light tanks, the 2nd Royal Tank Regiment with cruisers and the 7th Royal Tank Regiment with Matildas. The

first two joined the 7th Armoured Division, exchanging their respective B Squadrons as Creagh insisted that each of his armoured regiments should contain at least one cruiser squadron, and immediately became operational. The 7th Royal Tank Regiment, commanded by Lieutenant-Colonel R. M. Jerram, was retained under corps control, for Wavell not only did not wish to disclose that the regiment's Matildas, armoured with 78 mm frontal castings for their designated role of infantry support, were invulnerable to anything the Italians could fire at them, but also intended committing them *en masse* at the appropriate moment, thereby exploiting the element of surprise to the full. By the end of September, too, an air ferry route had been established across Africa from the Gold Coast to Egypt and the first Hurricane fighters began arriving in the Middle East.

The 25-pounder gun-howitzer was the mainstay of the British artillery during the Second World War. It had a range of 13,500 yd and in the Western Desert was often employed involuntarily in the anti-tank role, firing over open sights. These particular troops are engaging targets in Bardia, January 1941 (Imperial War Museum).

While Graziani argued with Rome about the difficulties of continuing his advance, events elsewhere began to have a significant bearing on the campaign. During their meeting at the Brenner Pass on 4 October, Hitler had not told Mussolini that he was on the point of occupying Romania. Outraged at this cavalier treatment by his fellow dictator, Mussolini chose not only to ignore the unresolved aspects of the war in North and East Africa, but also the fact that his Chiefs of Staff had warned him that the Italian armed services could not be equipped for a modern European conflict until 1942, announcing that he was going to 'occupy' Greece. The Greeks had their own ideas about that and when the Italian Ninth Army cross-

ed the frontier on 28 October it was subjected to a series of humiliating defeats and forced to withdraw into Albania. Worse was to follow, for on the night of 11/12 November Swordfish torpedo bombers, flying from the aircraft carrier HMS *Illustrious,* crippled the Italian battle fleet in its base at Taranto, radically altering the whole balance of naval power in the Mediterranean. This meant that supplying Graziani would become increasingly difficult and that the guns of Cunningham's battleships and other warships would be available to support Wavell with the accurate, shattering weight of their firepower.

In the desert itself there was little fighting. On 23 October a probing attack was made on the 1st Libyan Division's position at

Maktila by the 8th Hussars and the 1st Battalion Cameron Highlanders. The Italians had received ample warning from their many friends in Egypt and were able to beat off the assault without the slightest difficulty. Unfortunately for them, even this modest success tended to work against them, as thereafter, they complacently regarded their defence as adequate. The primary lesson for the British was the need for total security, and that was taken to heart. On 19 November, 2nd Libyan Division and Group Maletti, the latter with 27 M11/39 tanks of II Battalion 4th Tank Regiment, penetrated the Enba Gap but were mauled by a Jock Column, sustaining the loss of five tanks and 100 casualties for negligible return. After this, the Italians retired to their camps and stayed there.

The idea of a limited counter-offensive had been in Wavell's mind ever since Graziani's advance had run itself into the sand. What he envisaged was nothing more than a spoiling attack designed to last four or five days, intended to smash up the enemy's preparations for a further advance and cause him to withdraw. He was able to keep his thoughts from the politicians until early November, when Churchill demanded that he send aid to Greece. As the Greeks were more than holding ther own, Wavell felt that the Western Desert had priority and he was forced to declare his hand. Churchill was annoyed by the deception but gave the plan his enthusiastic endorsement. Wavell, O'Connor and Wilson then sat down to work out the details.

Despite the undoubted moral superiority which the British had attained, the odds against them had changed but slightly since the campaign began. In the air the Regia Aeronautica could put up 191 fighters against the RAF's 48, of which only 32 were modern Hurricanes, and 141 bombers against 116. The Italian artillery could muster 400 guns, the British 150, although the 25-pounder gun-howitzer was a better weapon than the Italian

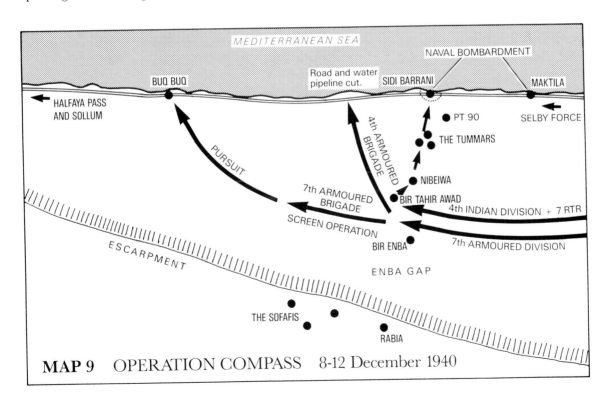

MAP 9 OPERATION COMPASS 8-12 December 1940

75 mm gun, and on occasion the imbalance could be corrected by naval gunfire support. As far as tanks were concerned, however, the Italians were now at a numerical as well as a qualitative disadvantage. Their 240 useless L3 tankettes were more or less balanced by the 200 British light tanks Mark VI, which were better fighting machines but still thinly armoured and armed only with machine-guns. The Italians also possessed 60 medium tanks and the British 75, but whereas 7th Armoured Division's A9, A10 and A13 cruisers were almost all runners, the only Italian medium tank unit deployed forward was the M11/39 battalion attached to Group Maletti; the other M11/39 battalion was in such poor mechanical shape that it had been withdrawn to refit in Libya, where a battalion of improved M13/40s was also forming. Again, Graziani had nothing to compare with the Matilda, which Wavell intended using as a mace to batter his

way into one position after another. In terms of manpower the Italians still dwarfed the small British corps which opposed them and the indications were that, while they had not distinguished themselves in open warfare, they would fight much harder behind their prepared defences.

Given O'Connor's understanding of the Italian psychology and Wavell's intimate knowledge of Allenby's tactics in Palestine, it was hardly surprising that the basic form of the British counter-offensive, codenamed Operation Compass, involved deep penetration of the Enba Gap followed by a wheel northwards to the coast which contained echoes of Megiddo. The 7th Armoured Division's tasks included the isolation of Sidi Barrani from the west by 4th Armoured Brigade (7th Hussars, 2nd and 6th Royal Tank Regiments) while 7th Armoured Brigade (3rd and 8th Hussars and 1st Royal Tank Regi-

Italian M11/39 Medium Tank, a badly-designed and unreliable vehicle with its main armament housed in a limited traverse mounting in the hull. It stood no chance at all against the British Cruisers and Matildas (Imperial War Museum).

ment) screened the whole operation against interference from the camps at Rabia and Sofafi, lying above the escarpment to the south-west of the Gap. Simultaneously, Major-General Noel Beresford-Peirse's 4th Indian Division, composed entirely of long-service professionals, would storm in succession the enemy camps at Nibeiwa, Tummar and Sidi Barrani, spearheaded by the Matildas of 7th Royal Tank Regiment. As a diversion part of the Mersa Matruh garrison, known as Selby Force, was to advance along the coast and attack Maktila, which would also be subjected to naval bombardment.

Only the most senior officers knew what was intended when serious training began in November. The troops involved believed that they were taking part in Exercise No 1, which was simply a rehearsal for a larger corps exercise to be known as Exercise No 2. Not until the night before the attack itself were they told that the latter was the real thing. During this period 7 RTR and 4th Indian Division practised on dummy camps which had been laid out to represent the Italian positions, using aerial reconnaissance photographs and patrol reports.

The accurate timing of the 70 mile approach march was essential. On 3 December, 7 RTR set out, the regiment's Matildas travelling at half their maximum speed of 15 mph so as to reduce the effects of wear and tear.

7th Armoured and 4th Indian Divisions began moving forward on 7 December, completing the journey by easy stages with regular halts for maintenance. By the night of 8/9 December the whole of O'Connor's corps had arrived in the Enba Gap undetected, the sound of thousands of engines and tank tracks being masked by aircraft flying low over the Italian positions, a device which had worked well during the First World War. On the northern horizon a low rumble and continuous flashes marked the naval bombardment of Maktila and Sidi Barrani, but none of this

Italian M13/40s advancing under fire (RAC Tank Museum).

seemed to disturb the sleeping enemy.

The first camp to be tackled was Nibeiwa, the home of Group Maletti, a rectangle measuring approximately 2,500 by 2,000 yards, ringed by dry-stone sangars containing automatic weapons and field artillery. Air reconnaissance had revealed that the camp was surrounded by a minefield, but an unmined approach was available from the west and it was decided to attack from this direction, despite the fact that the M11/39 battalion was leaguered directly in the path of the assault.

At 07:15 the 7th Medium Regiment, which provided Western Desert Force's corps artillery support, opened fire on the camp with its vintage 60-pounder guns and minutes later the divisional artillery regiments joined in with their 25-pounders, a total of 124 guns supplemented by the sustained fire of Vickers medium machine guns which combed the position from end to end. Before the Italians fully understood what was happening, the spearpoint of the British attack, A Squadron 7 RTR, commanded by Major Henry Rew, had struck them like a thunderbolt. The crews of the M11/39s were caught emerging from their blankets; those who managed to scramble aboard their vehicles were either killed or forced to abandon them as their flimsy armour was raked through and through by the Matilda's 2-pounder shot. Not one Italian tank succeeded in moving and within minutes the entire battalion had been reduced to burning wrecks. A Squadron ground on remorse-

Position held by the Italian rearguard at Buq Buq following their defeat during Operation Compass. The salt flat can be seen on the right of the picture with, barely discernible, one of 3rd Hussars' light tanks (Imperial War Museum).

lessley towards the perimeter, shrugging off direct hits from guns of every calibre present.

As the Matildas smashed their way into the camp the Italian gun crews fought to the bitter end, dying around their weapons, but once their artillery had been suppressed many of the infantry lost heart. There were, however, brave men who tried to tackle the invulnerable intruders with small arms or bundles of grenades and among them was Maletti himself, shot down as he emerged from his command dug-out with machine-pistol blazing. The second wave of the assault, consisting of 2nd Cameron Highlanders and 1st/6th Rajputana Rifles, led by B Squadron 7 RTR, now swamped the broken defences and by 10:00 the camp had fallen. Several hundred of the enemy had been killed or wounded and over 4,000 were captured, together with all their artillery and transport. British losses were light. 7 RTR's casualties amounted to two killed and six wounded; Major Rew died when he opened his cupola at the height of the action and four more casualties occurred in one tank when a burst from a 20 mm anti-aircraft gun entered the gap revealed by the driver sliding back his visor. A few tanks were temporarily out of action with mine damage to their tracks or hits on sprockets and idlers, but in no instance had a Matilda's armour been penetrated.

The next objective was the camp of Tummar West which, with the neighbouring camps of Tummar Central and Tummar East, contained Major-General Piscatori's 2nd Libyan Division. Leaving nine tanks and the non-runners at Nibeiwa as insurance against counter-attack, Jerram led the remainder of his regiment north, followed by the 5th Indian Infantry Brigade; the plan was for them to deliver the attack, while all round the artillery limbered up and moved to fresh fire positions. A sudden sandstorm restricted visibility but the route to the start-line was successfully calculated by dead reckoning.

Matildas show their paces. The Matilda's 78 mm armour was invulnerable to anything the Italians could fire at it and for a while the vehicle was known as The Queen of the Battlefield. With the arrival of better German anti-tank guns, particularly the dual-purpose 88 mm, the Matilda's importance began to decline (Imperial War Museum).

During the morning the garrison of Tummar West had been observed lining the walls of their sangars to watch the fighting at Nibeiwa through binoculars and to discourage any ideas they might have had of giving active assistance to their embattled comrades 7th Medium Regiment had sent over several rounds of 60-pounder shrapnel which 'swept the ground like a giant's broom'. Notwithstanding this experience and the object lesson of Nibeiwa, the Libyans were determined to make a fight of it. When the British attack went in at 13:00 it was led by D Squadron 7 RTR, followed by a composite squadron, giving a total of 22 Matildas. The infantry, 1st Royal Fusiliers and 3rd/1st Punjabis, were driven to within 150 yards of the camp's perimeter by New Zealand Service Corps drivers who snatched their rifles and joined the assault. As at Nibeiwa, the Matildas carried all before them and destroyed the enemy's heavy weapons but the Libyan infantry furiously contested each trench and dug-out, and it was only after two hours of close-quarter fighting with bayonet and grenade that the last resistance was crushed, yielding 2,000 prisoners including General Piscatori and his staff.

7 RTR still had to spearhead an attack on Tummar East, and Jerram was less than pleased to be told that 5th Indian Infantry Brigade intended retaining all but seven of his tanks in the counter-attack role. While these were replenishing their fuel and ammunition they were joined by two repaired mine casualties from Nibeiwa, enabling a composite three-troop squadron to be formed under Captain Badrock. The turrets of two of the tanks were jammed by shell splinters but it was decided to commit them for their effect on morale, and at 15:55 Badrock set off for Tummar East, accompanied by 4th/6th Rajputana Rifles and supporting artillery. On the way the column went slightly off course and found itself approaching the smaller camp of Tummar Central. This contained many shaken fugitives from Nibeiwa and Tummar West, all with terrifying tales to tell of the invincible Matilda, and the occupants were only too eager to surrender. Meanwhile, a major part of the garrison of Tummar East had set out in a motorized convoy to recapture Tummar West. The attempt foundered in a welter of concentrated artillery and machine-gun fire which inflicted 400 casualties, and the survivors scattered into the desert. Consequently, when Badrock's tanks and the Rajputs assaulted Tummar East in the failing light, they met minimal resistance.

If 4th Indian Division and 7 RTR had had a busy and successful day, the same was true of 7th Armoured Division, temporarily commanded by Brigadier Caunter while Creagh was on sick leave. 7th Armoured Brigade and the Support Group maintained their screening operation in the Enba Gap, but the 63rd Cirene Division, holding the camps at Rabia and Sofafi, made no attempt to intervene in the fighting. 11th Hussars reached the coast road at 09:00, ambushing a column of lorries. 4th Armoured Brigade was not far behind, cutting the water pipeline and telephone links to Sidi Barrani as well as overrunning an outpost of the 64th Catanzaro Division near Buq Buq. To the east the 1st Libyan Division, menaced by Selby Force and worried by the battles for the camps, began withdrawing from Maktila after dark. In Sidi Barrani itself, now isolated and waterless, the morale of 4th Blackshirt Division began to suffer as stragglers from the fighting stumbled in and General Gallina, commanding the Libyan Group of divisions, despatched a depressing signal to Graziani to the effect that he lacked adequate means to deal with the mechanized army which 'infested' the surrounding desert.

It had been the intention to storm Sidi Barrani at dawn next morning with the sort of set-piece attack which had captured Nibeiwa and the Tummars, using 7 RTR and 16th British Brigade. The latter, unfortunately, launched their assault prematurely and were pinned down by the Italian artillery, sustaining 250 casualties. Jerram, approaching with a composite squadron of eight Matildas under Major Hawthorn, decided to tackle the guns alone and conducted a 4,000 yard advance into the heart of the defences, destroying seven batteries in an hour's fighting. However, while tanks can take ground they cannot hold it unsupported, and at 09:30 the squadron returned to rally with 16th Brigade, accompanied by 200 prisoners. One tank had a track shot away, but fought on until its ammunition was expended. It was then set on fire by its crew, who later talked round a large number of their nervous captors, making it the only Matilda to be lost during the campaign.

A severe sand storm made further move-

Light Tank Mark VI beside an abandoned Caproni Ca309, El Adem airfield, January 1941. The tank carries the original 7th Armoured Division tactical sign, a red square enclosing a white circle; the more famous jerboa or Desert Rat began appearing in the centre of the circle shortly after (Imperial War Museum).

ment impossible and while this was raging the battle was re-planned. 16th Brigade were reinforced with 2nd Camerons and 4th/6th Rajputana Rifles and two of 4th Armoured Brigade's regiments were released from their blocking role at Buq Buq, 2 RTR to take part in the general attack on Sidi Barrani and 6 RTR to join Selby Force in its harassment of 1st Libyan Division, now strung out along the road from Maktila.

Jerram's attack had drawn the teeth of Sidi Barrani defences and when the assault was renewed at 16:00 resistance quickly collapsed, yielding 2,500 prisoners and 100 guns. 1st Libyan Division, utterly alone, fought on until the following morning. On 11 December the nearby camp at Point 90 was taken without incident and that evening 63rd Division slipped away from Rabia and Sofafi, and headed for the frontier under cover of darkness and dust storms.

In the air the RAF's Hurricanes,

Gauntlets and Gladiators had maintained a local superiority over the battlefield, defeating attempts by the Regia Aeronautics to assist their battered and bewildered ground troops. In any event, the fluid situation made the task of the Italian pilots all but impossible, for the desert surrounding Sidi Barrani resembled a disturbed ant-hill in which friend could not be distinguished from foe. Simultaneously, Wellington bombers flying from Malta raided airfields in Libya, inflicting further loss.

On the evening of 11 December Graziani sent a gloomy signal to Rome reporting the destruction of four divisions, complaining bitterly that he was being compelled to wage 'the war of the flea against the elephant'. Furthermore, the Commander-in-Chief continued, he was seriously considering a withdrawal to Tripoli 'in order to keep the flag flying over that fortress at least', adding in a note to his wife that 'one cannot break steel armour with finger nails alone'. Mussolini thought that he had gone mad, yet despite his talent for sombre histrionics Graziani was well aware of the facts of life and events were to justify his assessment of the situation.

O'Connor had fought a brilliant battle, exercising forward control of his formations through an efficient command radio net, and with the fall of Sidi Barrani the original aim of Operation Compass had been achieved. 4th Indian Division, urgently required for use against the Italian army in East Africa, was detached from Western Desert Force during the night of 10/11 December, leaving O'Connor with only 7th Armoured Division and 16th British Brigade to exploit his victory, although Wavell promised him Major-General Iven Mackay's 6th Australian Division as soon as it could be brought forward. Suddenly the transport services were stretched to the limit by the need to maintain the pursuit, remove thousands of prisoners to the rear, move 4th Indian Division to the railhead at Mersa Matruh and pick up the Australians. Even the acquisition of the enemy's lorries and some willing Italian drivers only permitted O'Connor to exploit his victory with the two armoured brigades by temporarily stripping 7th Armoured Division's Support Group of its transport.

On 12 December, 7th Armoured Brigade, hitherto only lightly engaged, was ordered to intercept the 64th Division as it withdrew from Buq Buq. The intention of the brigade commander was to cut the coast road behind the Italians but his hook landed short and a tail chase ensued. The leading British regiment, 3rd Hussars, found the massed artillery of the enemy's rearguard lining a semi-circle of dunes behind a salt-flat, across which it promptly launched its two light tank squadrons in a headlong charge. The tanks were soon floundering as they broke through the crust and the Italian guns, firing over open sights, began blowing them apart at will. The position was brought under fire by a battery of 4th RHA and a second attack was made by

8th Hussars and the Third's cruiser squadron (B Squadron 2 RTR), which worked their way round the flanks. The Italians swung their guns to meet the threat but were momentarily stunned when one of their ammunition lorries went up in a tremendous explostion. By the time the dust had settled the tanks were into the gun line and resistance collapsed.

The action at Buq Buq yielded 14,000 prisoners, bringing the four-day total to 38,000 including four generals, while enemy equipment captured or destroyed included 237 guns and 73 tankettes or medium tanks. Western Desert Force was now heavily outnumbered by its captives and a real danger existed that the administrative services would be swamped by the scale of the problem. Long columns trudged eastwards escorted by a handful of infantrymen, while elsewhere the prisoners organized convoys with their own lorries and ran an unescorted shuttle service to and from the prisoner of war compounds. It all made wonderful newsreel material, but the Italians instinctively recognized that their very survival depended upon the fullest co-operation.

Meanwhile, the pursuit continued across the frontier. Sollum was not defended and on the 14th a platoon holding the ruins of Fort Capuzzo surrendered to a solitary light tank of 3rd Hussars. Two days later a dashing attack on Sidi Omar by 4th Armoured Brigade ended dramatically when Captain P. R. C. Hobart, commanding C Squadron 2 RTR, smashed his way into the main fort, blazing away from the turret with his revolver, followed by a second tank. For the 900 defenders this was the last straw and they emerged from nooks and crannies with their hands up. With the fall of Sidi Omar the frontier zone was once again under British domination.

The Italian withdrawal was also harried from the sea by Force W, based on Mersa Matruh. This originally consisted of the Insect Class gunboats *Aphis* and *Ladybird*, armed with two 6 in guns, joined later by a third

Insect, *Gnat,* and the monitor *Terror,* which mounted two 15 in guns. As well as bombarding Maktila and Sidi Barrani during the opening phases of Operation Compass, Force W hammered Italian transport streaming along the Bardia road from Sollum and on the 17th *Aphis* impudently steamed into Bardia harbour and sank three freighters at point blank range. For a while, the Insects also delivered 100 tons of drinking water daily, ferried in reinforcements and shipped out prisoners.

A short period of comparative quiet followed as both sides prepared for the next round of the fighting. The Italians retired into Bardia, which was surrounded by a continuous 17-mile anti-tank ditch behind which lay barbed wire aprons, minefields, concrete emplacements and blockhouses with interlocking arcs of fire. The fortress was held by the 1st and 2nd Blackshirt Divisions, plus those elements of the 62nd, 63rd and 64th Divisions which had survived the débâcle in the desert, a total of 45,000 men supported by 400 guns and over 100 armoured vehicles. In command was one of Italy's most famous soldiers, General Bergonzoli, of whom Hegenreimer has left an interesting portrait, revealing that he was far from typical of the senior Italian officers of his day.

> I had known and been friendly with the old warrior in Spain, where he was to be found in the front line at all times. He lived for and with his men, ate and drank with them, and always slept in a tent despite his advanced years and the fact that he could have chosen the best quarters. His temperament and vitality, his curly grey beard framing a healthy reddish face with small, sparkling blue eyes, had brought him the nickname 'Electric Whiskers', which was known all over Italy. He emanated calm and humour even in the most difficult situations. He was certainly no genius and the tendency of the old trooper to simplify tactical procedures by launching frontal attacks quite frequently horrified the General Staff. But there were not many his equal in dependability and honesty toward friend and enemy alike.

Universal Carrier and Quod Artillery Tractor drive past a memorial erected by the Italians to commemorate their brief stay in Sidi Barrani, December 1940 (Imperial War Museum).

That the British intended assaulting Bardia was beyond reasonable doubt, for 7th Armoured Division quickly severed communications with Tobruk and 16th British Brigade ranged the perimeter until 6th Australian Division arrived on 20 December to impose a state of siege. Having only a month's water supply in hand, Bergonzoli knew that Bardia's days were numbered even if O'Connor did not attack and to Mussolini's exhortation to 'stand at whatever cost, faithful to the last', he responded with studied ambivalence, 'In Bardia we are, and here we stay.'

Mackay was not a professional soldier but he had emerged from the First World War as a brigadier and his Australians were every bit as formidable as their fathers who had fought under Allenby in Palestine. Furthermore, while Bardia was obviously a tougher nut to crack than the Sidi Barrani camps, his assault would be supported by Jerram's Matildas. Once he had selected the points at which he intended breaking into the defences his engineers constructed a full scale replica, including the anti-tank ditch, dummy mine fields and wire entanglements and during rehearsals a battle drill was established.

An hour before dawn on 3 January, 122 guns opened fire on the chosen sector of the perimeter, their shells falling in an area some 2,500 by 500 yards. Most of the enemy's counter-battery fire was badly ranged and did little damage. The morning was cold enough for the Australians to be wearing greatcoats and a slight mist enabled an infantry attack to rush three posts, closely followed by three parties of sappers, one to throw down the sides of the ditch, so creating causeways on which the tanks could cross, one to clear a path through the mines and one to cut the wire with Bangalore torpedoes. By 06:40 six causeways had been built and the 16th Australian Brigade went in, spearheaded by four troops of Matildas, the first two of which swung respectively left and right to roll up the perimeter, the second pair striking deeper to tackle the enemy artillery, the overall effect being of widening circles caused by a stone thrown into a pool. The Matildas immediately attracted the attention of every weapon within range, causing the infantry to follow at a respectful distance, but each enemy post was methodically eliminated, the Australians closing in with bayonet and grenade once the oc-

Two-pounder portée anti-tank gun. The gun was carried piggy-back on a cut down lorry, the idea being that this would eliminate the damage caused if the weapon was towed over bad going. The original idea was that it would be dismounted for use but in practice this rarely happened, partly because time would seldom permit, and partly because the ammunition was stowed in bins behind the mounting. The portée is said to have been conceived by a Rhodesian officer, Lieutenant Gillson (Imperial War Museum).

cupants' fire had been suppressed by the tanks. Soon a growing flood of prisoners was being directed back towards the gap in the perimeter, but the Italians' ordeal had only just begun. At 08:10 the battleships *Barham, Valiant* and *Warspite,* seven destroyers and Force W began a pulverizing bombardment of specific areas within the defences.

Despite this, the Italians were by no means the pushover the end result of the battle might suggest. On the southern sector of the perimeter a diversionary attack by the 2nd/6th Battalion was pinned down, and 16th Brigade was itself counter-attacked by a company of six M11 and M13 medium tanks which broke through the 2nd/3rd Battalion. One was eliminated by an Australian who jumped aboard and fired his machine-pistol into the open turret, but the remaining five rumbled on, temporarily releasing 500 prisoners. The affair began to assume serious proportions

when the nearest Matilda crews dismissed the report as a false alarm, but the timely arrival of three 2-pounder portees put an end to the matter, four of the tanks and two portees being knocked out in the ensuing exchange. Two battalions of 17th Brigade entered the fray about noon, wheeling to the south-east, but lacked tank support and made comparatively slow progress, at some cost. Nevertheless, by nightfall the defences had been all but cut in two and the back of the enemy's resistance had been broken.

Next morning 16th Brigade and two Matilda troops assaulted the town and harbour of Bardia and by 16:00 these had been secured. One of the more spectacular events of the day was a protracted duel between Second-Lieutenant Taylor's troop and a coast defence battery on the South Headland, the issue being finally resolved when the Matildas smashed their way through the gates of the

Dawn assault. Australian infantry storm the defences of Bardia, January 1941 (Imperial War Museum).

The Bardia garrison marches into captivity. The tiny escort could have been overwhelmed at any time, had not the prospect of unrelieved thirst provided a restraining influence (Imperial War Museum).

fort. The last struggles within the doomed fortress took place on 5 January when 19th Brigade, led by two troops of Matildas, passed through 17th Brigade and cleaned out the southern sector of the defences.

The capture of Bardia had cost XIII Corps, as O'Connor's command had become known on 1 January, 500 casualties, of whom 150 were killed. Once again, 7 RTR's Matildas had proved to be a decisive factor in the fighting and Mackay had placed the entire resources of his divisional workshops at the regiment's disposal so that damaged tanks could be got back into action with the minimum of delay, commenting that each Matilda was worth a battalion of infantry to him. O'Connor, already deeply immersed in planning the next operation, also found time to write Jerram a personal note of congratulation.

Bergonzoli evaded capture and walked to Tobruk, but a further 38,000 prisoners began

the long walk into Egypt leaving the victor to count the immense spoils, which included 700 wheeled vehicles, many in working order. The 6th Australian Divisional Cavalry Regiment decided to supplement its tracked carriers with captured medium tanks and formed three squadrons named Dingo, Rabbit and Wombat, Dingo having five M11s and one M13, Rabbit and Wombat two M13s each, all painted with prominent white kangaroos on the hull and turret.

O'Connor's next objective was Tobruk, which possessed far better harbour facilities than Bardia. Creagh had resumed command of 7th Armoured Division shortly after the Sidi Barrani battles and, even while the last shots were being fired in Bardia, he directed 7th Armoured Brigade westward, isolating Tobruk on 6 January. 6th Australian Division followed immediately and completed the investment.

The defences of Tobruk were very similar

to those of Bardia and were manned by the 61st Division, a 2,000-strong naval detachment and the survivors of vanished formations, a total of 25,000 men supported by 200 guns and 90 armoured vehicles. In command was General Pitassi Mannella, known among his peers as The King of Artillerymen, an elderly officer of great dignity overburdened by the responsibilities of an impossible situation, the essence of his problems being that he had to defend an area twice the size of Bardia with a force half the size of Bergonzoli's lost garrison. Relief was the remotest of possibilities for the nearest friendly troops, the 60th Division and General Babini's newly-formed armoured brigade, which Graziani was strangely unwilling to commit, were at Derna, 60 miles away. Nor could much air support be expected, as the Regia Aeronautica had been forced to abandon the nearby base of El Adem and was now operating from airfields 170 miles distant. There was little Mannella or his troops could do other than await the British attack with gloomy foreboding.

Notwithstanding the poor state of the enemy's morale, nothing was taken for granted by XIII Corps and the same meticulous preparation went into the taking of Tobruk as had gone into the capture of Bardia. The assault was to have commenced on 20 January but was postponed for 24 hours because of a severe sandstorm. Once again,

British medium artillery bombarding Tobruk, January 1941 (Imperial War Museum).

Tobruk harbour after its capture by XIII Corps. The tank on the left is an M13/40, that on the right an M11/39; both have been taken over by the 6th Australian Divisional Cavalry Regiment and painted with prominent white kangaroos to avoid recognition problems (Imperial War Museum).

bombardments from land and sea softened the defences and shortly after dawn the Australians went in, led by a composite five-troop Matilda squadron. The fighting took much the same form as in Bardia, the Italians being assisted for a while by the main and secondary armaments of the ancient cruiser *San Giorgio,* lying aground in the harbour, which, to the crew's discomfort and surprise, had already absorbed some punishment from the 4.5 in guns of 68 Medium Regiment. The 2nd/8th Battalion of 19th Brigade, advancing on Fort Pilastrino, was confronted by rows of dug-in L3 tankettes which were sweeping the ground with their fire and in an astonishing attack the Australians swept over these, receiving the surrender of their crews as they came to close quarters. During the afternoon the 2nd/8th, now supported by two Matildas, continued their advance but for a while were held up by a determined counter-attack delivered by nine medium tanks and several hundred men. After this had been broken up by the Matildas, some anti-tank guns and artillery concentrations the defence cracked and the Italians began surrendering *en masse.* General Mannella was captured in Fort Solaro and although he refused to order his troops to throw down their arms by nightfall the

Australians had reached the edge of the escarpment overlooking the town.

During the night the garrison attempted to destroy its stores and the grounded *San Giorgio* was set ablaze, sending a dismal smoke pall drifting across the harbour. Elsewhere, the ill-fated 4th Tank Regiment burned its standard. There was little fighting next day and by 10:00 the town had fallen. Among the acquisitions made by XIII Corps were refrigeration and water distillation plants and 10,000 tons of drinking water.

At this juncture a further factor influenced the strategy of the campaign. The Luftwaffe had begun attacking Malta and British shipping in the central Mediterranean from airfields in Sicily and to counter this development it was considered essential that the RAF should establish bases in the Benghazi Bulge. No sooner had Tobruk fallen than 7th Armoured Division was probing westward towards Derna. By now, numerous breakdowns caused by the continuous hard running were seriously eroding its tank strength and the personnel of two armoured regiments, 8th Hussars and 6th Royal Tank Regiment, returned to Egypt after handing over their remaining vehicles, leaving Creagh with about 40 cruisers and 80 light tanks split between four regiments. By way of contrast, substantial reinforcements had reached the Italians, who could field over 100 medium M13s, and it was only Graziani's reluctance to involve the Babini Armoured Brigade in offensive operations which concealed the fact.

The new Italian line ran south from the Wadi Derna, held by the 60th Division, to Mechili, where much of Babini's strength was concentrated. As 4th Armoured Brigade began approaching the latter General Tellera, who had assumed command of the Tenth Army some time previously, ordered Babini to counter-attack. Thus it was that when 7th Hussars attempted to cut the Mechili–Derna track on 24 January they were suddenly assailed by 14 M13s, firing on the move. Having only three cruisers which could engage on anything like equal terms, the Hussars were forced into a hasty withdrawal, losing several light tanks and a cruiser in the process. A second cruiser was damaged and although the third managed to knock out two M13s the outlook was bleak, for although brigade headquarters had acknowledged the contact report and instructed 2 RTR to despatch assistance, that regiment, like the Matilda crews in Bardia, found it difficult to accept the idea of Italian armour being handled aggressively and was slow to react. However, once a Hussar liaison officer arrived with details of the enemy's whereabouts two cruiser squadrons were manoeuvred to form a fire trap and, catching the M13s exposed on the crest of a ridge, they destroyed all but five of them in a matter of minutes without loss to themselves.

When 6th Australian Division reached the Wadi Derna position the following day, it met the most determined resistance and was unable to make headway in the face of heavy artillery fire and fierce local counter-attacks. 7 RTR was called forward from Tobruk but in the event its Matildas were not used as Tellera, unsettled by 7th Armoured Division's continued pressure on his southern flank and fearing that this might develop into an encirclement through the Djebel Akhdar massif, in which the 11th Hussars' cars were already operating, withdrew during the night of 28/29 January, burning his stores. Graziani, informed by his agents of the arrival of 2nd Armoured Division in Egypt, approved the move although it meant abandoning what remained of Cyrenaica, Benghazi being untenable as a defensive position.

The local Arabs were quick to inform the British of Tellera's departure, but it was Babini's retirement to the north-west to act as Tenth Army's rearguard which confirmed O'Connor's suspicions that the Italians would use the coast road through Benghazi for their retreat into Tripolitania and he realized at once that this presented him with an oppor-

tunity to administer the *coup de grâce* to his battered opponents. His plan, which by coincidence bore some resemblance to that employed at Khan-al-Baghdadi, required 6th Australian Division to maintain its pursuit along the coast while 7th Armoured Division cut across the base of the Benghazi Bulge south of the Djebel Akhdar along the axis Mechili–Msus–Antelat, reaching the coast at Beda Fomm and establishing a blocking position which would entrap Tenth Army between XIII Corps' two major formations.

Speed was essential and 7th Armoured Division's advance guard, called Combeforce after its commander and consisting of 11th Hussars, 2nd Battalion The Rifle Brigade, C Battery 4 RHA's 25-pounders and nine 37 mm *portée* anti-tank guns manned by 106 RHA, moved off on 4 February, followed by 4th Armoured Brigade with 3rd and 7th Hussars and 2nd Royal Tank Regiment, then 7th Armoured Brigade, reduced to 1st Royal Tank Regiment only, and finally the rump of the Support Group. The Italians had sown some mines but these proved to be less of an obstacle than the loose slab rock which covered part of the route, as this not only kept down the pace but also increased fuel consumption. The fuel situation, in fact, gave rise to serious concern, for the lumbering replenishment lorries had great difficulty in keeping up and the constant jostling of the flimsy 4 gallon petrol cans caused the seams of many to split and spill their contents.

Despite these difficulties, Combeforce succeeded in reaching Beda Fomm shortly after noon on the 5th and established a block astride the coast road. There was barely time for the infantry to dig in, for the guns to be sited and for a few mines to be laid when, at 14:30, the head of a long column began approaching from the north. This came to a standstill as soon as the leading vehicles went up on mines and others were set ablaze by the fire of the armoured cars and 25-pounders. The escorting Bersaglieri regiment tumbled

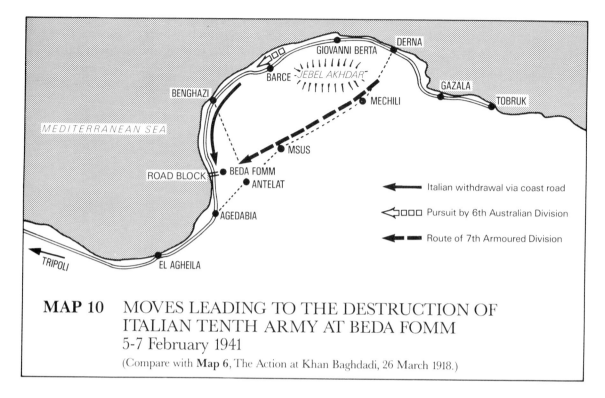

MAP 10 MOVES LEADING TO THE DESTRUCTION OF ITALIAN TENTH ARMY AT BEDA FOMM
5-7 February 1941
(Compare with **Map 6**, The Action at Khan Baghdadi, 26 March 1918.)

from its lorries and launched a series of disconnected attacks against the block, all of which were held without difficulty.

The bulk of the column consisted of administrative units which were leading the exodus from Benghazi, but as the afternoon wore on more fighting troops began to arrive and pressure on the block intensified. Combe was in radio contact with 4th Armoured Brigade and suggested to Brigadier Caunter that his tanks should engage the steadily lengthening enemy column from a series of ridges lying to the east of and parallel with the road. Caunter agreed and as evening approached he threw all three of his regiments against the Italians' flank. In the lead was B Squadron 7th Hussars, commanded by Major Ralph Younger:

At about 17:00 B Squadron was ordered to find out if Beda Fomm itself, a windmill on high ground, was held. In no time at all the leading troop leader reported it clear and that there was

a long column of transport halted on the road away to the west. We knew that Combeforce was in position a few miles to the south-west, across the road. In spite of the tanks being very low on petrol B and C Squadrons attacked the column and only darkness, partly relieved by a burning petrol tanker, saved much of it from being destroyed.

The Italians had believed that 7th Armoured Division was still two days' march distant, closing in on Benghazi from the north, and O'Connor's move had taken them completely by surprise. Although Tellera was with the column, the rearguard was commanded by Bergonzoli, upon whom responsibility now devolved for freeing the Tenth Army from the trap into which it had driven. The Babini Armoured Brigade, commanded by General Cona since 3 February, hurried forward from the rear while artillery and infantry were concentrated under cover of darkness for the breakout attempt. Bergonzoli intended mounting a holding attack against Combeforce while the bulk of his armour swung off the road at a point which would become known as The Pimple, smashing through 4th Armoured Brigade's cordon and then swinging south to assault the block from the flank and rear. The plan was sound and, in normal circumstances, stood every chance of succeeding.

Following a blustery, rain-laden dawn the Italian tank attacks began, supported by artillery fire. Despite their lack of experience the crews showed more determination than at any other time during the campaign, but each attack foundered under the steady fire of 2 RTR's hull-down cruisers. The principal reason for the failure of the Italian armour was that units were committed piecemeal as they arrived from the north, whereas a concentrated assault might well have broken through, albeit at heavy cost. There was also a lack of understanding of the principles of fire and movement, in which units provide mutual support for each other as they advance, and the practice of firing on the move produced poor results. Again, while all British tanks were fitted with radios, only the Italian battalion and company commanders' vehicles were so equipped, the result being that attacks were difficult to control once they had been launched.

The trapped column was now 11 miles long and while 3rd Hussars savaged its centre 7th Hussars fastened on to its rear. Even so, by evening vehicles were beginning to edge south in anticipation of the breakout, the reason being that continuous attacks had finally caused 2 RTR to give ground in the area of The Pimple. The Second's situation had indeed become critical as the regiment's 19 cruisers were reduced to seven, which between them possessed no more than a few rounds of 2-pounder ammunition. At this point, however, 1 RTR arrived from Antelat with 10 more cruisers and went straight into action. This provoked Italian suspicions that the British had ample reserves in hand and caused them to abandon their attacks,

although the truth was that at best 7th Armoured Division had never been able to field more than 32 cruisers and 50 light tanks.

Elsewhere on the 6th, the Support Group occupied Sceleidima and 6th Australian Division entered Benghazi, somewhat startled at the warmth of the welcome extended by the town's mayor, bishop and civic dignitaries who eagerly hailed the footsore infantrymen as 'gallant allies'. The noose was tightening around Tenth Army and hope began to fade with the evening light.

The day's fighting had reduced Bergonzoli's tank strength to 30. Quite probably these could have battered their way through Combeforce under cover of darkness, but instead it was decided to wait until dawn to deliver the attack. At first light, heavy artillery concentrations fell on the block and the tanks advanced, trading losses with 106 RHA's *portée* anti-tank guns. The latter's numbers were swiftly written down as the remaining M13s broke into the Rifle Brigade's positions which, as a matter of desperation and with full permission, were brought under fire by the 25-pounders of C Battery 4 RHA. As luck would have it, the moment produced the men. Only one *portée* remained to 106 RHA, manned by the anti-tank battery commander, his batman and a cook. The vehicle was driven to a flank from which it sent five successive rounds into five different M13s, the last of the tanks being dealt with by the 25-pounders and the Rifle Brigade's anti-tank rifles.

The failure of the tank attack was the last act in the drama. White flags began to flutter along the length of the column, signalling the end of Tenth Army. Bergonzoli surrendered to Colonel Combe, who gave him breakfast, but Tellera had been mortally wounded and died later in the day. In all, 25,000 prisoners were taken, as well as 1,500 wheeled vehicles, 216 guns and over 100 tanks, of which a number remained in working order. In Cairo, Wavell received the following brief signal from O'Connor, who had spent much of the battle at Creagh's headquarters: 'Fox killed in the open'.

Since Operation Compass had begun in December, O'Connor's corps had destroyed ten Italian divisions, taken over 130,000 prisoners, captured 380 tanks and 845 guns, advanced more than 500 miles and occupied half of Libya, all at a cost of 500 killed, 1,373 wounded, 55 missing and a handful of tanks written off. In the wider sphere the Italian Army's inability to fight a modern war had been ruthlessly exposed and Franco announced that he would remain neutral, rejecting a request that German troops be allowed passage through Spain to attack Gibraltar.

O'Connor himself emerged from the campaign as one of the great practitioners of mechanized warfare. He had studied the American Civil War in some detail, admired 'Stonewall' Jackson and approved of the manner in which Grant handled his cavalry, but was not influenced by contemporary theories on the employment of armour. He later commented that his tactics were simply dictated by common sense, adding that 'had they been incorrect the Italians would have fought a great deal better, slowed up our advance, and given us much heavier casualties'. O'Connor and his divisional commanders, Creagh, Beresford-Peirse and Mackay, were all knighted for their part in the campaign.

Because of subsequent events in the Western Desert, one question is always asked about the end of O'Connor's campaign. Could XIII Corps have gone on to capture distant Tripoli? In O'Connor's own words,

> I think we could have done so at once, or fairly shortly after (Beda Fomm), before the Luftwaffe came into the picture. Of course, the question of supplies would have been difficult. But this would have been greatly eased by the Italian rations which we could have picked up at Sirte and Tripoli. Like the rest of the campaign it would have been a risk, but I think personally not a dangerous one.

Should, then, the attempt have been made? The answer to this is only intelligible if one understands Wavell's priorities as they existed then. Once Graziani's army had been destroyed, its remnants in Tripolitania posed no threat and the decision to contain them with a small covering force at El Agheila was quite justifiable; furthermore, the acquisition of more territory was a luxury to which the over-extended British resources could not be committed. Churchill was anxious that troops should be sent to the aid of the hard-pressed Greeks, and as Wavell himself believed that the campaign in Greece stood a reasonable chance of success, this became his prime consideration on 7 February 1941. O'Connor has commented that had he had the slightest inkling of what was to follow, he would have continued his advance until he received the most firm and definite orders to halt.

CHAPTER 6

THE WESTERN DESERT 1941-42

Battles of manoeuvre

In Berlin, Adolf Hitler, already deeply immersed in his plans for an invasion of the Soviet Union, received the news of continued Italian defeats in Greece and North Africa with a growing sense of unease. The grand strategy of his Russian adventure, codenamed Barbarossa, demanded a secure southern flank in the Balkans and the Mediterranean and he had looked to Mussolini to provide

this. Now it seemed that the Italian dictator would face political extinction unless his fortunes were somewhat restored. On 5 February 1941 he again offered Mussolini military assistance in North Africa, and this time the offer was accepted.

Hitler was aware that the assault on Russia would absorb the bulk of the Wehrmacht's resources and he had no inten-

The Stuart was the first American tank to serve in North Africa and was much admired for its handling qualities. Note the battered state of the 'flimsy' petrol containers. Sand has accumulated around the vehicle during a recent dust storm, leaving the crew little room in which to work (Imperial War Museum).

Captured PzKw II in a British harbour area. Like the British, the Germans had little use for their light tanks after the early clashes. This particular example is still in its European colour scheme, indicating the speed with which German units were shipped to Africa (RAC Tank Museum).

German PaK 38 50 mm anti-tank gun on the move. The Afrika Korps's use of anti-tank guns was far more aggressive than that of the Eighth Army (Imperial War Museum).

tion of granting Mussolini an open licence to wage war in North Africa. Instead, he stressed that the objectives were to be limited first to containing the British within their advanced positions at El Agheila, then to providing stiffening and technical advice for the Italians, and finally to recovering the province of Cyrenaica in a joint advance. At this stage the prospect of a drive into Egypt was not even on the agenda.

German staffs set to work with their customary efficiency. The Luftwaffe was already operating against British shipping from Italian airfields, and in March began flying from bases in Tripolitania. The first German troops, belonging to the 5th Light Division, a formation based on a cadre supplied by the experienced 3rd Panzer Division, began disembarking at Tripoli on 14 February. The 5th Light, which itself became 21st Panzer Division in October, was joined in April by the 15th Panzer Division and together these two formed the Deutches Afrika Korps (DAK). In August a number of independent motorized infantry units were amalgamated as the Afrika Division, re-named 90th Light

on 27 November. From 15 August these formations were known together as Panzer Group Afrika.

The Germans differed from their opponents in a number of respects which had an important bearing on the conduct of subsequent operations. With the exception of several hundred former members of the French Foreign Legion they were, of course, initially less desert-wise than the British, and although they learned very quickly they were less inclined to use the huge open spaces to the south of the main battlefront. Many were veterans of the campaigns in Poland and France and were thoroughly experienced in the conduct of mechanized warfare. Their primary loyalty was to their division and they were used to working in all-arms battlegroups. In particular they were adept at combining the movement of tanks with that of anti-tank guns so that the former could retire on the latter if pressed too hard. These 'sword-and-shield' tactics left British tank crews with the uneasy feeling that they were permanently outgunned, but the truth was that most of the damage was caused by all-but-invisible anti-tank gun screens. Most important of all, the Germans appreciated that success in mechanized warfare is obtained at the operative or corps level of command and they therefore fought with their forces concentrated whenever possible. O'Connor had grasped this instinctively, but a full 18 months were to pass before other British commanders did likewise.

For their part, the British possessed a priceless asset in their fierce regimental pride and German ambitions would often founder on this rock when logic dictated a quite different result. Yet in many ways this very asset was also a serious liability because units did not work easily with strangers, particularly if they came from other arms whose problems were unfamiliar to them. Thus, admirable as it might be, this sense of family did little to generate an understanding of the details of mechanized warfare and therefore made the concept of the all-arms battlegroup that much more difficult to implement. Again, the handling of such groups was not always a comfortable experience for commanders who had been brought up in this strictly tribal background.

This flaw would, perhaps, have been less apparent had not the British also been obsessed by dispersion. Something of Lawrence's thoughts on the subject has already been mentioned, and to these Basil Liddell Hart, the eminent military journalist, had added some comments of his own in 1935.

> The dangers of air attack, the aim of mystification, and the need of drawing full value from mechanized mobility, suggest that advancing forces should not only be distributed as widely as is compatible with combined action, but should also be dispersed as much as is compatible with cohesion. Fluidity of force may succeed where concentration of force merely entails a helpless rigidity.

Lawrence, of course, had been speaking of irregular operations, but Liddell Hart was referring to the conduct of regular, mechanized warfare. Unfortunately many British officers failed to see that there was not quite a *consensus ad idem* and chose to regard the remarks of these distinguished commentators as being valid in either context. The basic

fallacy of this view was later concisely expressed by Field Marshal Lord Carver in his book *Tobruk*.

> The problem was to judge what was 'compatible'. Those who believed that mobility alone could achieve a decision had found their faith fully justified in the early desert campaign against the Italians. A wide degree of dispersion, adopted originally for sheer lack of numbers and accentuated both as a means of reducing vulnerability to air attack and of deception where concealment was impossible, became the hallmark of desert veterans; the touchstones by which they judged the degree of 'desert worthiness' of new arrivals. Long after the situation in the air had rendered it unnecessary, this exaggerated dispersion continued undisputed and had, I now believe, a pernicious influence on tactics. The Germans certainly never practised it to the same degree and, although it is true that at times they suffered heavily from air attack, their tactical concentration on the battlefield paid a dividend time and time again.

The most obvious aspect of this policy of dispersion was the Jock Column, which had proved its worth against the unmechanized Italians but could hardly be expected to obtain similar results against the better equipped and more professional Germans. Moreover, the continued employment of Jock Columns, which were understandably popular as they provided a degree of temporary in-

Close-up of the German PaK 38 50 mm anti-tank gun (Imperial War Museum).

Forward tactical headquarters of the 21st Panzer Division showing, left, an SdKfz 250/3 communications half-track, centre, a command version of the PzKw III, and right, the divisional commander's Horch staff car. At the critical command levels the Afrika Korps's forward control of the battle was more efficient than that of the Eighth Army (Bundesarchiv).

dependence, had the effect of weakening the divisional artillery and anti-tank gun assets, often at a time when these should have been concentrated.

Rather more insidious was the effect of dispersion on command, control and communications. Speech communication using the vehicle radios of the day was seldom possible beyond the range of a very few miles. The sets themselves picked up chatter from neighbouring frequencies, Morse from all over the ionosphere, and continuous distorted sound. This in itself made speech difficult, and in the desert it often became impossible after sunset. Thus the transmission of vital information and orders took time, especially if the message was encoded or conditions demanded the use of the 'words twice' procedure. Carrier wave Morse signals could penetrate

the cacophony over longer distance, but again this method took time. As both sides monitored the other's frequencies security became a problem, too. In this respect senior British officers, unused to secure voice procedure, were sometimes the worst offenders, using their radios much as they would a private telephone. These factors resulted not only in perpetuating the issue of detailed written orders which took time to write, time to deliver by despatch rider, and time to digest and disseminate, but also in unit and formation commanders travelling miles to attend briefings at the next higher headquarters, then returning to brief their own troops, which consumed yet more time. By way of contrast the Germans, whose unit and formation headquarters were seldom far from each other, relied to a much greater extent on verbal directives given on the spot at *ad hoc* briefings, a tradition known as 'Saddle Orders'. Inevitably, their decision-making process tended to be much the faster.

The personality which would dominate this, the first desert war between two mechanized armies, was that of Lieutenant-General Erwin Rommel, the 49-year-old officer selected by Hitler to command the German troops in North Africa. An infantryman, Rommel had served with distinction during the First World War and as a company commander had been awarded Imperial Germany's highest decoration, the *Pour le Mérite*, for his part in the Battle of Caporetto. He was less than popular with the upper echelons of the German military establishment, but he had enjoyed Hitler's favour ever since the latter had read his textbook *Infanterie Greift An* (Infantry Assault) and at one stage he had even commanded his personal bodyguard, the Führerbegleitabteilung. During the 1940 campaign in the West he had commanded the 7th Panzer Division with style and dash although he had been thrown momentarily off balance by the British counter-attack at Arras. A

Vickers medium machine-gun team in action. The Vickers was a recoil, gas-assisted, water-cooled weapon with a rate of fire of 450 rounds per minute, although a lower rate was set when the gun was used in the sustained fire role. The water in the cooling jacket boiled after 600 rounds continuous firing, the steam being led off by hose to a condenser can, whence it could be used again on cooling. The gun was very suitable for use in the indirect fire role against distant reverse slopes and suspected enemy concentrations and, using streamlined ammunition, could engage targets up to a maximum range of 4,500 yd. It remained in service with the British Army until the 1960s (Imperial War Museum).

master of his craft, Rommel possessed immense drive, energy and ambition. He was also impatient with higher authority and inclined to take risks which could not be justified. On the other hand, he was frequently blessed with luck and, as Napoleon had said, it was possession of this quality which separated the outstanding commander from the merely competent.

Rommel arrived in Tripoli on 12 February and immediately flew up to the front to assess the situation, leaving orders for 5th Light to follow as soon as its units disembarked, together with the Italian reinforcements which were being shipped to Libya. In Cairo, Wavell was advised of this development but thought it unlikely that the Axis forces would be capable of offensive action before the end of May. In Berlin the Army High Command (Oberkommando des Heer or OKH) had already reached a similar conclusion and had actually forbidden any advance before that date. Rommel, however, decided to act on his own initiative and attack at once, relying on his influence with Hitler to protect him from the wrath of OKH, simultaneously dismissing the nominal authority of Marshal Italo Garibaldi, who had replaced the unhappy Graziani as Italian Commander-in-Chief North Africa after Beda Fomm.

While Rommel's instinct may have been correct, he could not have been fully aware of the inherent weakness of the British position. O'Connor had gone on sick leave and the British troops in Cyrenaica were now commanded by Lieutenant-General Sir Philip Neame, a fighting soldier and a holder of the Victoria Cross who nevertheless lacked experience of senior command. The 7th Armoured and 6th Australian Divisions had also returned to Egypt and been replaced by Major-General M. D. Gambier-Parry's 2nd Armoured Division, which held the forward positions, and Major-General Leslie Morshead's 9th Australian Division, which was in immediate reserve with brigades in Benghazi

and Tobruk. Both of these formations were under-equipped, only partially trained and, with a few exceptions, new to the desert. The situation of 2nd Armoured Division was particularly unsatisfactory for one of its armoured brigades and part of its support group had been detached for service in Greece. The remaining armoured brigade—the 3rd—consisted of 5 RTR with 23 worn-out cruisers and 3rd Hussars and 6 RTR equipped with light tanks and Italian M13s captured at Beda Fomm.

By the end of the third week in March Rommel had in hand Major-General Johannes Streich's 5th Light Division, spearheaded by 70 light and 80 medium tanks, plus three Italian infantry divisions and part of the Italian *Ariete* Armoured Division. On 24 March, a German reconnaissance unit attacked the British advanced post at El Agheila, situated in a neck of land between the sea and an extensive salt marsh. This was held by an armoured car patrol of the King's Dragoon Guards, which withdrew to the main British position, located in a similar defile at Mersa Brega. Thereafter, events moved with bewildering rapidity. On 31 March 5th Light attacked Mersa Brega but were held by 2nd Armoured Division's Support Group. It is possible that the status quo could have been maintained, for a while at least, had Gambier-Parry accepted a suggestion that 3rd Armoured Brigade should counter-attack at once, but he chose to rely on standing orders which required him simply to impose delay, and withdrew from the position.

The effect of this was to invite the same sort of drive across the base of the Benghazi Bulge as that with which O'Connor had destroyed the Italian Tenth Army, and Rommel wasted no time in seizing the opportunity. Having taken Agedabia on 2 April, he sent a reconnaissance battalion north along the coast road to Benghazi, which was entered unopposed two days later, and directed two battlegroups to converge on Mechili, one by way of Sceleidima and Msus and the other along a little used desert track that passed through Ben Gania and Tengeder. To the annoyance of his staff, who often had no idea where he was, he exercised forward control of the advance from his Fieseler Storch light aircraft, landing beside his column commanders to spur them on.

It was now the turn of the British to learn the painful lesson that even a modest reverse in the desert could result in catastrophic consequences in the twinkling of an eye, just as the proximate cause of an avalanche might be the accidental disturbance of a comparatively small stone. The 9th Australian Division avoided being caught in the trap and withdrew into Tobruk, but elsewhere the story was one of unrelieved disaster. 2nd Armoured Division, already suffering from communication difficulties, was subjected to order and counter-order and soon became fragmented, never to reform. Its 3rd Armoured Brigade, short of petrol for its British vehicles and diesel for its M13s, imposed what checks it could but shed broken-down tanks at an average rate of one for every ten miles of movement until by 5 April it had all but ceased to exist as a fighting formation. The following day Rommel's columns reached Mechili, capturing Gambier-Parry and his staff as well as overrunning the independent 3rd Indian Motor Brigade. This attack is of some interest in that the Germans used trucks to raise dust as a means of concealing the paucity of their numbers but in the event such precautions proved unnecessary as the brigade consisted solely of lorried infantry battalions and lacked artillery support and anti-tank guns. Even so, almost one third of its members managed to evade capture and reached Tobruk.

In the longer term much worse was to follow. Wavell, whose own reaction to the Axis offensive had been ambivalent, lost confidence in Neame and asked O'Connor to take over. O'Connor declined but offered to act as Neame's adviser and flew to the front. On 7

April Neame and O'Connor, travelling in the same unescorted staff car, were captured by German motorcycle troops near Derna. It was a loss from which the British Army would be slow to recover. Also captured were Brigadier Rimington, the commander of 3rd Armoured Brigade, and Brigadier Combe, the former commanding officer of the 11th Hussars, who had accompanied O'Connor forward.

Having been advised by Admiral Cunningham that Tobruk could be supplied by sea, Wavell decided that the fortress would be held. A fourth Australian brigade and 1 RTR, equipped with cruisers, were shipped in to reinforce the garrison, bringing its strength to 25,000 men, five field artillery regiments (one 18-pounder and four 25-pounders), one medium regiment, 25 cruiser tanks, four Matildas, 15 light tanks and the King's Dragoon Guards' 30 Marmon Herrington armoured cars. Only sixteen 2-pounder anti-tank guns were available and it was decided that these would be supplemented by 25-pounders firing armour-piercing shot over open sights as the situation demanded. The garrison's major asset, however, lay in the steely determination of its commander, Major-General Leslie Morshead, that Tobruk was not going to fall. Morshead, a veteran of the First World War and a shipping executive in civilian life, represented the Australian ideal of a citizen general and was affectionately known to his men as Ming the Merciless, the original Emperor Ming being the cruel, ruthless opponent of the science-fiction film hero Flash Gordon. As 5th Light and the Italian divisions closed in around the perimeter Morshead tersely informed his senior officers: 'We'll have no Dunkirk here. If we get out of here, it will be down a road we have cleared for ourselves in battle. But there will be no surrender and no retreat.'

As there were insufficient troops present to man the whole of the 30 mile perimeter in strength, Morshead decided to employ a mobile defence, channelling any penetration on to tank killing grounds by a combination of minefields and natural obstacles. The infantry manning the outer defences, lacking adequate anti-tank protection, were instructed to let the enemy's armour roll past them and then surface to tackle his own infantry. When major assaults were not in progress aggressive patrolling was to be the order of the day, a policy which the Italians in particular found most unsettling.

For his part Rommel believed that the increased number of ships heading for Tobruk could only mean that an evacuation was being planned. He was already considering crossing the Egyptian frontier and although he was aware that he would require the logistic support which the deep-water harbour could provide were he to do so, he was for the present more intent on preventing the British embarkation, just as he had prevented that of the crack 51st Highland Division at St Valéry on the coast of France, 10 months earlier. It seemed unlikely that the British, caught wrong-footed by his advance, could have recovered their balance and the prospect of eliminating their presence in Cyrenaica by repeating this spectacular achievement was a temptation too great to be resisted.

On 11 April the defences on the central sector were probed with the loss of several Italian tanks, destroyed in a gunnery duel across the wire and anti-tank ditch by 1 RTR's cruisers. Three days later a more determined effort was made in the same area, using the 5th Panzer Regiment, the 8th Motor-Cycle Battalion, which had captured Neame and O'Connor, and part of the *Ariete* Armoured Division which, to Rommel's fury, arrived late and contributed little. Having secured a crossing of the anti-tank ditch the German tanks drove on for two miles only to find themselves on a killing ground with a line of 25-pounders ahead and *portée* anti-tank guns on either flank. Tanks were already erupting in smoke and flame when 1 RTR counter-attacked from the east, all but invisible in the glare of the early

morning sun. Having lost 17 of his tanks Colonel Olbricht, commanding 5th Panzer Regiment, decided that enough was enough and embarked on a hasty withdrawal, harried by 1 RTR as far as the perimeter. The German crews, having enjoyed easy victories in Poland, France and thus far in Africa, were badly shaken by their ordeal and the reaction of the survivors varied between dumb disbelief and hysterical panic. The 8th Motor-Cycle Battalion, fighting as dismounted infantry, was left to its fate. Those of its men who attempted to scramble aboard their retreating tanks were quickly shot off; the remainder were pinned down and wiped out by an Australian counter-attack. The 5th Light, which believed its opponent to be groggy and on the ropes, had suddenly been sent reeling back across the ring with a bloody nose. Streich, its commander, believed himself incredibly fortunate that Morshead did not choose to follow up his victory. When ordered by Rommel to resume the attack that afternoon he asked, with what? With his 19 remaining tanks and the five officers and 92 men that were all that was left of the 8th Motor-Cycle Battalion? The assault was not renewed, but Rommel characteristically blamed Streich and Olbricht for the failure and decided privately that they would have to go at the earliest possible opportunity.

One reason for the low German tank strength was that the desert had also caught up with 5th Light. There had, of course, been some battle casualties during the long advance from El Agheila, but the number of breakdowns had soared as engine air filters clogged with sand, while in many cases the strain on transmissions and running gear had proved intolerable. 5th Panzer Regiment desperately needed time to put its house in order before the next assault but while its tank crews worked hard their efforts were balanced by the arrival of D Squadron 7 RTR in Tobruk, bringing with them 14 of the formidable Matildas.

A Valentine crew change a roadwheel with assistance from the squadron fitters, whose mobile workshop is in the background (Imperial War Museum).

The arrival of 15th Panzer Division's infantry element from Tripoli enabled Rommel to launch a second assault. This was directed at the south-western corner of the perimeter and began during the night of 30 April with an infantry attack which secured a breach one-and-a-half miles wide in the outer defence. Through this passed the 5th Panzer Regiment, now restored to a tank strength of 70. The regiment's leading battalion, some 40 strong, headed due east towards Tobruk but had covered only a mile when it rolled on to a newly-laid minefield. Seventeen of its tanks were disabled and although all but five were repaired under fire further progress along this axis was clearly barred. Meanwhile the second battalion had turned right and begun rolling up the Australian line of defence posts. After five posts had been overrun and the attack had covered three miles in the face of a growing artillery response, the German tanks were halted by 1 RTR, firing from the front and flank. They withdrew after losing three of their

number in exchange for one cruiser but, having replenished their fuel and ammunition they came on again in the afternoon, only to be brought to a standstill by concentrated artillery fire. 1 RTR, reinforced by D Squadron 7 RTR with five Matildas, then counter-attacked and by dusk had recovered four of the five posts. They were then assailed by both of 5th Panzer Regiment's battalions and lost two cruisers and two Matildas in a furious tank battle which lasted until darkness made shooting impossible.

The following day Rommel decided to break off the attack, which had resulted in the net gain of a useless toe-hold. 5th Panzer Regiment's strength had fallen to 35 tanks and 1,200 casualties had been incurred, the majority among the inexperienced German infantry. With British forces active on the frontier similar expensive assaults on the fortress could not be contemplated for the present. Nor were Rommel's superiors inclined to leave him a free hand. Brauchitsch, the Army's Commander-in-Chief, could hardly punish him for recovering most of Cyrenaica at such little cost, but the fact was that Rommel had flagrantly disobeyed orders. Halder, the Chief of General Staff, described his actions as those of a soldier gone 'stark mad' and sent over his deputy, von Paulus, to exercise a restraining influence.

Von Paulus, who was to command the German Sixth Army at Stalingrad, arrived at Rommel's command post in time to witness the second assault on Tobruk and the result convinced him that there was a real danger that Axis resources in Africa were being stretched beyond their limit. He advised Rommel that he should remain on the strategic defensive and even be prepared to abandon the siege of Tobruk in the event of a major British offensive. His report to OKH echoed that of von Thoma, stressing that the difficulties of sea-borne communications imposed a physical limit on the number of troops which could be supported in Africa and, with the exception of units already on their way, he saw no point in reinforcing Rommel. Subsequently, Rommel was to complain that OKH repeatedly denied him the resources that would have enabled him to secure a decisive victory. This begged the question that however vital the campaign might be to British interests, for the German Army it was a sideshow made necessary by the need to prop up its tottering allies and tie down British divisions where they could do least harm to the Reich. Again, even if OKH had been favourably disposed, such a view took little account of whatever thoughts the Royal Navy or the Royal Air Force might have on the subject.

Rommel's situation was indeed far from enviable, since he was forced to divide his attention between the static siege of Tobruk and mobile warfare on the frontier. In the latter area German reconnaissance units had brawled with light forces commanded by Brigadier W. H. E. Gott but had established themselves at Capuzzo, Sollum and Halfaya Pass. Wavell

was determined to recapture these positions as a springboard for the relief of Tobruk and reinforced Gott until his command consisted of 22nd Guards Brigade, 7th Armoured Division's Support Group, 4 RTR with two Matilda squadrons, 2 RTR with 29 reconditioned cruisers, and the 11th Hussars.

The British attack, codenamed Brevity, began at dawn on 15 May with an assault by C Squadron 4 RTR and 2nd Scots Guards on the position covering the head of Halfaya Pass, which was held by a company of the German 15th Motorized Light Infantry Battalion and a battery of Italian artillery. Despite being taken by surprise the Italian gunners put up a stiff fight and they had clearly given some thought to the problem of how best to deal with the Matildas. As the leading wave of tanks reared over their sangar walls they manhandled their guns a few paces to the rear and sent rounds through the vulnerable belly plates. Seven tanks were knocked out in this way, but the remainder had overwhelmed the opposition before the infantry arrived to round up the prisoners, many of whom had been cooking their breakfast. Sollum fell to a second attack led by a single troop of Matildas.

The sound of fighting on the coastal sector had alerted the German battle-group holding Capuzzo. When A Squadron 4 RTR and 1st Durham Light Infantry arrived they met fierce resistance. Seven Matildas were disabled with track and suspension damage but two more led the infantry's successful attack on the fort. The Germans counterattacked with II Battalion 5th Panzer Regiment and re-took the position later in the day, both sides sustaining heavy casualties in the process. To the south 2 RTR was still intact after a day spent skirmishing on the open desert flank, but the mechanical state of the regiment's cruisers was beginning to cause serious concern.

At dusk, Gott concluded that further progress could not be achieved with his slender resources and withdrew, leaving 3rd Cold-stream Guards and a composite squadron of nine Matildas to hold Halfaya Pass. By coincidence Colonel von Herff, commanding the force at Capuzzo, was also withdrawing in the belief that his badly-mauled troops could not withstand another assault. The result was that a reinforcement battlegroup, despatched by a thoroughly alarmed Rommel, arrived to find the battlefield deserted.

Rommel had no intention of leaving Halfaya Pass in Wavell's hands and he promptly began planning its recapture. 5th Panzer Regiment was detailed to provide a diversion while an infantry holding attack was launched at the centre of the position, but the *coup de grâce* was to be delivered by the 8th Panzer Regiment from 15th Panzer Division, attacking from the east accompanied by motorized infantry, the whole operation being supported by the fire of several artillery and anti-aircraft units. Altogether, 160 tanks would be used to defeat nine in a startling demonstration of the technique of overkill.

However, when the attack began on 27 May, the nut refused to be intimidated by the sledgehammer. In response to 5th Panzer Regiment's demonstration, the Matilda squadron, commanded by Major G. C. Miles, sallied forth and proceeded to lay about them. 5th Panzer Regiment had unhappy memories of its encounters with the Matilda within the Tobruk perimeter and at Capuzzo, and one of its battalions shied away. Rommel, beside himself with rage, used the occasion to rid himself of Streich and Olbricht; they were lucky, for the unfortunate battalion commander received a court martial for his pains. Nevertheless, the ultimate outcome of the battle was never in doubt. Gott ordered Lieutenant-Colonel Moubray, commanding the Coldstream Guards, to disengage and the Matildas covered the withdrawal of the battalion, and such of the artillery's guns as could be got away, down the Pass and on to the coastal plain; British losses amounted to 150 men, six tanks and several guns.

Rommel now reorganized his forces to

A9 Cruiser Tank aboard a tank transporter. The use of tank transporters saved track mileage and therefore increased operational endurance, particularly in a harsh environment like the desert (Imperial War Museum).

SdKfz 222 light armoured car. The initial contacts between British and German troops in North Africa were made by reconnaissance units (RAC Tank Museum).

meet the possibility of being attacked on two fronts simultaneously. The Italians, with the *Ariete* Armoured Division in support, maintained the siege of Tobruk while 5th Light, under the command of Major-General Johannes von Ravenstein, licked its wounds in the desert south of the fortress and Major-General Walter Neumann-Silkow's 15th Panzer Division assumed responsibility for the defence of the frontier.

The German commander was right to be cautious for in April Churchill, determined to restore British fortunes in North Africa, had taken the daring step of despatching a fast convoy of five ships, loaded with tanks and aircraft, through the Mediterranean under the operational codename of Tiger. One ship was sunk by mines off Malta but on 12 May the remainder reached Alexandria, where 238 tanks and 43 Hurricanes were unloaded. Disappointed by the result of Brevity, Churchill urged Wavell to make prompt use of what he called his 'Tiger Cubs' and mount a fresh offensive at the earliest possible moment. Most of the 'Tiger Cubs' were Matildas but there

were enough of the new—and unfortunately untried—Crusader cruiser tanks to equip 6 RTR.

Wavell planned a scaled-up version of Brevity, codenamed Battleaxe, the objects of which were the recapture of the frontier positions, the destruction of the German armour, the relief of Tobruk and exploitation as far as Derna. The operation would involve the whole of XIII Corps, commanded by Beresford-Peirse, which consisted of 7th Armoured Division under Creagh and 4th Indian Division, recently returned from its successful campaign in East Africa, under Major-General F. W. Messervy. 7th Armoured Division possessed two armoured brigades, the 4th and 7th, the former consisting of 4 RTR and A and B Squadrons 7 RTR, equipped with Matildas throughout, while the latter contained 2 RTR, still with A.9, A.10 and A.13 cruisers, and 6 RTR. The 4th Indian Division contained only two infantry bridges, 22nd Guards and 11th Indian. During the first phase of the operation 4th Indian Division, with the infantry tanks of 4th Armoured Brigade under command, would capture Halfaya Pass, Point 206 six miles inland, and Fort Capuzzo. Simultaneously 7th Armoured Division would advance on Hafid Ridge to the south, hoping to attract the bulk of the enemy's armour, being rejoined by 4th Armoured Brigade once this had been released by Messervy.

Battleaxe began at 05:45 on 15 June with an unsuccessful attack by two Indian battalions on the Axis positions at the foot of Halfaya Pass. On the escarpment above, C Squadron 4 RTR, commanded by Major Miles, advanced on the heavily-fortified head of the pass with 2nd Cameron Highlanders but was shot to pieces by five dug-in dual-purpose 88 mm anti-aircraft/ anti-tank guns. Miles was killed and only one of his Matildas survived the encounter. The Germans had also received new 50 mm anti-tank guns and some of these took part in the defence of Point 206, which did not fall until dusk, and then at some cost to A and B Squadrons 4 RTR. At Capuzzo 7 RTR and 22nd Guards Brigade smashed their way into the fort, overcoming fierce resistance. On 7th Armoured Division's sector there was some initial confusion as to the location of Hafid Ridge. When this was resolved both cruiser regiments attacked in turn but could make little progress against a defence in depth which included four Eighty-Eights. Nor did the attack succeed in attracting most of the German armour, although Rommel sent down a battalion of 5th Panzer Regiment and towards evening this engaged 7th Armoured Brigade in a long-range gunnery duel. 2 RTR had begun the day with 38 tanks and 6 RTR with 50, but when they disengaged at last light these figures had been reduced to 28 and 20 respectively. The major cause of vehicle loss was breakdown and in this respect the new Crusader was a serious disappointment, its principal faults being an inadequate air filter, weak fan drive and an unreliable gear selector.

There had been much careless talk on the radio and this had given Rommel an accurate picture of the British dispositions. He decided that the following day 15th Panzer would counter-attack at Capuzzo while 5th Light executed a wide flanking march through the desert and then swung north towards the escarpment and Halfaya Pass, effectively trapping most of XIII Corps within a pocket.

The attack on Capuzzo was met by Messervy's artillery and the accurate fire of 7 RTR's hull-down Matildas. By noon the 8th Panzer Regiment had hauled off with 50 of its 80 tanks out of action. Its commander decided to bypass the position but abandoned the move when 4 RTR was encountered at Point 206.

Nonetheless, the attack did pay dividends in other areas. Creagh had intended renewing his attack on Hafid Ridge once Messervy had released 4th Armoured Brigade, but this Messervy felt unable to do. Instead, 7th Armoured Brigade found itself engaged with 5th

The Crusader Cruiser Tank had a disastrous operational début during Operation Battleaxe (RAC Tank Museum).

Panzer Regiment in a running fight which took it towards the frontier. The effect of this was to reduce 2 RTR's tank strength to 15 and that of 6 RTR to 10.

During the early hours of 17 June, Creagh called Beresford-Peirse and asked him to fly up as an important decision was required. The German intercept operators were listening and Rommel deduced, correctly, that Creagh no longer felt capable of handling the situation. He therefore ordered 15th Panzer Division to conform to 5th Light's northward movement toward the escarpment.

Messervy was soon in no doubt as to the enemy's intentions. At 10:45 he spoke to Creagh and told him that he was abandoning Capuzzo to avoid being cut off. For the sake of security the conversation was held in Urdu, the Indian Army's lingua franca. An hour later Beresford-Peirse arrived at Creagh's headquarters with Wavell, tacitly accepting the decision.

The safe withdrawal of 4th Indian Division through the narrowing corridor between the German spearheads and the escarpment depended upon Brigadier Alec Gatehouse's

Turret-down Crusader squadron keeps watch across a crest line while infantry dig in (National Army Museum).

4th Armoured Brigade. Both Matilda regiments were much reduced in strength but each formed a composite squadron. In an epic fight lasting six hours, the two squadrons held off a German division apiece. When the last of the infantry had been seen through the gap they broke contact and disappeared eastwards into the gathering dusk. The Fourth's squadron, which had halted 5th Light, was reduced to six tanks; the Seventh's, which had be engaged with 15th Panzer Division, was down to five.

This was the last act in the drama of Battleaxe. The three-day battle had cost the British 969 casualties, including 381 killed and missing, and 91 tanks, of which 64 were Matildas, a high proportion of the tank loss having been caused by mechanical failure. German personnel casualties amounted to 678, including 328 killed and missing. The British claim to have disabled approximately 100 enemy tanks was probably close to the truth, but as the Germans retained the battlefield they were able to recover all but 12 burned-out hulks.

The most notable casualties, however,

were the senior British commanders. Churchill, extremely bitter about the squandering of his 'Tiger Cubs', ordered Wavell to exchange appointments with General Sir Claude Auchinleck, the Commander-in-Chief India. For the moment Wavell's victories over Graziani and in East Africa, Syria and Iraq counted for less than his defeats in Greece, Crete and on the frontier, but in later years Churchill's views mellowed somewhat and he was to comment that 'We had ridden a willing horse to a standstill'. For his part Wavell, tired and depressed, was not sorry to leave.

Beresford-Peirse and Creagh were dismissed. The former, despite his experience during Operation Compass, had not emulated O'Connor's forward style of command. Instead, he had established his Corps headquarters at Sidi Barrani, 60 miles behind the fighting, where poor communications had resulted in his being out of touch at critical periods and his control of the operation had been uncertain. Creagh, with only two armoured regiments in hand, was handicapped by 4th Indian Division's unavoidable retention of 4th Armoured Brigade, but on this occasion there was no gainsaying the fact that 7th Armoured Division had not performed well under his command.

For the British, the major lesson of Battleaxe was that, given the Germans' integrated style of fighting, the enemy's armour could not be brought to battle unless his anti-tank guns were engaged simultaneously. This took a very long time to assimilate. Moreover, it was a task which the majority of British tanks were unable to perform because their 2-pounder guns fired only a solid armour-piercing shot and were outranged by the anti-tank guns. Close support versions, armed with a howitzer firing a high explosive shell with the necessary reach, did exist but were normally issued at the scale of one or two per squadron and were not always available. In structuring their armoured forces, the Germans had foreseen this problem and the PzKw IV, armed with a 75 mm howitzer, was present in much greater numbers in their tank regiments. The situation contained two ironies, the first of which was that the greatest tank killer of all, the Eighty-Eight, was high-standing and terribly vulnerable to shellfire. The second was that the British 3.7 in anti-aircraft gun was equally potent and had actually undergone trials in the anti-tank role earlier in the year, but increased Luftwaffe activity had resulted in these weapons being concentrated for the air defence of Alexandria. The key to the British problem lay in a much tighter interlock between armoured formations and their supporting artillery, but this was seldom developed adequately.

After Battleaxe the Western Desert remained quiet for five months. The investment of Tobruk continued and both sides maintained a wary watch on each other across the frontier, settling into a daily routine. Initially the Germans had been fed a diet of black bread, tinned sardines in oil and sausage from which the fat oozed in the heat. This was quite unsuitable for a hot climate and soon gave rise to dysentery and other disorders. Rather more palatable if extremely monotonous was the tinned beef bearing the monogram AM, standing for *Administrazione Militare,* but which Germans said really stood for *Alter Mann* (Old Man) and the Italians *Arabo Morte* (Dead Arab). On the whole the British fared rather better with hard tack biscuits, corned beef and composite ration packs.

As the sweltering days of high summer merged together and those at the front grumbled about the food, caught up on their sleep and looked forward to mail deliveries which punctuated the monotony, there were major developments behind the scenes. During September and October most of the Tobruk garrison was relieved by sea, the 9th Australian Division being replaced by Major-General R. Scobie's 70th Division and the Polish Carpathian Brigade. The garrison was additionally reinforced with 4 RTR which, together with 1 RTR and D Squadron 7 RTR, formed 32nd Army Tank Brigade under Brigadier A. C. Willison. The tank brigade differed from the armoured brigade in that it was equipped with heavily armoured infantry tanks and generally fought dispersed in direct support of infantry operations. In this instance 4 RTR and D Squadron 7 RTR possessed a total of 69 Matildas, but 1 RTR was still armed with 32 old cruisers and 25 light tanks.

Reinforcements also reached Egypt in the form of Major-General Bernard Freyberg's 2nd New Zealand Division, already blooded in Greece and Crete, the 1st and 2nd South African Divisions, commanded respectively by Major-Generals G. L. Brink and H. B. Klopper, plus 1st Army Tank Brigade and 22nd Armoured Brigade. Churchill wasted no time in urging the new Commander-in-Chief to resume the offensive but Auchinleck was not to be hurried and despatched a pointed signal to the Prime Minister:

> It is quite clear to me that infantry divisions, however well equipped and trained, are no good for offensive operations in this terrain

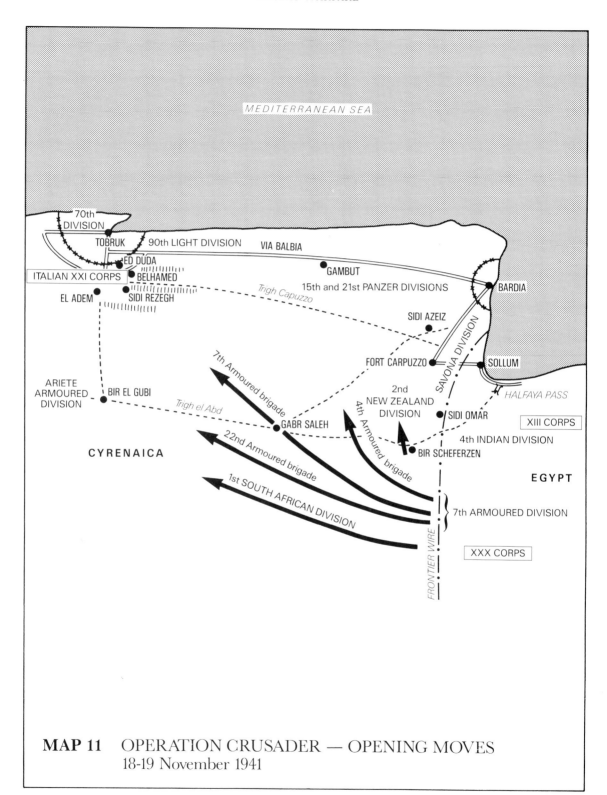

MAP 11 OPERATION CRUSADER — OPENING MOVES
18-19 November 1941

against enemy armoured forces. Infantry divisions are and will be needed to hold defended localities after enemy armoured forces have been neutralized and destroyed, but the main offensive must be carried out by armoured formations supported by motorized formations.

There were, however, inter-service considerations to be taken into account as well. Admiral Cunningham had been as good as his word and kept Tobruk supplied in the face of heavy Axis air attacks, but the cost in warships and merchant vessels sunk or damaged was high and he was anxious to be rid of the burden. Similarly, Air Marshal Tedder required the airfields in Cyrenaica so that air cover could be provided for Malta's vital supply convoys. Although neither brought undue pressure to bear on the Commander-in-Chief these considerations, coupled with the recognition that the enemy had also been reinforced, led Auchinleck to choose 18 November as the date upon which he would launch a fresh offensive, codenamed Crusader, in preference to his original choice of January 1942, by which time the whole of 1st Armoured Division would have reached Egypt.

The British troops in the Western Desert were now elevated to the status of being the Eighth Army, commanded by Lieutenant-General Sir Alan Cunningham, the Admiral's younger brother, who had distinguished himself during the campaign in East Africa. The Army consisted of two corps, XIII under Lieutenant-General A. R. Godwin-Austen, who had also served in East Africa, and XXX under Major-General Willoughby Norrie. During Crusader XIII Corps, consisting of 4th Indian Division, 2nd New Zealand Division and 1st Army Tank Brigade, was to bypass the frontier defences to the south, containing some positions and assaulting others from the rear, and strike north to the Via Balbia, along which it would advance towards Tobruk. Further south XXX Corps, containing 7th Armoured Division, 1st South African Division and 22nd Guards Brigade, was to strike

north-westwards across the desert, destroy the enemy's armour and effect a junction with the Tobruk garrison, which would simultaneously effect a breakout in the area Belhamed/Ed Duda. The 2nd South African Division was to remain in Army reserve for the moment. Discounting light tanks, which were of little use, the total British tank strength in Tobruk and on the frontier amounted to 201 infantry tanks and 523 cruisers. The latter included Crusaders, modified since their dismal performance in Battleaxe, and American Stuarts which, while extremely reliable, were driven by fuel-hungry radial engines and consequently had a restricted range of about 40 miles. With the exception of a few close support models, all were armed with the 2-pounder or its equivalent the American 37 mm, giving approximate parity with the 37 mm or short 50 mm guns mounted by the PzKw III.

Before discussing the course of Crusader, a battle so fluid and confused that at times commanders and troops on both sides had little idea of the general situation, it is necessary to examine what had been taking place on the Axis side of the lines. The invasion of Russia had absorbed the bulk of German resources since June but Rommel had been reinforced to the point where 5th Light became 21st Panzer Division and it was possible to form the Special Service Afrika Division, which contained most of the old Foreign Legion hands. In addition to the Afrika Korps under Lieutenant-General Ludwig Crüwell, Rommel also had under command Lieutenant-General Enea Navarini's XXI Italian Corps, containing the *Brescia, Pavia, Trento* and *Bologna* Infantry Divisions, deployed around the Tobruk perimeter, and the *Savona* Infantry Division which, with German support, was manning the frontier defences. Outside Rommel's immediate control and responsible directly to General Ettore Bastico, Garibaldi's successor as Commander-in-Chief, was Lieutenant-General Gastone Gambara's XX Mobile Corps with the *Ariete* Armoured Division at Bir el Gubi and the *Trieste* Motorized Division at Bir Hacheim. After deducting the light PzKw IIs, the German tank strength amounted to 139 PzKw IIIs and 35 PzKw IVs, while the Italians could field 146 of the unreliable M13s. Superficially, therefore, it seemed that in the coming battle the Axis would be heavily outnumbered, but the balance was redressed by the German anti-tank guns. The Afrika Korps possessed no fewer than 96 of the excellent 50 mm PAK 38s, which were longer and more powerful weapons than the gun of the same calibre fitted to the PzKw III, and 12 of the formidable Eighty-Eights; a further 23 Eighty-Eights were dug in on the frontier in support of the *Savona* Division.

Encouraged by his early successes in Russia, Hitler now extended his ambitions to the Middle East and Rommel was invited to submit plans for the capture of Tobruk and the invasion of Egypt. Both undertakings would be difficult, for Malta was proving to be a major thorn in the side of the Axis. Operating from the island the RAF, the 10th Submarine Flotilla and surface units were littering the sea bed with sunken ships, tanks, guns, ammunition and stores of every kind bound for Tripoli. On average, one third of all cargoes loaded in southern Italian ports failed to reach their destination. One consequence of this was that the Axis armies in North Africa were perpetually short of fuel. Another was that the Italian Merchant Marine was losing ships faster than they could be replaced and this led to a request that Tobruk should be captured as quickly as possible, not only to provide a more secure sea passage but also to ease the logistic burden considerably. Rommel therefore began training the Afrika Korps for a major assault on the fortress, to be delivered against the southeastern sector of the defences with the support of a specially assembled artillery group which included nine 210 mm, 38 150 mm and 12 105 mm howitzers. Unfortunately for him, dur-

ing the night of 8/9 November Force K from Malta, commanded by Captain William Agnew RN and consisting of two cruisers and two destroyers, sank an entire convoy of seven ships without loss to itself although it was heavily outnumbered by the Italian naval escort. As a direct result of this only 2,500 tons of fuel reached North Africa that month and the assault on Tobruk had to be postponed. By coincidence, however, it also left the Afrika Korps ideally positioned to meet both the Crusader offensive and the Tobruk garrison's breakout.

So efficient was the Eighth Army's security that when its leading elements crossed the frontier on 18 November Rommel at first refused to believe that General Cunningham contemplated anything more serious than the sort of reconnaissance in force he had himself conducted in September, with negative results. As the Luftwaffe's airfields were unusable for the moment after torrential rain, it was some time before the truth was discovered and XXX Corps enjoyed a day's free running, its left flank protected by 1st South African Division.

7th Armoured Division, now commanded by Gott, contained no less than three armoured brigades. On the left was Brigadier J. Scott-Cockburn's newly arrived and completely inexperienced 22nd Armoured Brigade (3rd and 4th County of London Yeomanry and 2nd Royal Gloucestershire Hussars) with 158 Crusaders; in the centre was Brigadier G. Davy's veteran 7th Armoured Brigade (7th Hussars, 2 and 6 RTR) with 26 A.10s, 71 A.13s and 71 Crusaders; and on the right, covering the left flank of XIII Corps, was Brigadier A. H. Gatehouse's equally experienced 4th Armoured Brigade (8th Hussars, 3 and 5 RTR) with 165 Stuarts. Impressive as this might be on paper, it diluted the division's artillery and infantry resources to the point at which none of the brigades was adequately supported. Furthermore, there was a gap of 20 miles between the 22nd and the 7th, and a further gap of 35 miles between the 7th and the 4th, which meant that each armoured brigade was working in virtual isolation.

Shortly after noon on the 19th, Scott-Cockburn's brigade made contact with Italian troops in a position which it believed was five miles east of Bir el Gubi. Gott was visiting Scott-Cockburn at the time and ordered him to attack, despite warnings from the 11th Hussars that the position was Bir el Gubi itself and that it was heavily defended. The assault was delivered by the Gloucestershire Hussars and 4 CLY, supported by the brigade's single battery of 25-pounders. The Italians, however, could not be taken for granted and had dug in their anti-tank guns, carefully siting dummies and derelict vehicles to draw the tanks' fire. The *Ariete's* armoured regiment mounted a counter-attack and although 12 anti-tank guns and 35 M13s were knocked out in exchange for 25 Crusaders the objective remained in Italian hands.

On the division's right flank, 4th Armoured Brigade had been shadowed by German armoured cars and as the afternoon wore on Gatehouse ordered 3 RTR to chase them away to the north. This the regiment achieved without difficulty, its pursuit bringing it within sight of Bardia. At DAK head-quarters Crüwell overestimated the significance of this development and began moving 15th Panzer Division into a blocking position. Meanwhile, the remainder of the brigade was heavily dive-bombed and then counter-attacked by 21st Panzer Division. As dispersion was practised within brigades as well as divisions, the brunt of this was borne by 8th Hussars, who had lost 20 tanks by nightfall.

On the morning of the 20th the contest was renewed until 21st Panzer disappeared to the north-west, but during the afternoon 15th Panzer, released from its task of guarding an empty stretch of desert, closed in on the brigade and in heavy fighting forced its three regiments to give ground. By the end of the day 4th Armoured's strength had been reduced to 98; the destruction of some 50 enemy tanks was claimed, although the number actually written off was only seven. Nevertheless, during the evening Gott switched 22nd Armoured across the battlefield and there was

The Sidi Rezegh battlefield showing a wrecked PzKw III and a 2-pounder portée (Col P.W.H. Whiteley).

genuine optimism that on the morrow the two armoured brigades would together finish 15th Panzer.

When the 21st dawned, however, it revealed a desert on which the only German tanks to be seen were wrecks from the previous day's fighting. The unopposed thrust by 7th Armoured Brigade and 7th Armoured Division's Support Group towards Sidi Rezegh airfield had seriously alarmed Rommel and he had ordered Crüwell to despatch both panzer divisions there as quickly as possible. Over the next two days the battlefield became an inextricable tangle of friend and foe in which formations of both sides found themselves simultaneously attacking in one direction and maintaining a desperate defence in another. For the sake of simplicity this phase of Crusader is usually referred to as the Multi-Layer Battle, but for those involved it lacked any sort of form and was an apparently chaotic jumble of ferocious tactical battles inducing stark terror and utter fatigue. In the north the Tobruk garrison had begun to break out against opposition from the Afrika Division, which was also trying to defend Sidi Rezegh against 7th Armoured Brigade and the Support Group, who were in turn under attack from the south-east by DAK, whose anti-tank gunners were doing their best to hold off the pursuit by 4th and 22nd Armoured Brigades.

At 08:30 on the 21st the infantry of Brigadier Campbell's Support Group, consisting of three King's Royal Rifle Corps companies and one company of the Rifle Brigade, launched an attack on Sidi Rezegh ridge across the airfield, taking their objective with heavy casualties. Two squadrons of 6 RTR then crossed the ridge and headed straight for Ed Duda, but as they approached Belhamed they drove into a half-circle of anti-tank guns, including four Eighty-Eights which Rommel had personally brought up, and were wiped out.

While the Support Group's assault was in progress Davy, warned of the approach of 15th and 21st Panzer Divisions, had turned round 7th Hussars and 2 RTR to meet the threat. Few of those watching the oncoming dust clouds retained any illusions about survival but one Hussar officer saw no point in brooding on the fact and speculated casually on whether he had time for a shave. He had but, tragically, it was his last for 7th Hussars were assailed first by the full force of 21st Panzer and then by 15th Panzer, which shouldered its way past 2 RTR. Within 30 minutes the Hussars had lost their commanding officer and all but ten of their tanks. 2 RTR drove to the assistance of their embattled comrades and succeeded in inflicting some loss but were held off by the Germans' rapidly deployed anti-tank gun screen.

7th Armoured Brigade had been virtually eliminated from the contest but a lull ensued while the panzer divisions replenished their fuel and ammunition. When they came on again at 11:30 it was clear that they intended to recapture Sidi Rezegh airfield and destroy the Support Group, which was already being dive-bombed and was under fire from Rommel's artillery group, located at Belhamed. They were met by a furious response from the 25-pounders of 60th Field Regiment and part of 4 RHA, firing over open sights, and the 2-pounder *portées* of 3 RHA, and fought to a standstill. The German artillery and mortars joined in until, as an officer of the Rifle Brigade put it, 'to look over the edge of a slit trench was suicidal'. The gunners gave as good as they got and were occasionally rewarded by the sight of their victims erupting in smoke and flames. Typical of the spirit of Sidi Rezegh was the action of Second Lieutenant Ward Gunn, who commanded a troop of four *portées* in Major Bernard Pinney's J Battery 3 RHA. At the height of the battle Gunn edged his vehicles out to bring them within killing range of the enemy tanks. Through the enveloping smother of drifting dust, smoke and exploding shells he was seen directing the fire of his guns on foot, an observer commenting that 'never was there a clearer case of a man possessed with the joy of battle'. Two of the *portées* succumbed quickly to direct hits, followed by a third some minutes later. The fourth continued firing until only one man remained alive, and he began to drive it out of action. Pinney told Gunn to halt the vehicle, which he did, then manned the 2-pounder after removing the dead crew. The major joined him but was immediately compelled to deal with a fire in an ammunition bin. Gunn kept firing until he was killed. Pinney moved his body and took over the gun himself until further hits rendered it unusable, then joined another of his troops which was concentrating its fire on a group of tanks trying to work its

way round the battery's flank. This move was defeated and the remainder of the enemy armour retired. Pinney was killed by a stray shell next morning; both he and Gunn were recommended for the posthumous award of the Victoria Cross, but it was granted only to Gunn. J Battery, however, received the Royal Artillery's rarest distinction, an Honour Title, *Sidi Rezegh,* only one of five awarded during the Second World War.

The situation was further eased by the arrival of 22nd Armoured Brigade, which reached the battlefield late that afternoon. Next morning the contest was renewed when 21st Panzer Division attacked the Support Group

Defusing mines lifted by hand (Imperial War Museum).

again, this time from the west. Campbell was the soul of the defence, darting here and there in his open car, manning weapons, rounding up small groups of tanks from the remnants of 7th Armoured Brigade and leading them into action in person. 22nd Armoured Brigade mounted an uncoordinated series of counter-attacks from the south but was forced to retreat with serious tank losses.

A more promising counter-attack, launched by 4th Armoured Brigade with 3 and 5 RTR across Sidi Rezegh airfield from the east, broke down amid dust, smoke and general confusion in the mistaken belief that it was being fired on by 22nd Armoured Brigade, although it did cause 21st Panzer Division to retire from the immediate area. Nevertheless, the German infantry were now bringing intense pressure to bear on Campbell's handful of riflemen and with great reluctance the Support Group's commander decided that he would have to abandon the airfield and retire over the escarpment to the south. The withdrawal was covered successfully by 3 and 5 RTR, the operation being marred by a communications failure which meant that many Stuarts failed to reach their regimental rally points that night. 3 RTR rallied with only five, joined by five more at first light, and only 26 of 5 RTR's 40 tanks could be accounted for. The 8th Hussars had not been committed to the counter-attack and at dusk had gone into leaguer with brigade headquarters. Shortly after 15th Panzer Division, which had spent the day refitting and reorganizing and was now returning to the battle, overran the position. A close-quarter fight raged for 45 minutes by the light of flares. Some of the Hussars' tanks worked their way clear of the mêlée but others were knocked out or captured where they stood. Gatehouse was fortunately absent at the time and escaped the destruction of his headquarters.

Meanwhile Norrie had begun moving 1st South African Division north towards Sidi Rezegh, leaving 22nd Guards Brigade to

screen Bir el Gubi. By the morning of 23 November the 5th South African Brigade, under Brigadier B. F. Armstrong, had established itself several miles short of the southern escarpment, where Gott reinforced it with an infantry battalion and some guns. Rommel immediately made the brigade his next target, using 15th Panzer Division reinforced with 5th Panzer Regiment, plus the *Ariete* Armoured Division which the Italians had made available and which was moving north from Bir el Gubi to join him. As the Germans headed south they fended off weak attempts to interfere by the remnants of the Support Group and 7th Armoured Brigade, stampeding Campbell's and Armstrong's transport echelons in the process. By noon they were in position south of 5th South African Brigade and *Ariete* came up on their left flank; at 15:00 Crüwell gave the order to attack. *Ariete* did not press home their assault and this enabled 22nd Armoured Brigade, now reduced to a single composite regiment, to harry the Germans' left. Similarly the Support Group, with elements of 3 and 5 RTR, engaged their right rear. Despite these distractions and the fact that Gott had persuaded Armstrong to strengthen his southern perimeter the brigade was overrun with the loss of 224 killed, 379 wounded and 2,000 prisoners, including Armstrong himself. The cost had been prohibitively high, for Crüwell's tank strength was written down from 162 to 90, a figure which included the remaining light PzKw IIs.

Nevertheless, Rommel was jubilant, believing that he had destroyed XXX Corps. 'What difference does it make if you have two tanks to my one when you spread them out and let me smash them in detail?' he asked a captured senior officer. 'You presented me with three armoured brigades in succession.' This was actually something of an oversimplification, as DAK had not always fought as a complete entity, nor had its tank strength always been superior at the point of contact.

On the other hand, it could hardly be denied that Gott's three armoured brigades had been defeated on separate occasions, or that by the evening of the 23rd his division was in serious disarray. 4th Armoured Brigade was still comparatively strong but its tanks were widely dispersed and it would not become a fighting formation again until its command structure was rebuilt. 7th Armoured Brigade was finished, and after handing over its 15 surviving tanks its personnel returned to Egypt; 22nd Armoured Brigade was down to 34 tanks, and the Support Group had been severely mauled during its heroic struggle on Sidi Rezegh airfield. Finally, the destruction of 5th South African Brigade had so weakened Norrie's corps that it no longer possessed the capacity to break through to Tobruk.

Rommel therefore had ample cause for satisfaction, but on the 24th he made a mistake which cost him the battle. Crüwell had wanted to spend the day reorganizing his divisions and eliminating the last British presence in the battlefield, but instead Rommel planned to lead the DAK and *Ariete* eastwards in a lightning foray to the frontier which would re-establish contact with his garrisons there and, he hoped, pose such a threat to British communications that Cunningham would abandon Operation Crusader. This decision was based on the defeat of XXX Corps, but took little or no account of XIII Corps' activities.

In fact XIII Corps, supported by Brigadier H. R. B. Watkins' 1st Army Tank Brigade (8 RTR with Valentines, 42 and 44 RTR with Matildas), was making excellent progress and Cunningham had already transferred responsibility for effecting a junction with the Tobruk garrison from Norrie to Godwin-Austen. On 22 November 7th Indian Infantry Brigade had successfully assaulted two of the *Savona* Division's fortified camps, known as Omar Nuovo and Libyan Omar, spearheaded by two squadrons from 42 RTR and one from 44 RTR. In each case the tanks'

leading wave suffered losses from a troop of dug-in Eighty-Eights, which were tackled from the rear by the second wave. Fort Capuzzo fell to an attack by 5th New Zealand Brigade and B Squadron 8 RTR, delivered from the west, and the Bardia garrison's water supply was cut. The remainder of 2nd New Zealand Division and the tank brigade continued westwards towards Tobruk, 6th New Zealand Brigade overrunning Crüwell's field headquarters during the night. On the 23rd Freyberg's men entered the eastern edge of the dismal Sidi Rezegh battlefield, littered with wrecked aircraft, gutted tank hulks, smashed guns and unburied bodies, and during the next two days forced the Axis infantry back against the Tobruk perimeter.

In Tobruk the garrison's breakout attempt had been suspended until the situation at Sidi Rezegh was resolved, but with the approach of the New Zealanders it was renewed, reaching a climax on the night of 25 November with an attack on Strongpoint *Wolf* by A Company 2nd York and Lancaster Regiment, with 4 RTR in support, the course of which is described by the former's historian.

> As the ground was flat and open it was decided to launch the attack under cover of darkness. As time for reconnaissance was short, the start-line and forming up position outside *Tiger* were laid out and marked for A Company by the Black Watch. The plan of attack, in co-operation with the tanks, was that the enemy's position was to be subjected to a heavy artillery concentration for an hour. During this time A Company was to advance as close up to *Wolf* as possible and then, the moment the guns lifted, to go in to the assault. Meanwhile the tanks, using the same start-line but on a different timing owing to their greater speed, were to assault simultaneously on the right of A Company. All went like clockwork. A Company's leading wave got within 50 yards of *Wolf* with a couple of minutes to spare and, the moment the guns lifted, the roar was heard of the tanks coming up right on time. The rapidity of the attack caught the enemy with his head still down and large numbers of them fell to the bayonet and Tommy-gun as they crawled from

their trenches. During this the tanks put down a withering fire on the back regions which effectively kept down that of the enemy. For a time there existed that measure of confusion inevitable in any night attack. Captain Keymer very soon realized that the enemy was still in great strength and the position much larger than had been anticipated. He therefore wisely called a halt and consolidated what he then held.

The half-moon which had enabled the tanks to operate now went down and they therefore withdrew, except for two which had run into a minefield. These remained fully manned and eager to help in any way they could. The enemy's troops, realizing the comparatively weak numbers of those who had attacked them, took heart and subjected A Company to heavy mortaring and also shouted insults and threats of what they would do to them at dawn. A Company, knowing that the tanks would return to their assistance as soon as the light permitted, dug in and grimly waited. At first light the enemy attacked and were met with heavy fire from the rifles and Bren guns of the company, ably assisted by the Besas of the disabled tanks. Nevertheless the enemy, being in strength, still came on. At this moment the tank squadron arrived and, sweeping in from the flank with its Besas blazing, caught the enemy in the open and the counter-attack collapsed.

Some of the enemy who attempted to escape to the south were soon rounded up by a section of tanks. The rest surrendered and soon a column of some 350 of them were wending their way under escort to the prison cages in Tobruk. A Company spent the rest of the day in consolidating; over 150 enemy dead were buried and quite an arsenal of enemy weapons collected. During the whole of this fierce, but completely successful, operation for the capture of *Wolf*, the total casualties suffered by A Company amounted to only about thirty.

Wolf was the last obstacle separating the garrison from its final objective, the escarpment at Ed Duda. This was secured by 4 RTR in a 20 minute attack shortly after noon on the 26th and the position was consolidated under artillery fire by the 1st Essex Regiment.

It fell to Brigadier L. M. Inglis's 4th New Zealand Brigade, then engaged at Belhamed,

to effect a junction that night. Inglis detailed Lieutenant-Colonel S. F. Hartnell's 19th Battalion for the attack, which would be led by 44 RTR under Lieutenant-Colonel H. C. J. Yeo, who had trained his regiment in night-fighting techniques. Yeo planned to advance on a one-squadron frontage, the leading squadron being followed after an interval of ten minutes by a second squadron, which would be accompanied by 19th Battalion. The advance would be made at walking pace with the infantry company commanders walking alongside the tanks of the troop leaders who had been detailed to support them. The tanks of the second squadron would carry pin-head tail lights which would act as guides for the infantry following in the dark and dust.

There was no preliminary bombardment and the first the Axis defenders knew of the operation was the arrival of the leading squadron's Matildas in their positions. Tracks squealing, engines rumbling just above tick-over, the dark shapes pressed on slowly to the rear, spattering the ground ahead with the fire of their machine-guns. No sooner had they disappeared into the gloom than further tanks were heard approaching from the east. The defenders simply melted away and 45 minutes after they had crossed their start-line the crews of the leading tanks were shaking hands with the men of the Essex. By 01:00 on the 27th the entire 19th Battalion was through; the cost of this brilliantly conceived action was one infantryman wounded.

Meanwhile, Rommel's drive to the frontier, often referred to as the Dash to the Wire, had not reaped the dividends he anticipated. *Ariete*'s half-hearted participation ended when the division found 1st South African Brigade blocking its path east of Bir el Gubi. For 5th Panzer Regiment the 25 November began badly when its commander was killed during a low-level strafing attack. Already seriously reduced in strength, the regiment was worsted in a spectacular duel with the 25-pounders of 1st Field Regiment at Sidi Omar and forced to turn away. Having been replenished, it then attempted to drive north again but ran straight into 7th Indian Brigade's positions, was halted by a minefield and sustained a further battering from 25th Field Regiment's 25-pounders, 68th Medium Regiment's 5.5 in howitzers, the Bofors guns of 57th Light Anti-Aircraft Regiment and a troop of 2-pounder *portées* belonging to 2nd South African Anti-Tank Regiment. Again 5th Panzer was forced to retire, going into leaguer that night with ten tanks, of which only three remained battleworthy.

Elsewhere little was achieved save that 15th Panzer Division temporarily eliminated 1st Army Tank Brigade's workshops at Sidi Azeiz, where 16 of 42 and 44 RTR's Matildas were undergoing repairs after their battle at the Omars some days previously. The crews of these manned their vehicles and fought back until overwhelmed, destroying several enemy tanks. There were no survivors and there was some evidence that the prisoners had been shot. This was an uncharacteristic departure from the 'clean' war which both sides fought in the desert and it was not repeated when 15th Panzer overran the headquarters of 5th New Zealand Brigade after a fierce struggle the following day. Rommel himself again came close to being captured when his British-built command vehicle broke down near the Wire and for several hours he was surrounded by unsuspecting Indian troops.

The Dash to the Wire had consumed much priceless fuel and cost tanks which could not be replaced, but it did have one notable consequence. Cunningham had flown across the battlefield at a time when the transport of both British corps was scattering in all directions before the eastwards rush of the panzer divisions. As Rommel hoped, he began to have doubts about the wisdom of continuing Crusader and communicated these to Auchinleck. The latter did not share his views and on 26 November he replaced him as Army Commander with his own Deputy Chief of Staff, Major-General Neil Ritchie, who had served with the Black Watch in Mesopotamia during the First World War.

The news that Tobruk had been relieved brought Rommel racing back from the frontier on the 27th, to find the overall situation radically altered. 7th Armoured Division had used the respite to good effect, repairing cripples and collecting stragglers so that 4th Armoured Brigade now had 77 Stuarts and 22nd Armoured Brigade 45 Crusaders, with the promise of more tanks on their way forward. Rommel was thus forced to hold off Gott's armour while he strove simultaneously to sever the link between 2nd New Zealand Division and Tobruk. He succeeded in both respects, but the scales began to tilt irrevocably against him, for although heavy casualties forced the New Zealanders to withdraw, the 4th Indian Division was moving up to replace it, having been relieved on the frontier by 2nd South African Division. Furthermore, the British armoured brigades could no longer be tempted on to anti-tank gun screens and it mattered little if they lost a few tanks in each of a series of inconclusive engagements; for the DAK the loss of a similar number was a very serious matter, as they could not be replaced. On 29 November von Ravenstein, commanding 21st Panzer Division, was captured while conducting a reconnaissance in person, his place being taken by Major-General Bottcher, the commander of Rommel's artillery group. On 3 December two supply columns despatched to the frontier garrisons were ambushed and destroyed. At Bir el Gubi a Young Fascist battlegroup had successfully held off a series of attacks by 11th Indian Brigade and 8 RTR but on 5 December a major Axis effort to relieve this isolated post was abandoned, partly because *Ariete,* bombed by both sides and under artillery fire, was delayed, and partly because Neumann-Silkow, commanding 15th Panzer Division, was mortally wounded. Later that day an 11th Hussar patrol re-established contact with Tobruk west of Ed

Duda.

The DAK's tank strength had now dropped to 40, one-third of its artillery weapons had been lost and its fuel supply was critically low. There was no immediate prospect of reinforcement and re-supply and with extreme reluctance Rommel accepted that if he remained in the area of Tobruk his army would be destroyed. Despite vociferous protests from his Italian superiors he also recognized that he would have to abandon Cyrenaica and on 7 December began to withdraw westwards, the first step of a well-ordered retreat to El Agheila.

Logistics reduced Ritchie's pursuit to XIII Corps, the major formations of which were now 4th Indian and 7th Armoured Divisions. On 16 December an attempt was made to entrap the Axis army between a thrust by 4th Armoured Brigade across the enemy's rear at Tmimi and the main body of XIII Corps, advancing from the east. This was foiled by the Stuart's greedy fuel consumption, which made frequent replenishment essential, plus determined resistance by the Italian infantry divisions on the coastal sector and an armoured counter-attack at Alam Hamza which temporarily overran one battery of 25th Field Regiment. The withdrawal continued, the Italians streaming through Benghazi while the DAK went straight back to Agedabia, a second attempt to intercept the latter at Mechili again being frustrated by fuel shortage. Serious endeavours were now being made to reinforce Rommel and although two ships with 45 tanks aboard were sent to the bottom on 13 December, six days later 22 reached Benghazi and 23 were unloaded at Tripoli. On 28 December Crüwell, with 44 mediums and 16 lights, struck back at 22nd Armoured Brigade near Agedabia. The Germans had much the better of the engagement, losing only seven tanks, battle casualties and breakdowns combining to reduce Scott-Cockburn's strength from 90 to 53 by the end of the day. On the 30th Crüwell struck again,

knocking out 23 of Scott-Cockburn's 62 in exchange for a further seven of his own. Having imposed these checks the DAK began slipping through the El Agheila defile on 1 January 1942, and there the British pursuit ended.

There remained some tidying up to do and this was undertaken by Norrie's XXX Corps, which now contained the bulk of the infantry. Bardia was assaulted on 31 December by the 2nd South African Division, supported by 8 and 44 RTR, the fire of the massed British artillery being supplemented by that of the cruiser HMS *Ajax* of River Plate fame, and the gunboat HMS *Aphis*. Using the same methods which had proved so successful almost a year earlier, the attackers worked their way steadily into the defences until the 8,000-strong garrison surrendered at dawn on 2 January. Sollum also fell to the South Africans but the Axis battlegroup at Halfaya Pass held out until 17 January, by which time many of its members were close to dying of thirst.

Crusader had succeeded in relieving Tobruk, mauling the enemy's army, and forcing its remnants to evacuate Cyrenaica, but it had proved to be a far tougher struggle than anyone had imagined. Axis casualties amounted to 38,000 killed, wounded and missing as against 18,000 British and Commonwealth, many South African and New Zealand prisoners being released when Bardia was captured. Some 300 German and Italian tanks had been destroyed compared with 278 British, but a high proportion of the latter could be recovered and repaired.

The immediate sequel to Crusader was less satisfactory and bore an uncanny similarity to the events of the previous March. Just as Wavell had been required to despatch assistance to Greece after Beda Fomm, now Auchinleck was forced to strip his command and send substantial reinforcements to the Far East, where the Japanese had invaded Hong Kong, Malaya and Burma. These included the

70th Division, 6th and 7th Australian Divisions, 7th Armoured Brigade (7th Hussars and 2 RTR), supporting artillery and several RAF squadrons. Likewise, in the Benghazi Bulge 7th Armoured Division was replaced by the inexperienced 1st Armoured Division under Messervy, who had taken over when its original commander was wounded shortly after he had arrived. The front itself lay east of Mersa Brega and was thinly held by 200th (formerly 22nd) Guards Brigade and Messervy's Support Group. Eighty miles to the rear and dispersed for training with little fuel in hand was 2nd Armoured Brigade, consisting of the Queen's Bays, 9th Lancers and 10th Hussars. In the Djebel Akhdar and at Benghazi was 4th Indian Division, now commanded by Major-General Francis Tuker.

On 5 January a further convoy reached Tripoli with an additional 55 tanks, 20 armoured cars, replacement anti-tank guns and more supplies than had once seemed possible. Rommel knew that the British logistic system was stretched to its limits and when his excellent radio interception unit revealed Godwin-Austen's dispositions he again defied his superiors and attacked with 110 tanks on 21 January. He not only gained an immediate local superiority over the scattered components of 1st Armoured Division but instinctively recognized that he was no longer dealing with the veterans who had fought Crusader. Both panzer divisions, the 90th Light (formerly Afrika) Division and the mechanized Italian XX Corps all emerged from the El Agheila gap and advanced into the Bulge. Agedabia and Antelat fell on the 22nd but the following day Rommel was visited by Luftwaffe Field Marshal Albert Kesselring, who had recently been appointed German Commander-in-Chief South with special responsibility for the security of communications between Italy and Africa, Marshal Ugo Cavallero, the Italian Chief of General Staff, and General Bastico, all of whom urged him to abandon the offensive on the grounds that

it could not be supported with the resources available. Rommel dismissed their recommendations, commenting tartly that only Hitler could stop him.

Msus was taken on the 25th and further moves initiated which resulted in Benghazi being outflanked. The port was held by 7th Indian Brigade under Brigadier H. Briggs, who had no intention of being cut off and broke out into the desert to the south, swinging north-east to drive across the Axis rear, his columns eventually reaching safety at Mechili and El Adem. On the 29th Rommel entered Benghazi, where he learned of his promotion to Colonel-General.

The British response to these reverses was more controlled than it had been the previous year, although both Auchinleck and Ritchie seriously underestimated the situation at first. After Benghazi had fallen, however, it was clear that the Bulge could not be held and a withdrawal was sanctioned to the line Gazala–Bir Hacheim, the DAK and the Italians conforming to the movement. Godwin-Austen had not shared Ritchie's initial optimism and he had resented the Army Commander's meddling in the conduct of XIII Corps' operations. At Gazala he asked to be relieved of his command and his place was taken by Gott.

During Crusader a feeling had developed throughout the Eighth Army that Rommel was a commander in a class of his own, always able to turn the tables with some totally unexpected and ingenious move, although the truth was that it had been his own mistakes which led to his eventual defeat. Nevertheless, his latest counter-stroke tended to reinforce that opinion and so was born the legend of the wily Desert Fox. Nor did it help that Churchill should comment in the House of Commons itself: 'We have a very daring and skilful opponent against us and, may I say across the havoc of war, a great general.' Auchinleck, far from pleased that his opponent should occupy so prominent a place in the thoughts of his men, despatched a circular to unit and formation commanders, instructing them 'to dispel the idea that Rommel is anything but an ordinary German general, and a pretty unpleasant one at that, as we know from the mouths of his own officers.'

Another four months were to pass before the contest was renewed, and by then its nature had altered subtly. It remained to be seen whether the Desert Fox would destroy the Eighth Army, or whether he would hang himself with the rope of his insubordinate ambition. By the end of the year the answer would be clear.

CHAPTER 7

THE WESTERN DESERT 1942-43

Battles of position

During the spring of 1942 both armies prepared for a renewed offensive the object of which was to eject its opponents from Cyrenaica. Logistics, of course, imposed their iron will on all aspects of planning, and the British solved their problems by the traditional means of building a railway.

At the beginning of the war the Western Desert Railway ran from Alexandria to Mersa Matruh. An extension to Sollum had been contemplated and a rough survey had been made by Egyptian State Railways. With the advance of our forces into Cyrenaica (following the success of Operation Compass), plans were prepared for the extension of the line to Bomba via Capuzzo and Tobruk. The biggest problem was not so much railway construction as water supply. The Western Desert is practically a waterless waste from the borders of the Nile Valley to the hills of Cyrenaica; such water as is found along the route is brackish and unsuitable for locomotive consumption. A pipeline to serve all military purposes was laid along the railway to Dabaa, whilst water trains of tank wagons were run to supplement this supply and carry water to the Mersa Matruh garrison. Early in 1941 work was started on the difficult section to Mohalfa, at the top of the escarpment above Mersa Matruh. The first retreat caused a stoppage of the work, but following the successful advance later in the year (ie Operation Crusader), rapid progress was made with the railway. Rates of track-laying up to two miles a day were achieved by the New Zealand Railway Construction Group, which was primarily responsible for the work. Lorries and tractors were used to haul material

forward across the open desert from the railhead. The rate of laying was controlled by the rate at which material could be forwarded along the line of communications and at times rails were loaded direct from ships at Alexandria into the construction trains. By mid-June 1942 the railhead had reached Belhamed, a few miles east of Tobruk. While construction of the railway was in progress the pipeline was extended to Mersa Matruh and later to Mishaifa. Even this was not sufficient for locomotive

The Grant, armed with a sponson-mounted 75 mm gun and a 37 mm gun in the turret, provided an unpleasant surprise for the Afrika Korps during the Gazala/Knightsbridge battles and also distinguished itself at Alam Halfa, where it was known as Egypt's Last Hope (RAC Tank Museum).

needs and water trains still had to be run from Alexandria until the arrival of diesel engines from America. (Official History *Transportation in the Second World War.*)

Together, the railway and supplies delivered by sea enabled the Eighth Army to establish a large base complex south-east of Tobruk. This was intended to support the planned offensive, although Ritchie's deployment along the line Gazala–Bir Hacheim was actually designed to protect it from Axis incursions.

In the technical sphere, both sides received improved equipment during the long pause. The Grant tank, armed with a turret-mounted 37 mm gun and a 75 mm in a sponson, began reaching the desert in quantity so that by May Eighth Army had 167 available. Although the sponson mounting made it virtually impossible for the tank to fight hull-

down the 75 mm gun was capable of penetrating even up-armoured German tanks at ranges up to 850 yards and was also able to fire a high explosive shell, while the Grant's own armour was proof against the 50 mm anti-tank gun at 1,000 yards. Another weapon new to the desert was the 6-pounder anti-tank, which had a performance far superior to the old 2-pounder.

On the German side of the lines the majority of the medium PzKw IIIs and IVs had been up-armoured and a handful of PzKw III Model Js, armed with the longer 50 mm L/60 gun, had arrived, as had four PzKw IV Model F2s, armed with a 75 mm L/43 high velocity gun in place of the normal howitzer, although there was as yet no ammunition available for the latter. Often forgotten, however, are the 117 *Marder* III tank destroyers sent to Africa in May. These vehicles were based on the

Marder tank destroyer, based on the chassis of an obsolete Czech tank and armed with a captured Russian 76.2 mm gun rechambered to take German 75 mm ammunition (Bundesarchiv).

chassis of the obsolete PzKw 38T light tank and were armed with a captured Russian 76.2 mm anti-tank gun re-chambered to take German 75 mm ammunition. These weapons were so successful that for a while the British believed they were faced by a mechanized version of the dreaded Eighty-Eight and as they reached the front they did much to balance the qualitative superiority possessed by the Eighth Army. Also despatched to Africa were a number of self-propelled 150 mm howitzers mounted on PzKw II or obsolete French chassis, but these proved to be something of a disappointment.

All of these developments were logical evolutions based on experience, but the weapon which was to have a profound influence on the conduct of future operations was the mine, both anti-personnel and anti-tank, many thousands of which were laid bet-

ween the two armies when the front became static. At first this prodigal use of mines was, on the British side at least, unscientific, as there were large areas of minebelt that were not covered by defensive fire and which in consequence could be cleared at leisure.

Another product of static warfare, and one which was to exert a malign influence on the Eighth Army, was the concept of the box, an area held in brigade strength. Its principal defences would consist of field and anti-tank artillery and might or might not include a minebelt, depending upon how close it was to the front and how long its tenants had been in occupation. The problem with boxes was that while they offered some of the benefits of the zariba, namely a comparatively secure operational and administrative base in which troops could obtain some rest, their disadvantages were that they were not mutually sup-

Dual purpose 88 mm anti-aircraft/anti-tank gun and tractor unit. The high-standing Eighty-Eight was a fearsome weapon but both it and its crew were terribly vulnerable to shellfire (Imperial War Museum).

Crusader and Grant aboard tank transporters (National Army Museum).

porting and as they provided a tempting target for enemy armour it was often necessary to despatch friendly armour to their assistance. In such circumstances, boxes tended to be a liability rather than an asset.

By the middle of May it became apparent that it would be Rommel who struck the first blow. The overall Axis strategy involved two major phases. In the first, *Venezia,* the Eighth Army was to be decisively defeated and Tobruk captured. This would be followed by a further operational pause in the desert during which *Herakles,* the airborne and amphibious invasion of Malta, was to take place. In Kesselring's opinion the capture of Tobruk meant little unless Malta, the perpetual threat to Axis communications, could be secured as well. Only when Malta had been suppressed could sound plans be made for further operations against the weakened British presence in the Middle East. Hitler accepted this view, as did Goering and, for the moment, Rommel himself.

Rommel's tank strength amounted to a total of 560, including 50 PzKw IIs, 223 up-armoured PzKw III 50 mm L/42s, 19 PzKw III 50 mm L/60 Model Js, 40 howitzer-armed PzKw IVs and the *Ariete* Armoured Division's 228 M13s. The DAK and the Italian XX Mechanized Corps assembled south-east of Rotunda Sagnali prior to commencing a drive which would take them round the southern end of the British positions and then northeast in the general direction of Tobruk. Simultaneously the four infantry divisions of the Italian X and XXI Corps would mount diversionary attacks against the northern sector of the British defences.

Ritchie's army contained two corps, XIII under Gott and XXX under Norrie. XIII Corps consisted of 1st South African and 50th Northumbrian Division in the line and 2nd South African Division in Tobruk, and was supported by 1st and 32nd Army Tank Brigades with 110 Matildas and 166 Valentines between them. XXX Corps consisted of the 1st and 7th Armoured Divisions plus a number of infantry brigades, including General Pierre Koenig's 1st Free French Brigade occupying a box at Bir Hacheim.

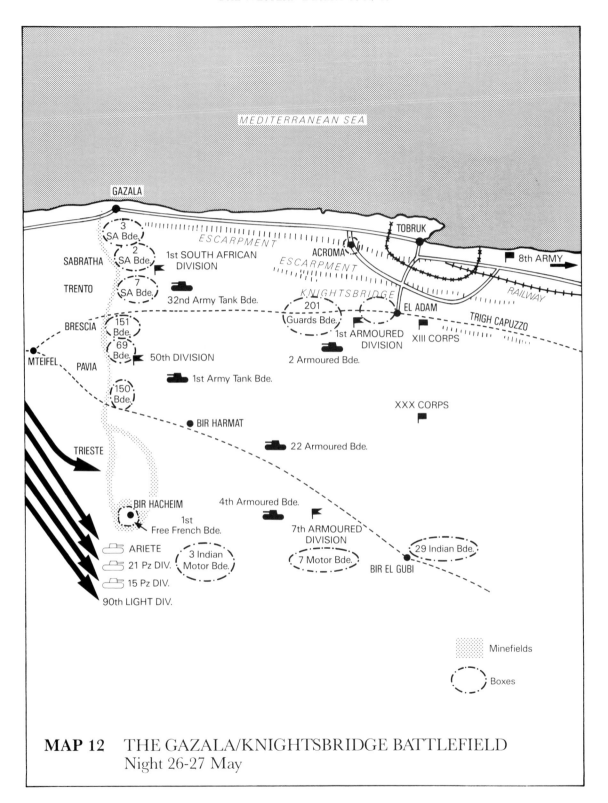

MAP 12   THE GAZALA/KNIGHTSBRIDGE BATTLEFIELD
Night 26-27 May

Bishop self-propelled gun, armed with a 25-pounder gun-howitzer and based on the chassis of the Valentine tank. Note how the 'sunshade' rail has been used to stow a bivouac sheet and the replacement of 'filmsies' with sturdier jerrycans. The crew have augmented their frontal armour with sandbags (Imperial War Museum).

Major-General Herbert Lumsden's 1st Armoured Division contained two armoured brigades, the 2nd (The Queen's Bays, 9th Lancers and 10th Hussars) and the 22nd (2nd Royal Gloucestershire Hussars, 3rd and 4th County of London Yeomanry), its regiments being equipped on the scale of one Grant and two Crusader squadrons each. Messervy's 7th Armoured Division contained a single armoured brigade, the 4th (8th Hussars, 3rd and 5th Royal Tank Regiments), but in this case regiments possessed one Stuart and two Grant squadrons each, so that in effect both divisions were able to produce six Grant squadrons apiece. Excluding the two Army Tank Brigades, the Eighth Army could muster 167 Grants, 149 Stuarts and 257 Crusaders, plus a further 75 Grants and 70 Stuarts which would become available when 1st Armoured Brigade reached the front. The British, therefore, possessed a numerical as well as a qualitative superiority which should have enabled them to win the subsequent battle with comparative ease.

Ritchie believed that Rommel would open his offensive with a sweep round the southern flank. Auchinleck, however, was of the opinion that he would make a concentrated thrust through the centre of the British line. The two armoured divisions were therefore deployed some way back, with the 7th within striking distance of Bir Hacheim, so enabling them to deal with either eventuality. Both generals were agreed that wherever the enemy's main thrust was delivered, there were bound to be feint attacks; the essential problem, therefore, was to identify which was which in time to allow units to proceed to their pre-designated battle positions.

Operation *Venezia* began during the afternoon of 26 May. Crüwell, who had handed over command of the DAK to Lieutenant-General Walther Nehring in March, was responsible for the diversionary attacks on the northern sector of the front, but these coincided with a sandstorm and made little impression. At about 16:00 reports were received from aircraft and prowling armoured cars that there was considerable movement in the area of Rotunda Sagnali. After dusk and throughout the night, a series of signals from the 4th South African Armoured Car Regiment monitored the progress of the Axis columns as they ground their way to the south-east, although it was impossible in the darkness and dust to gauge their size. At the highest British command levels, there was a reluctance to accept unreservedly that this was the enemy's major effort, but at 02:00 a warning order was despatched to Brigadier G. W. Richards, commanding 4th Armoured Brigade, telling him that his regiments must be prepared to move at dawn; where was not stated. At 06:00 the cat suddenly leapt out of the bag when, south of Bir Hacheim, an aircraft spotted several thousand vehicles spearheaded by an estimated 400 tanks. Rommel's night march had achieved complete strategic surprise.

The first blow fell on the 3rd Indian Motor Brigade, which had recently established a box five miles south-east of Bir Hacheim. The brigade consisted of three Indian cavalry regiments (2nd Royal Lancers (Gardner's Horse), 11th Prince Albert Victor's Own Cavalry, and 18th King Edward VII's Own Cavalry), for the moment fighting as mechanized infantry. Its artillery was incomplete and only 30 of its 64 2-pounder anti-tank guns had arrived. Nevertheless, at 06:40 it opened fire on *Ariete* which, together with part of 21st Panzer Division, swung left towards it and at 07:15 closed in to attack. The troopers put up a terrific fight but went down under the tidal wave of advancing armour. Over 200 were killed, perhaps twice that number wounded and nearly 1,000 were captured, but the remainder escaped and managed to reach 29th Indian Brigade's box at Bir el Gubi. In exchange, they knocked out no less than 54 tanks, the majority belonging to *Ariete*.

The campaign in the Western Desert is sometimes referred to as The Last of the Gentlemen's Wars and this particular engagement gave rise to two incidents which might endorse such a view. The first involved the remarkable Admiral Sir Walter Cowan, many of whose decorations had been earned as a junior officer during Queen Victoria's reign. Despite his 72 years Cowan possessed an unquenchable thirst for action and his present appointment was that of Naval Liaison Officer to 18th Cavalry, a none too demanding task as the regiment was operating some 40 miles from the sea. Summoned to surrender by a German tank, he emptied his revolver at it. The tank crew declined to respond and he was led off with the respect appropriate to his rank. The news that an admiral had been captured resulted in a premature German announcement that Tobruk had fallen.

The second incident related to the 11th Cavalry, most of whom were captured. The regiment's British officers were immediately separated from their men and marched off. The Indian officers, however, persuaded their Italian captors that their soldiers would starve in the prisoner of war cages, as their religion forbade their eating normal European rations. It was certainly true that since the Great Mutiny each Indian cavalry regiment's three sabre squadrons were recruited from different races which, because of their religious beliefs, ate or were denied certain diets, but the argument was something of an overstatement. Be that as it may, the Italians accepted it and the regiment was released upon receiving a parole that the men would not fight again in the Middle East. After marching across the desert to the British lines the regiment was returned to India and, equipped with armoured cars, played a distinguished part in the campaign in Burma.

Meanwhile, the senior officers of XXX Corps remained unconvinced by the stream of reports which had come in throughout the night, but by 07:00 there could be no mistaking the fact that they had a fight on their hands. Norrie, the corps commander, telephoned Lumsden at 1st Armoured Division and ordered him to despatch 22nd Armoured Brigade to 7th Armoured Division's assistance; an acrimonious discussion followed which was, sadly, to be representative of the British higher direction of the entire battle. At about the same time Messervy at 7th Armoured Division ordered Richards' 4th Armoured Brigade to move at once to its battle position.

It was too late. The tragedy was that Richards knew the ground well from his experience with the Light Car Patrols during the First World War and he had chosen an excellent position in which his brigade could have met the enemy. There was, however, barely time for him to issue the necessary orders before 15th Panzer Division swung north to engage his regiments in turn.

The 8th Hussars were actually breaking leaguer when the head of the German column appeared. The Stuart squadron, commanded by Major (later General Sir John) Hackett, was clear first and attempted to buy time while the Grant squadrons shook out, then moved on to the regiment's flanks as they went into action. During the next 15 minutes they destroyed some 30 of the estimated 150 enemy tanks facing them, plus at least one Eighty-Eight. At the end of this period, however, they had been reduced to a single Grant each and the regiment was forced to retire. Significantly, the Grant's main armour had withstood multiple impacts from the fire of the enemy's tanks and was only penetrated by his anti-tank guns.

Meanwhile, the 3rd Royal Tank Regiment under Lieutenant-Colonel G. P. B. Roberts, who began the war as a captain and finished it as a major-general commanding the 11th Armoured Division, had broken leaguer at 07:30 and was moving south towards its battle station, screened by its Stuart squadron. At about 07:40 the Stuarts observed dust and movement about three miles ahead and this

soon resolved itself into 15th Panzer Division, resuming its northward thrust. Roberts brought up his Grant squadrons and was interested to see that the German tanks, deployed eight ranks deep, halted 1,300 yards distant, well beyond what had been the usual battle range. The Grants immediately began slamming 75 mm rounds at them, and the 25-pounders of the accompanying Chestnut Troop, 1st Royal Horse Artillery, joined in with high explosive. The Germans were forced to shuffle forward to make effective reply and lost about 20 tanks in the process, replacing these from their rear ranks as the head of their column was shot away. Roberts' own strength was being eroded, however, and he was concerned by the absence of 8th Hussars on his left and 5 RTR on his right. In addition von Vaerst, the German commander, had begun detaching tanks and anti-tank guns and sending them in a wide hook around the regiment's right flank. For the moment this threat was being contained by the Stuart squadron but Roberts was becoming worried that his regiment, even if it was not destroyed where it stood, would be cut off. The situation was resolved when, after an hour's heavy fighting, the remaining Grants exhausted their ammunition and he had no alternative other than to order the regiment to withdraw.

Further north, 5 RTR had also broken leaguer, becoming involved almost immediately with the right flank of von Bismarck's 21st Panzer Division, driving northwards towards the coast. The Germans shied away to the west but by the time contact was broken events elsewhere prevented the regiment going to the assistance of Roberts's embattled squadrons.

On the outer flank of the great Axis wheel around Bir Hacheim was the 90th Light Division, whose objective was El Adem. As its columns moved north-east, one of its reconnaissance units ran down a group of British vehicles heading in the same direction. They formed part of the headquarters of 7th

Armoured Division and, unknown to the Germans, their prisoners included Messervy and his Chief of Staff, who had removed their badges of rank. The two escaped that night but as a result of their capture the vital link in the chain of command between Norrie at XXX Corps and Richards' 4th Armoured Brigade was broken at about 10:00.

Richards did the only thing possible in the circumstances and ordered his regiments to pull back and concentrate three miles southeast of El Adem. 8th Hussars could produce a Stuart squadron and a couple of Grants; 3 RTR could also produce a Stuart squadron and a weak Grant squadron; and 5 RTR were almost complete. Richards despatched a liaison officer to establish a direct link with Norrie and towards evening the brigade mounted a counter-attack on 90th Light, driving it away from Ed Duda, before going into leaguer near Sidi Rezegh at about midnight.

As Richards's brigade had moved towards its rally point, its path was crossed by hundreds of lorries, travelling singly and in groups at top speed in different directions. The whole of Eighth Army's rear area was in complete uproar and Roberts commented that the effect reminded him of a disorganized musical ride. The principal reason for such apparent chaos was that the layout of the army's infrastructure had been designed with an offensive in mind. As Richards put it, 'Supplies, repair units and hospitals were moved into the forward area. This would lead to disaster if we lost the opening battle, as all these vital support arrangements would be exposed to the enemy. If the Eighth Army had been planning a *defensive* battle all the administrative organization behind the fighting troops would have been built up further back.'

The opening battle, however, was far from over. At about 09:00 21st Panzer clashed with Brigadier E. H. Carr's 22nd Armoured Brigade, which was at last preparing to move south. After losing 30 tanks but inflicting some loss in return, Carr's regiments

withdrew a short distance in the direction of the Knightsbridge box. At 11:00 Briggs' 2nd Armoured Brigade was sent forward in support and came in on Carr's left, facing west. At 14:00 a co-ordinated attack was launched which inflicted heavy casualties on 15th Panzer Division's mechanized infantry regiment. Shortly afterwards, 44 RTR smashed into the Germans' western flank and virtually destroyed a second mechanized infantry regiment, this time belonging to 21st Panzer Division, albeit at a cost of 18 Matildas.

Thus, when both panzer divisions went into leaguer near Bir el Harmat at last light, Rommel's own situation was a matter for serious concern. He had himself narrowly escaped capture while trying to visit 90th Light, now lying isolated in the desert to the east, and he was forced to admit that he had not allowed for the Grant in his calculations. He had lost some 200 tanks, amounting to one third of his total strength, and at the end of the day the ratio of British to German tanks was actually higher than it had been at the beginning. Again, the condition and dispersed state of his divisions inhibited further offensive operations. 15th Panzer Division had only 29 tanks fit for action, plus 14 more undergoing repair, and was almost out of petrol and ammunition. 21st Panzer Division still had 80 tanks but also needed replenishment. The *Ariete* Armoured Division had been repulsed by the Free French at Bir Hacheim with the loss of yet more of its tanks and the latter's aggressive defence had resulted in the liberation of many prisoners from 3rd Indian Motor Brigade. Finally the *Trieste* Mechanized Division had taken a wrong turning during the night and was still west of the minefields.

During the next two days Rommel managed to concentrate the DAK but was pressed back against the British minefields, and in particular against the box manned by 150th Brigade. Isolated and lacking supplies of every kind, including water, his situation became so desperate that he told a captured British officer that unless it improved quickly he would have to ask Ritchie for terms. In the nick of time *Trieste* managed to gap the minefields and a convoy got through. Even so, the fate of the Afrika Korps hung in the balance for a while and, to add to its misfortunes, Crüwell's light aircraft was shot down over 150th Brigade's box and the general was captured. His place as commander of the static northern sector of the front was temporarily taken by Kesselring, who had flown in from Italy to observe at first hand the progress of *Venezia*.

Notwithstanding the criticisms levelled at Ritchie's initial dispositions in subsequent years, the fact was that they had sufficed despite the mistakes which had been made. There now existed a real opportunity for the destruction of the Afrika Korps and since the Italians could not stand without their allies the war in the Western Desert could be brought to a rapid conclusion, provided it was grasped firmly and decisively. It was not, and the result was the worst defeat in the Eighth Army's history.

It was a dictum of Clausewitz that an army commander's personal authority tended to diminish in proportion to the number of command levels interposed between him and his troops. Writing the previous century, he had commented that 'an order loses in rapidity, force and exactness if the graduation ladder down which it has to descend is long, and this must be the case if there are Corps Commanders between the Division Leaders and the Chief.' Some would argue that this could hardly apply in an era of rapid communications, yet those who support the theory have only to contrast the opposing command systems during the Gazala battles.

The nub of the problem for the British was that Ritchie, the Eighth Army's commander, was subjected to a needless degree of close supervision by Auchinleck, the Commander-in-Chief. Typical of this was the exchange of signals between the two on 27 May, during which Auchinleck acknowledged that Ritchie had been correct in his forecast as to the form Rommel's offensive would take, but warned the Army Commander twice to beware of the possibility of a second major attack on the northern sector of the front. This, as we know, was not within the capacity of the Axis to deliver, but Ritchie was well aware that the Commander-in-Chief, sitting at the centre of the intelligence gathering net in Cairo, was privy to information he did not personally possess and was greatly influenced by the fact. Auchinleck's intelligence sources included, *inter alia,* the high level Ultra interceptions, but as far as the war in the Western Desert was concerned these required careful handling. There could, for example, be no guarantee that a commander as independently minded as Rommel would conform to higher directives, nor were resources always available to deal with altered circumstances if he did. Again, once battle had been joined Ultra was of little use as the time involved in deciphering transmissions and forwarding them from the United Kingdom to Egypt often meant that they were out of date.

Be that as it may, Ritchie loyally attempted to implement Auchinleck's wishes and this brought him into conflict with his corps commanders, Norrie and Gott, who were both personal friends but nominally senior to him in the Army List. In their view the orders received sometimes bore no relation to the situation as it was and the result was debate, delay and local interpretation which spread downwards to divisional level. As General Sir David Fraser comments in his book *And We Shall Shock Them,* there was indiscipline at the top and because of it the command apparatus could not generate the drive and speed necessary for victory. There were days when discussions were so protracted that nothing was attempted until late afternoon, the effect being that little could be achieved before dusk thus putting an end to the fighting. Perhaps the worst feature of all this was that the troops themselves sensed instinctively what was wrong. Jake Wardrop, a regular soldier serving as a tank driver with 5 RTR, committed his thoughts to his diary: 'It seemed to me that if they [the generals] had got a lot of kit together and had one big push in one place, we could have done something definite. As it was, the units were just battering themselves to pieces in a lot of little scraps which were getting us nowhere.'

Unfortunately for Wardrop and his comrades, the German command situation was the exact antithesis of the British. Rommel may have been responsible for the predicament in which he found himself, but in the days that followed his divisions functioned solely in response to his own directing intelligence and will, exercised in the heart of the battle, the consequence being that he won the greatest victory of his career.

It occurred to at least one German officer that the best way to eliminate the Cauldron, as the area occupied by the stranded DAK became known, was for XIII Corps to mount holding attacks against its northern perimeter while XXX Corps, with most of the armour, reversed the move with which Rommel had begun the battle and, having entered 150th Brigade's box, overran the German position from the rear. This alternative was apparently not considered and, in General Fraser's opinion, was probably beyond British capacity or imagination.

For several days Rommel recovered his strength behind his defensive cordon of anti-tank guns. Then on 30 May, he launched an all-out assault on 150th Brigade's box. Bat-

British 6-pounder anti-tank gun crew engaged in live ammunition training (Imperial War Museum).

tered by dive bombers and concentrated artillery, assailed by tanks and infantry, Brigadier C. W. Haydon's three battalions (4th East Yorkshire Regiment and 4th and 5th Green Howards), supported by the 25-pounders of 72 Field Regiment, Matilda squadrons from 42 and 44 RTR, and 232 Company Royal Engineers fighting as infantry, fought grimly on under a lowering pall of dust and smoke. Not until shortly after 14:00 on 1 June were the last remnants overwhelmed, their ammunition expended. Rommel had needed to win this battle—and in the circumstances could hardly have lost it—but he was deeply impressed by the brigade's tenacious stand against odds and later wrote that his troops 'had met the toughest resistance imaginable. The defence was conducted with marked skill and as usual the British fought to the end'. Hoping to meet a man whom he considered to be a gallant and resourceful foe, he entered the shattered defences, but it was not to be; Haydon lay dead among his men.

It had not escaped Rommel that the Eighth Army had done little or nothing to assist 150th Brigade in its death struggle, and as his opponents had apparently changed little since Crusader he reasoned that it would be to his advantage to let them smash themselves against the constantly strengthening defences of the Cauldron.

At dawn on 5 June, Ritchie at last made a determined effort to break into the Cauldron, employing converging but disconnected attacks against its northern and eastern perimeter. The northern attack was delivered by 32nd Army Tank Brigade and was led by the Matildas of 7 and 42 RTR, followed by a Valentine squadron from 8 RTR and a lorried infantry batallion, the 7th Green Howards. A smoke screen was laid by the artillery to mask the approach to the objective, Sidra Ridge, but several tanks were lost when they crossed a hitherto unsuspected minefield. The remainder pressed on and emerged from

the smoke. They were immediately engaged by invisible 88 mm and 50 mm anti-tank guns firing from the east, with the rising sun behind them. Silhouetted against the dispersing white fog, the Matildas provided perfect targets and were unable to make effective reply because of the glare. 21st Panzer Division joined in the battle but the brigade held its ground until noon, when it was ordered to withdraw. Fifty of its tanks had to be left on the battlefield and only 12 reached the rally point.

The eastern attack fared even worse and was marred from the outset by faulty reconnaissance. The break-in objective was easily secured by 4 RTR's Valentines and 10th Indian Infantry Brigade, the reason being that it lay short of the enemy's real position. 22nd Armoured Brigade and 9th Indian Infantry Brigade passed through but after the former had pushed *Ariete* off Aslagh Ridge it ran into an anti-tank gun screen and was eventually forced to withdraw having lost 60 tanks.

The following day Rommel counterattacked and overran most of 10th and part of 9th Indian Infantry Brigades, taking 3,000 prisoners. Also captured was the entire artillery of 5th Indian Division, Ritchie's Army Reserve. As always the gunners fought to the muzzle, but by the end of the day 96 25-pounders and 37 anti-tank guns had to be added to the total of equipment lost. Operation Aberdeen, as Ritchie's assault on the Cauldron was known, had been a ghastly failure, relieved only by many acts of individual heroism.

In the aftermath of Aberdeen, Ritchie had wanted to evacuate the Free French Brigade from its box at Bir Hacheim, but Auchinleck insisted that it must be held. The 90th Light and *Trieste* were already investing the box and on 8 June Rommel despatched 15th Panzer to join them in administering the *coup de grâce*. Koenig's Foreign Legionnaires, Fusiliers Marins and native colonial troops drawn from all over France's empire threw back one attack after another with the fire of their famed 'Seventy-Fives'. However, by the afternoon of 9 June it was apparent that the box could not survive much longer and Koenig obtained Ritchie's permission to break out. This was achieved successfully during the night of 10/11 June, 2,700 men of the garrison's 3,600 reaching safety.

Having cleared this last obstacle across his rear, Rommel repeated the north-easterly thrust with which he had begun the battle. His tank strength amounted to 128 German mediums, plus a score of light tanks, while the Italians could produce 70 M13s. Despite the losses he had inflicted he was still outnumbered, for Norrie's two armoured divisions possessed 200 tanks between them, including 83 Grants, while Gott could dispose of 63 Matildas and Valentines.

The critical fighting took place on 12 June when Norrie's three armoured brigades were defeated in detail in a manner reminiscent of the opening stages of Crusader, losing 90 tanks. The situation was additionally complicated when Messervy was forced to take refuge inside a bir to avoid capture by a German reconnaissance unit. In view of his absence Norrie issued orders for all the armoured brigades to pass under Lumsden's control, but by the time this had taken place the damage had been done.

Next day both panzer divisions attempted to isolate the Knightsbridge box, held by 201st Guards Brigade, the eastern and western claws of their pincer being contained respectively by 2nd and 22nd Armoured Brigades until the former began to run out of ammunition, when it was relieved by 32nd Army Tank Brigade. By evening the Eighth Army had only 70 battleworthy tanks left and the Guards were withdrawn during the night.

It was now apparent that, with the DAK pressing ever closer to the coast, the remaining fragment of the Gazala Line could not be held and, early on the 14th, Gott received permission to withdraw his two divisions. None too soon, Pienaar's South Africans began

streaming back along the coast road while 8 RTR held a corridor open for them under tremendous pressure. Major-General W. H. Ramsden's 50th Division, now reduced to two brigades, could expect no such luck as its boxes lay further south, but solved its problem by attacking westwards through the Italian infantry, then driving round Bir Hacheim and on to the Egyptian frontier.

Hopes of holding a new line running south from Tobruk were dashed almost at once. The armoured brigades' surviving tanks were concentrated under Richards in 4th Armoured Brigade. By 17 June 90 had been assembled but they were as weary as their crews so that during the next few days the total fluctuated wildly in spite of comparatively light battle casualties. However, the general movement of Eighth Army continued to be eastwards across the frontier and at dawn on the 20th Richards was ordered to conform to this, reaching Khireigat, 12 miles east of the Wire, about noon. Within 24 hours came the shattering news that Tobruk had been stormed.

It had not been Auchinleck's intention that Tobruk should undergo a second siege, but the speed with which the Eighth Army had been separated from the fortress ensured that it would be invested. Within the defences were 2nd South African Division, 201st Guards Brigade, 11th Indian Infantry Brigade and 32nd Army Tank Brigade, the last consisting of 4 and 7 RTR equipped with Valentines, plus a handful of Matildas and Grants, overall command being exercised by Major-General Klopper.

The Germans were as desperately tired as the British, but they had just won a major victory which Rommel was determined to crown. Selecting the same area of the perimeter which he had intended assaulting the previous autumn, he mounted a whirlwind demonstration of the blitzkrieg technique, using ammunition which had been dumped there at the time. At 05:20 on the 20th, dive-bombers and artillery began pounding a narrow sector of the defences while engineers filled in the silted-up anti-tank ditch and cleared lanes through the mines and barbed wire. By 08:30 both panzer divisions had broken through 2/5th Mahrattas and were pushing steadily north. Klopper's response was tardy and unco-ordinated. 32nd Army Tank Brigade counter-attacked and fought to the last tank when its regiments became the focus of a hail of fire from tanks, anti-tank guns and dive-bombers. By 13:30 the Germans had reached the escarpment overlooking the harbour and at 18:00 21st Panzer entered the town.

Klopper now faced three alternatives. He could continue the fight in the western half of the defences, a course of action which would end inevitably in his defeat but which would buy time for the Eighth Army and write down the DAK; or he could order his men to break out, knowing that while many would be captured many would also reach safety; or he could surrender. He chose the third course and early the following morning concluded the formalities; unlike Manella in January 1941, however, he consented to a general surrender. The majority of his units, barely touched by the fighting and still manning their positions on the perimeter, found this hard to stomach and some refused to accept it. 2/7th Gurkha Rifles went on fighting until the evening of the 21st. The veteran 2nd Camerons refused to lay down their arms until the 22nd, and then only after they had been threatened with extermination. A large party of 199 Coldstream Guardsmen and 188 men from other units, commanded by Major H. M. Sainthill, drove out into the desert and made contact with South African armoured cars near the old Knightsbridge box. A smaller party of Kaffrarian Rifles also broke out and reached the El Alamein position after a remarkable desert journey of 38 days. As for the rest, 32,000 men marched into captivity, 19,000 of them British.

Some destruction of stores had taken place but Tobruk proved to be a veritable treasure trove containing 2,000 vehicles in working order, 1,400 tons of priceless petrol and 5,000 tons of food. The capture of the fortress brought Rommel to the pinnacle of his career and his reward was a field marshal's baton presented by a grateful Hitler.

For the British, the bitter paradox was that during the Gazala/Knightsbridge battles, regiments and their supporting services had functioned at the peak of efficiency. It was no accident that, despite the grievous losses incurred, the Eighth Army's tank strength actually rose during the concluding phase and its immediate aftermath, from 70 on the evening of 13 June to 90 on the 17th and approximately 170 on the 26th, and for this the vehicle recovery organization, manned by the Royal Army Ordnance Corps until the Royal Electrical and Mechanical Engineers were formed on 1 October 1942, was responsible.

Much progress in this area had been made since the early encounters with the Afrika Korps, which often resulted in many repairable tanks being left on the enemy dominated battlefield. In simple terms the RAOC's recovery organization paralleled the Royal Army Medical Corps' casualty clearance procedure in which wounded men were passed back through the Regimental Aid Post, Advanced Dressing Station, Forward Surgical Unit and on to the Base Hospital, with each stage absorbing a higher level of injury. As far as tanks were concerned the first stage was the armoured regiment's Light Aid Detachment. If the damage was too serious for the LAD to cope with, the regiment's technical adjutant would signal the brigade recovery officer giving the vehicle's serial number, which would identify its type, its location and a lettered code which summarized the damage. Thus 'T24700 G125474 MSRTQ' would be understood by the Brigade Recovery Section as Tank No 24700 (a Grant) at Grid Reference 125474 with mine damage to suspension, right track blown off and unserviceable transmission. The Recovery Section was then despatched, together with a detachment from Brigade Workshops which would assist in on-site repairs to tracks, suspension and engine until the tank could be driven or towed to ground accessible to tank transporters and then back-loaded to the workshops themselves. Burned-out tanks would be abandoned unless their suspensions would support towing, although repairable turrets were salvaged and suspension parts would be cannibalized to get other tanks moving. Repairs beyond the capacity of Brigade Workshops, generally involving transmission damage, were back-loaded to a 3rd Echelon unit, the Tank Troops Workshop, and the most serious casualties of all were generally back-loaded by rail to Base Workshops. Collecting points were established at every level, the location of these being carefully selected to provide transporters with hard going and plenty of space in which derelicts could be winched aboard. Most recovery operations took place at night, as did most back-loading, to fit in with Corps movement control timetables. When things were going badly the tempo of back-loading had to be accelerated sharply.

At the start of the Gazala fighting Colonel P. W. H. Whiteley was appointed Army Recovery Officer and given a radio net which monitored divisional, brigade and regimental frequencies, enabling him to apply his resources quickly where they were most needed. His principal problems, particularly after the battle had begun to swing Rommel's way, lay in handling the third and fourth line casualties, and these he tackled in two ways. First, the seriously damaged tanks were taken to the rail-heads at Capuzzo or Fuka and shipped on flat-cars back to the base area production line facilities. Secondly, tanks which were clearly beyond repair were concentrated as far forward as possible, with the minimum of back-loading. These tank graveyards were called 'Help Yourself Dumps' and apart from

providing cannibalization facilities they caused the enemy to waste precious ammunition on what he imagined were leaguer areas. Whiteley also established a logical working relationship with the commander of the Royal Army Service Corps tank transporter column, simultaneously solving problems for both organizations. The RASC transporters saved track-mileage by bringing regiments forward from rail-heads to their operational areas, and also delivered new and repaired tanks to the armoured formations' Tank Delivery Squadrons, but would then return empty. There was seldom time for the tired drivers to ballast the empty trailers, the noisy vibration of which caused numerous weld failures. At Whiteley's suggestion, therefore, the transporters proceeded to the recovery collecting points after they had made their forward deliveries, and were there loaded with cripples destined for rail-head. The result was a sharp increase in the number of tanks back-loaded, coupled with a drop in the incidence of trailer failures.

Following the fall of Tobruk, decisions were taken by the Axis commanders which ensured that the war in the Western Desert entered its final decisive phase. *Venezia* was to have been followed by *Herakles*, the invasion of Malta, and on this issue Rommel and Kesselring were at odds. Rommel wanted to pursue the Eighth Army into Egypt, denying it the time and space in which to recover and reorganize. This made good sense, but only in the short term, for as Kesselring pointed out, Rommel lacked the resources, particularly air support, which would enable him to break through to Cairo and the Suez Canal, whereas the British would be fighting close to their bases and become progressively stronger as the days passed. Rommel, of course, needed no lessons in the economics of desert warfare but, driven by burning ambition that was itself fuelled by victory and his ability to overcome apparently insuperable difficulties, he set off into Egypt on 23 June, confident that

Hitler would support him. Hitler did and *Herakles* was cancelled, although in the light of subsequent events the Fuhrer was to plead that it was his lack of confidence in the Italian Navy which influenced his decision to abandon the invasion of Malta.

Ritchie did not attempt to hold the frontier. XXX Corps had already been sent back to reorganize and Gott's XIII Corps, with Richards' 4th Armoured Brigade under command, withdrew to Mersa Matruh where the new X Corps, including 2nd New Zealand Division, had been formed under Lieutenant-General Sir William Holmes. On 25 June Auchinleck relieved Ritchie and assumed personal command of the Eighth Army. The following evening the DAK effected a penetration between X Corps and XIII Corps, lying beyond the escarpment to the south. Confused orders and a breakdown in communications led to a disorderly and acrimonious retreat in which Freyberg, the New Zealand commander, was wounded. During the day Rommel had been visited by Kesselring, Cavallero and Bastico, who expressed serious concern about the wisdom of continuing his advance. Rommel was able to point to the fact that this latest victory had been won with approximately 50 tanks and 2,500 infantrymen in the face of greatly superior odds, and was reluctantly allowed to proceed.

Jumbled together, the two armies straggled eastwards. At this period about 85 per cent of Rommel's transport was of British manufacture and his artillery included captured field and anti-tank guns. Behind trundled *Ariete* and the recently arrived *Littorio* Armoured Division with about 70 tanks between them, followed by *Trieste* and 6,000 men of the Italian infantry divisions. In Cairo and Alexandria the Axis advance generated such alarm that part of General Headquarters was evacuated to Palestine and the Mediterranean Fleet was temporarily dispersed, while on what became known as 'Ash Wednesday' confidential files were burned by the score. The

uproar was sincerely enjoyed by those fighting troops privileged to witness it, and it was relished by the Egyptian Nationalists, whose ranks included such junior officers as Gamal Abdel Nasser and Anwar Sadat. On 29 June Mussolini flew into Tripoli and made preparations to enter Cairo on a white charger. As he did so 4th Armoured Brigade, operating behind the German spearheads, administered a sharp lesson to *Littorio* at Bir el Tamr, destroying 20 of its 30 tanks.

The British retreat ended at El Alamein, a little town lying on the railway some 60 miles west of Alexandria. Here the negotiable desert narrowed to a 35 mile strip bounded on the north by the sea and on the south by the impassable shifting sands and salt marshes of the humid Quattara Depression, lying below sea level. Within this strip were three ridges running roughly from east to west, Meteiriya in the north, Ruweisat some miles to the south, and Alam Halfa to the south-east; none were more than a swelling in the stony desert but the overview they offered made their possession extremely important. The defensive potential of the position had been evaluated in 1940 and now the conclusions were put to good use.

Auchinleck deployed XXX Corps (1st South African and 10th Indian Divisions, joined later by 9th Australian Division) on the northern sector while XIII Corps (2nd New Zealand and 5th Indian Divisions) covered the south, supported by the remnants of 1st and 7th Armoured Divisions. For those involved in the long retreat it had been an utterly exhausting experience. 'After that,' wrote Brigadier Richards, 'I came to the conclusion that no officer knew what war meant until he had experienced a defeat and forced withdrawal.' When, eventually, he found time to sleep, he did not wake for 48 hours.

There was never the slightest doubt that the troops would fight, but the Eighth Army was pervaded by a sour miasma of defeat and recrimination. The Commonwealth divisions resented the fact that, with the exception of divisional cavalry and armoured car regiments, the armour was in British hands. The infantry in general had, *force majeure,* played the role of hostages to fortune in their static boxes while the armour fought and lost its battles, and they felt that somehow they had been let down. As for the tank crews, they were tired of fighting for senior officers who always seemed to be one jump behind the enemy; tired of being sacrificed in badly-planned operations; and tired of standing to for attacks which were cancelled at the last minute. They were stale, or 'canny' as Wardrop puts it, unwilling to take risks without good reason. Throughout the army a dangerous cynicism had taken root, based on the assumption that whatever operations were planned, events would see to it that they never took place.

The protracted series of actions known as the First Battle of Alamein began on 1 July with an attack by 90th Light on the South African box enclosing El Alamein itself. The Germans were just as weary as the British and after their assault had foundered in a storm of shellfire they refused to renew it, despite the personal intervention of Rommel. Further south the panzer divisions ran into an unsuspected box at Deir el Shein, a hollow feature at the western end of Ruweisat Ridge. This was held by the 18th Indian Infantry Brigade, an *ad hoc* artillery regiment and nine Matildas, and by the time it was subdued 15th Panzer Division were down to 25 tanks and 21st Panzer to 12.

On 2 July Auchinleck, warned by Ultra that Rommel intended isolating the El Alamein box, was able to thwart this move by moving 1st Armoured Division into a blocking position. The following day both panzer divisions pushed east along Ruweisat Ridge but were again met by 1st Armoured, which lost 39 of its 119 tanks but halted the German advance and reduced the DAK's tank strength to 26. Rommel now accepted reluctantly that his army had shot its bolt and the DAK was pulled out of the line, its place being taken by the Italian infantry as they came up.

The battle was to rage for a further three weeks with attack followed by counter-attack along the front as Auchinleck strove to gain the initiative and Rommel fought to maintain

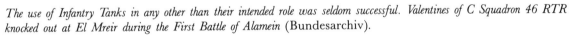

The use of Infantry Tanks in any other than their intended role was seldom successful. Valentines of C Squadron 46 RTR knocked out at El Mreir during the First Battle of Alamein (Bundesarchiv).

his position. Both sides recovered their strength but neither was quite strong enough to inflict a major defeat on the other, and as the front solidified both armies began laying defensive minebelts.

Much of the fighting centred on Ruweisat Ridge, which an Australian raid revealed was held by Gioda's Italian X Corps, consisting of the *Brescia* and *Pavia* Infantry Divisions. On the night of 14 July, therefore, a major operation was mounted by both British corps to capture the feature. 5th Indian Division was to capture Point 64, at the eastern end of the ridge, while 2nd New Zealand Division was to take Point 63, lying further west. The general direction of the attack was north-west and 22nd Armoured Brigade was to protect the exposed left flank. Both objectives were secured and some 2,000 prisoners were taken, but at first light on the 15th things began to go wrong. The advance had by-passed the night leaguer of part of 8th Panzer Regiment, and shortly after dawn the German tanks attacked 5th New Zealand Brigade, overrunning one battalion before making off to the southwest. Unfortunately, 22nd Armoured Brigade was late arriving and was unable to intervene. Rommel, seriously alarmed by this thrust at his centre, hastily formed a DAK battlegroup and launched a counter-attack at 17:00. The 22nd Armoured Brigade was again slow to react but came into action at 18:15, halting further German progress eastwards; by then the 4th New Zealand Brigade had been overwhelmed and Point 63 was once more in enemy hands. The German attack was resumed on the 16th but was broken up with the loss of 24 tanks by the combined efforts of 5th Indian and 1st Armoured Divisions, supported by the corps artillery.

Rommel's sensitivity was duly noted by Auchinleck, who decided to repeat the Ruweisat attack at the earliest possible moment in the hope that he would be able to break through to El Daba or even Fuka. The breakthrough phase presented something of

a problem because the experienced armoured brigades, well aware of the risks involved and having seen too many ambitious schemes shot to tatters, were unlikely to possess the necessary aggression. What was needed were completely fresh troops who knew nothing of the dangers and still retained their illusions, and as luck would have it such a formation had disembarked at Port Tewfik on 6 July. This was Brigadier Lawrence Misa's Valentine-equipped 23rd Armoured Brigade (40, 46 and 50 RTR) which, together with 24th Armoured Brigade, formed part of the 8th Armoured Division and had been at sea for two months. The 24th Armoured Brigade had still to complete its journey, its ship having broken down at Durban.

The operation was to start on the night of 21/22 July and would be controlled by Gott's XIII Corps. 5th Indian and 2nd New Zealand Division were to mount converging attacks on Point 63, the left flank of the latter being protected by 22nd Armoured Brigade. Simultaneously, gaps were to be made in the enemy minefield which would permit two of Misa's regiments (40 and 46 RTR) to advance along the southern edge of the ridge, break the anti-tank gun screen and capture El Mreir, a hollow feature lying to the south-west. 2nd Armoured Brigade would then pass through and exploit towards El Daba.

Unfortunately, the defences were now much stronger than they had been a week earlier. They were manned by German infantry who had increased the density of the minebelt and thickened up their anti-tank guns, while both panzer regiments lay on call just behind the front. Nevertheless, the attack began well with the Indians and New Zealanders both taking their objectives. At first light, however, they were heavily counterattacked and forced to relinquish their gains, the 6th New Zealand Brigade being overrun. Once again, 22nd Armoured Brigade had failed to turn up on time, its commander pleading lamely that his tanks were unable to move at night. For the New Zealanders, who had sustained 2,000 casualties since the Ruweisat operations began, this was the last straw, and for the moment their dislike of the armour amounted to something approaching hatred. This opinion would be modified somewhat during the next two hours.

Despite these reverses and the fact that the minefield remained ungapped, radio intercepts convinced Gott that the Germans were in disarray and he insisted that 23rd Armoured Brigade's attack must go in, although he permitted a more southerly axis through what he believed was an area clear of mines. This information was never received by Misa and at 08:00 his regiments moved off in accordance with the original orders, 40 RTR on the right and 46 RTR on the left. The 5th New Zealand Brigade was impressed by their evident determination and its historian commented that they 'thundered past our northern flank at a great pace—a real Balaclava charge'.

About one-and-a-half miles out from its startline the brigade crossed the minefield, losing about 20 tanks in the process. Undeterred, the remainder pressed on but suddenly found themselves on a tank killing ground, laced with armour-piercing shot and pounded by artillery. What followed amounted to a massacre. Private Günther Halm, manning a captured Russian 76.2 mm anti-tank gun on Panzergrenadier Regiment 104's sector, personally accounted for ten tanks before his weapon was smashed by return fire; his feat earned him the Knights' Cross and a commission. A handful survived the carnage and reached their objective, causing a panic at the nearby DAK headquarters until they were destroyed or driven off by local anti-tank guns and a counter-attack by 5th Panzer Regiment. Of the 97 tanks which had taken part in the attack, only 11 returned. During the afternoon 2nd Armoured Brigade penetrated beyond the minefield but were forced to withdraw after an action lasting 40 minutes, having lost 21

tanks. Further north 50 RTR supported an evening attack by 9th Australian Division on the Tel el Eisa (Jesus Hill) sector, losing 23 tanks on the objective, bringing the British total for the day to 132.

The battle smouldered on until 27 July without apparent result, yet many regard it as a turning point. German tank losses had been negligible but casualties among the infantry had been heavy and Rommel was desperate for reinforcements. First to arrive was the 164th Infantry Division from Crete, followed by the Ramcke Parachute Brigade and the Italian *Folgore* Parachute Division, none of which possessed their own transport; the paratroop formations were to have been dropped during the invasion of Malta and their diversion to the desert was clear proof that *Herakles* was dead. Moreover, while he had been able to contain Auchinleck's attacks, Rommel was faced with the unpleasant fact that he and his men were captives of his decision to penetrate so far into Egypt. The stores acquired in Tobruk had gone and with them went any further chance of resuming his advance, yet retreat would induce the sort of mobile battle which the Axis armour lacked the resources to sustain. Because of continuous raids by the RAF on the ports of Benghazi, Derna, Tobruk and Bardia, most of his supplies still passed through Tripoli, 1,000 long miles to the west, the result being that the amount of fuel reaching the front was barely sufficient to meet daily requirements. Such fuel as did arrive was allocated to the armoured formations at the expense of the Luftwaffe, the consequence being a reduction in the level of air support which had served him so well at Tobruk. The situation would have been even worse had it not been for the Western Desert Railway, which was extended from Belhamed to Tobruk. Even so, the line was subject to air attack and the attentions of the Special Air Service Regiment and was not used east of Mersa Matruh. To add to these difficulties Malta had recovered its offensive capacity. Submarines began operating from the island again and during August these sank four supply ships while aircraft accounted for a further three, a total of 40,043 tons.

On 3 August Churchill arrived in Egypt, accompanied by General Sir Alan Brooke, the Chief of the Imperial General Staff. The Prime Minister felt that change was needed at the top and General Sir Harold Alexander was appointed Commander-in-Chief Middle East while Gott was designated commander of the Eighth Army. Gott himself did not want the job. He had been in the thick of the desert war since its beginning and was now very tired. He told Brooke that new blood and new ideas were needed, but Churchill insisted. Fate now took a hand, for on 7 August his aircraft was forced down by German fighters; Gott survived the crash and was helping to free trapped passengers when he was killed by a second attack. Churchill then agreed to Brooke's personal choice, Lieutenant-General Bernard Montgomery, who immediately flew out from the United Kingdom and assumed command of the Eighth Army on 13 August.

Montgomery had served in France throughout the First World War, both as a regimental officer and in various staff appointments. In 1940 he had commanded the 3rd Division in France and gone on to command a corps and then the important South-Eastern Command. His name meant little to the general public but within the Army he was known for his orthodoxy, meticulous preparation and iron will. He was also known for his abrupt manner, his ruthlessness with those who opposed him and, less widely, for his kindness and loyalty to those who supported him. It has been said that he would not have performed well in a mêlée such as Crusader or Gazala, but he was not confronted with such a situation, nor did he intend becoming involved in one. He arrived in Egypt with a clear perception of what he had to do and subsequently recorded his attitude in his book *A History of Warfare.*

One point was very firmly fixed in my mind—desert warfare was not suited to remote control. I decided to give a clear lead and to take a firm grip on the Eighth Army from above; there must be no uncertainty about anything. My determination to deal firmly with Rommel and his army once and for all was clearly expressed: to hit the Axis forces right out of Africa. But I was equally determined not to begin the attempt until we were fully prepared, and I said as much to officers and men.

Recognizing the need to establish his own personality rather than Rommel's in the minds of his men, Montgomery discarded his general's cap and toured units wearing the Royal Tank Regiment's famous black beret, adding his insignia to the regiment's badge. In his incisive manner he told the troops that further withdrawals were out of the question; the army would fight where it stood, and the army would win. These were words which any new commander might have used yet their effect, even among the most cynical and jaded, was remarkable. It was not the words themselves, but rather an instinctive recognition that Montgomery knew his business and was capable of delivering what he promised.

In the meantime Rommel had decided on a last desperate gamble. The pause had allowed him to accumulate just sufficient stores to mount one major attack and, conscious that the British were being reinforced at a rate he could not hope to match, he knew that he must make the attempt as soon as possible, using the same right hook with which he had opened the Gazala Battle. By the end of August he had 203 German tanks, including 74 PzKw III Model Js and 27 PzKw IV F2s, the latter now the most powerful tanks on the battlefield, while *Ariete* and *Littorio* possessed a total of 243 M13s.

The attack, and its timing, had been predicted by Auchinleck's staff as early as 27 July and since then Ultra and other intelligence sources had confirmed the enemy's intentions. From north to south the British line was held by the 9th Australian, 1st South

African, 5th Indian and 2nd New Zealand Divisions. To the left of the New Zealanders deep minebelts stretched south towards the Quattara Depression, covered by the 7th Light Armoured Division, which mustered 122 Stuarts and Crusaders as well as armoured cars. However, Montgomery recognized that his opponent's wheel to the north would lead him towards Alam Halfa Ridge and he decided to fight a purely defensive battle based on this feature, bringing forward the 44th Division from the Delta for the purpose. The hard shell of the defence would be provided by Major-General Gatehouse's 10th Armoured Division, with 23rd Armoured Brigade covering the gap between the western end of the ridge and the New Zealanders, 22nd Armoured Brigade on the forward slopes of the ridge itself, and 8th Armoured Brigade east of the ridge. Altogether, the three brigades possessed about 500 tanks, including 164 Grants, which were now referred to as ELH (Egypt's Last Hope).

Rommel's attack began during the night of 30/31 August and ran into difficulties immediately. The minebelts were denser than had been anticipated and the fire of 7th Light Armoured Division, supplemented by that of the New Zealand artillery, caused heavy casualties among the mine-lifting parties and their covering infantry. With first light came the RAF to add to the torment and Rommel was on the point of cancelling the whole operation when his leading elements at last broke through. By then General Nehring, commanding the DAK, had been wounded, as had Major-General Kleeman, the commander of 90th Light; Major-General von Bismarck of 21st Panzer Division was killed by mortar fire in the minefields. Further delay was caused by a fierce sandstorm and then by an area of soft sand so that it was not until late afternoon that the German spearheads began approaching Alam Halfa.

The 22nd Armoured Brigade, commanded by the recently promoted Brigadier G. P.

B. Roberts since 29 July, was deployed around Point 102 with 1 RTR on the right, 4th County of London Yeomanry in the centre and 5 RTR on the left; in reserve were the as yet unb]ooded Royal Scots Greys, lying on the reverse slopes. Each regiment consisted of two Grant squadrons and one light squadron and the brigade's front was approximately three miles long, many of the tanks' hull-down positions having been excavated by bulldozers. A number of 6-pounder anti-tank guns were also dug in and concealed, and the fire of 1st Royal Horse Artillery's 25-pounders was on call.

Roberts had been kept fully informed as to the progress of the battle and during the afternoon sent out two of his light squadrons to look for the enemy. By 15:30 they were exchanging shots with 21st Panzer Division and began retiring, swinging wide to avoid disclosing the main position. Through his binoculars Roberts watched the serried German ranks grind steadily on, led by the PzKw IV F2s which, he noted with concern, were armed with 'the devil of a gun'. At 18:00, with the range closing slowly, he ordered his regiments not to engage above 1,000 yards; at 18:10 the CLY opened fire. The response was immediate and within minutes one of the regiment's squadrons had ceased to exist. There were also gaps in the German lines but, sensing victory, the mass began edging forward, only to run into the concealed positions of 1st Rifle Brigade's anti-tank guns, which held their fire until the tanks were within 300 yards. The Riflemen took a steady toll but some of their guns were overrun by sheer weight of numbers. The battle now rested on a knife edge. Lieutenant-Colonel Sir Ranulph Fiennes, commanding the Greys, was ordered by Roberts to bring his regiment forward with all speed and fill the breach which had been made in the brigade's centre. For the moment the Germans were stalled by 1 RHA's concentrations, which fell squarely on top of their tanks, but Roberts was becoming terribly anxious. Then, like their forebears at Waterloo, the Greys were thundering down the forward slope, closing the gap and letting drive with every gun they possessed. This crisis over, Roberts was able to turn his attention to a number of enemy tanks which had worked their way round 5 RTR's left flank and were being engaged over open sights by one battery of 1 RHA. He pulled out what remained of the CLY from the now secure but crowded centre and sent them across to his extreme left, where they contained the threat until darkness put an end to the fighting.

Next morning 15th Panzer Division attempted to slide past 5 RTR. From his driving seat Wardrop had a grandstand view of the action: 'It was just breaking light and there in front of us, about 2,000 yards away, was a great heap of tanks. They must have halted there the night before and were shaking out. I wakened the gunner and we started to go to town on them with the 75; we couldn't miss them, they were so bunched up. It was alright while it lasted, but they started to give us a lacing in return—it was quite a morning.'

Before long, Brigadier E. C. N. Custance's 8th Armoured Brigade (3 RTR, Sherwood Rangers and Staffordshire Yeomanry) closed in from the east and although the subsequent engagement was inconclusive Rommel was forced to accept that with his dwindling fuel reserves he was unable to fight his way through the wall of tanks and artillery which faced him every time he turned north. He cancelled the operation and during the next few days retired behind his own minebelts, bombed regularly by the RAF's Wellingtons and Albacores, harassed from the south by 7th Light Armoured Division and from the north by 2nd New Zealand Division and part of 23rd Armoured Brigade. The Battle of Alam Halfa had cost him 49 tanks and other AFVs, 60 guns of various type, about 400 transport vehicles and some 2,800 casualties, the major part of the loss falling on his German troops. The Eighth Army lost 67 tanks, including 31 Grants, but many of these were

repairable.

Alam Halfa restored the Eighth Army's confidence in itself and in its aftermath Montgomery began preparing for the battle which he promised would destroy his opponent. Because the front was now firmly established on both sides it would, in many respects, be a battle that had much in common with those of 1918, fought with modern weapons. It would, above all, be a battle of attrition or, as Montgomery himself put it, 'a killing match'. The British were much the stronger and were being reinforced daily but the Army Commander was only too aware that in the past numerical superiority had not always been sufficient to guarantee victory. With inexorable determination he began eliminating the heresies which had bedevilled the army for more than a year, replacing them with a strict orthodoxy the canon of which was sustained co-operation between arms at every level. Those commanders who were unable to adapt were removed; simultaneously, it was made plain that such terms as box, battlegroup and Jock column belonged to the past and had nothing to do with current thinking.

It was clear from the outset that in the coming battle the infantry would play a more important role than ever before. It would be they who protected the mineclearing sappers as they worked, and it would be they who fought to secure breaches in the enemy defences through which the armoured formations were to pass and write down their opponents. The infantry, therefore, must have the maximum assistance possible, including their own specialist armoured support.

In this respect Brigadier Richards made a most important contribution. Reserved almost to the point of diffidence, he was nonetheless extremely shrewd and Montgomery valued his opinion so highly that he employed him in an advisory capacity as Major-General Royal Armoured Corps during the campaign in North-West Europe. He had taken over 23rd Armoured Brigade short-

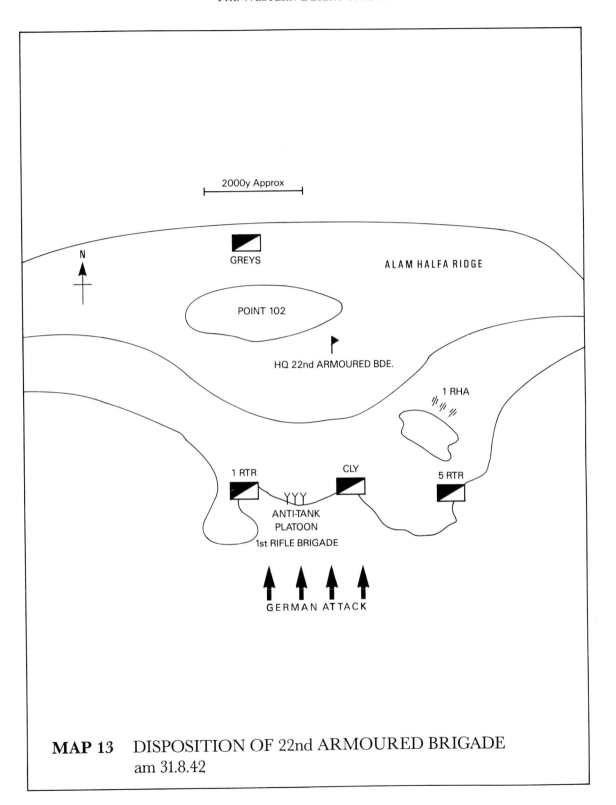

2000y Approx

N

GREYS

ALAM HALFA RIDGE

POINT 102

HQ 22nd ARMOURED BDE.

1 RHA

1 RTR

CLY

5 RTR

ANTI-TANK
PLATOON

1st RIFLE BRIGADE

GERMAN ATTACK

MAP 13   DISPOSITION OF 22nd ARMOURED BRIGADE
am 31.8.42

The Sherman, armed with a turret-mounted 75 mm gun, entered service with the Eighth Army shortly before Second Alamein (National Army Museum).

infantry leading with the tanks following close behind. When the objective had been taken the tanks remained with the infantry to break up the inevitable counter-attack and did not leave until the latter's 6-pounder anti-tank guns had been brought forward and dug in. During the weeks that followed the method was carefully rehearsed with 1st South African Division, 2nd New Zealand Division, 4th Indian Division, 9th Australian Division and Major-General Douglas Wimberley's newly arrived 51st Highland Division. The sustained contact broke down many of the prejudices held by the infantry and developed a mutual understanding of the problems faced by each arm. If, for example, the infantry were held up by machine-gun posts, the tanks would deal with them; if the tanks were held up by an anti-tank gun, it would be eliminated by the infantry.

Within the artillery, too, there was a return to an orthodoxy not seen since O'Connor's day, a process actually begun during First Alamein. Divisional and corps artillery were again concentrated so that the fire of large numbers of guns could be switched from area to area by means of an efficient command and control system established by Brigadier Sidney Kirkman, the army's senior artillery officer, who had flown out from the United Kingdom at Montgomery's request. Even the Bofors light anti-aircraft guns were required to contribute to Kirkman's fire plan, firing short bursts of tracer at regular intervals during night attacks to mark the axes of advance and the boundaries between brigades.

Of the new weapons reaching the Eighth Army, the Sherman medium tank was the most significant. Like the Grant, the Sherman was armed with a 75 mm gun, but this was mounted in a turret with all-round traverse and therefore offered numerous advantages, including the capacity to fight fully hull-down. Churchill had been visiting Roosevelt in Washington when he received the horrifying news that Tobruk had fallen. With typical

ly after the Ruweisat débâcle and promptly opposed its further employment in roles for which its Valentine infantry tanks were unsuited. Instead he proposed that the brigade should become an independent formation specializing in infantry support, its regiments living and training with the infantry divisions with whom they were to fight. Montgomery agreed and added a fourth regiment, 8 RTR, to its establishment, giving it a tank strength in excess of 200. In addition to training for the usual daylight infantry/tank attack, Richards was ordered to work out suitable tactics for night attacks. These consisted of the generosity, the President immediately offered to make his 2nd Armored Division available. It was, however, pointed out by General George Marshall, the US Army's Chief of Staff, that it would take up to five months for the division to reach the Middle East and it was decided instead to send 300 Shermans, plus 100 M7 (Priest) 105 mm howitzer motor carriages. These left America on 15 July and arrived in Egypt shortly after Alam Halfa. Also available were the Bishop 25-pounder self-propelled gun, based on the Valentine chassis, one regiment of which was logically allocated to 23rd Armoured Brigade, and the Deacon 6-pounder self-propelled anti-tank gun, which equipped one battery within anti-tank regiments.

Montgomery knew that he would be unable to achieve strategic surprise, but was determined to obtain tactical surprise if it was at all possible. His object was to convince Rommel that he intended striking his major blow on the southern sector of the front and to this end he set in motion the largest deception plan of the desert war, codenamed Bertram, under the overal control of Lieutenant-Colonel Charles Richardson, a member of his staff. Richardson's plan was similar to that employed by Allenby at Megiddo in that it relied on dummies to achieve its effect, but was far more elaborate in its scope. Closely involved in the day-to-day preparations was a Royal Engineer officer named Jasper Maskelyne who in civilian life had been a stage magician and was now a camouflage expert. Maskelyne's deceptions had proved effective on a number of occasions but his most notable invention was the 'sunshade', a wood and canvas lorry canopy and cab which could be mounted on a tank and quickly removed when the need arose. The device had been used before on a small scale but Bertram required the construction of hundreds. Thus, the appearance of seemingly harmless lorry parks in the north actually concealed the concentration areas of armoured formations, the tank tracks being obliterated by real lorries. Conversely, in the south the number of tank leaguers began to increase, but many of the tanks were expertly painted dummies

B-25 Mitchell bomber over-flying a Sherman squadron in the Western desert, 1942 (National Army Museum).

mounted on truck chassis, their tell-tale tyre marks masked by weighted trailers with track links fitted to the wheels.

Guns were similarly concealed and duplicated on the vital northern sector and no increase in the routine daily expenditure of ammunition was permitted. In the north, more sunshields and bivouac tents hid stockpiled stores, while in the south the enemy's air reconnaissance was given just sufficient clues to identify fuel and ammunition dumps that were merely stage props. Fresh tracks were constructed leading from the base areas to the southern sector, as was a 'water pipeline' made from fuel drums, complete with 'pumping stations' and 'storage towers' which were serviced daily by real transport vehicles and labour gangs. Nor was Richardson's activity confined solely to visual deception. The signals personnel of the now defunct 8th Armoured Division sent out a stream of transmissions from among the dummy formations to simulate the normal traffic of real units and in this way the Axis intercept

Up-gunned PzKw IV, known to the Eighth Army as the Mark IV Special, knocked out during the Second Battle of Alamein. This was the most powerful tank possessed by either side, but comparatively few were present (Author).

operators were able to report, *inter alia*, that the fictional 74th Armoured Brigade, consisting of the imaginary 39, 118 and 124 RTR, was now in the line and preparing for operations. Finally, to prevent the enemy's intelligence services from discovering the truth,

Matilda Scorpion. The flail was driven by a Ford or Bedford engine mounted on the right of the hull and exploded mines in the vehicle's path. The twin, antennae-mounted, rear-facing red lights which acted as a guide for troops following in the dust and darkness. Twelve of these vehicles were used at Second Alamein (Imperial War Museum).

the Eighth Army was virtually sealed off during the last phases of preparation.

Rommel could only await the assault and offer the best defence possible in circumstances which left him with little more than a day or two's fuel in reserve at any one time. His minebelt was extended to between two and five miles in depth and along the length of the front German units were interposed with Italian to provide a stiffening. The infantry was ordered to hold its forward line with the minimum of troops and to occupy a main position well to the rear, where it would escape the worst effects of the British bombardment. The four armoured divisions were disposed in two groups, 15th Panzer and *Littorio* in the north and 21st Panzer and *Ariete* in the south. If the British armour did succeed in emerging from the minefields it was to be halted by dug-in anti-tank gun screens and promptly counter-attacked before it could deploy its superior numbers. Having done what he could, Rommel, now tired and ill, left for home and sick leave on 23 September, handing over temporary command of Panzerarmee Afrika to General Georg Stumme.

For the forthcoming battle the Eighth Army had over 1,000 tanks, including 252 Shermans and 170 Grants, in first-line service, plus 200 in immediate reserve and approximately 1,000 more in workshops. Against these Stumme could deploy only 520 tanks, including 88 PzKw III Model Js and 30 PzKw IV F2s, the bulk of the remainder consisting of 85 short 50 mm PzKw IIIs and 278 M13s; in workshops there were a further 32 tanks, mostly PzKw IIIs. In other areas the contrast was equally marked, 435 British and Commonwealth armoured cars being opposed by 192; 908 field and medium artillery weapons compared with 500 field and 18 heavy guns; and 1,451 anti-tank guns compared with 500 German (including 86 Eighty-Eights) and 300 Italian. In the air the Western Desert Air Force had been joined by a number of US Army Air Force fighter and bomber squadrons, equipped respectively with Kittyhawks and Mitchells, and possessed a numerical superiority

Latterly the Italians placed greater reliance on their Semoventi assault guns than they did on their obsolete tanks. The fixed superstructure enabled a larger weapon to be mounted, in this instance a 75 mm gun. The crew have supplemented their 50 mm frontal armour with track links and sandbags (Imperial War Museum).

over the Luftwaffe and *Regia Aeronautica* in the ratio of five aircraft to three.

Montgomery's army now consisted of three corps. XXX Corps, commanded by Lieutenant-General Sir Oliver Leese, was deployed on the northern sector of the front and consisted of 23rd Armoured Brigade Group, 9th Australian Division (Lieutenant-General Sir Leslie Morshead), 51st Highland Division (Major-General Douglas Wimberley), 2nd New Zealand Division (Lieutenant-General Sir Bernard Freyberg, VC), containing two infantry brigades and 9th Armoured Brigade, 1st South African Divi-

sion (Major-General D. H. Pienaar), and 4th Indian Division (Major-General F. I. S. Tuker). To the south was Lieutenant-General B. G. Horrocks' XIII Corps, consisting of 7th Armoured Division (Major-General A. F. Harding), 50th Division (Major-General J. S. Nichols) and 44th Division (Major-General I. T. P. Hughes); the 1st and 2nd Fighting French Brigade Groups were integrated respectively with 7th Armoured and 50th Divisions, the latter also being supplemented by the 1st Greek Infantry Brigade Group. Behind XXX Corps and overlaying its rear areas was Lieutenant-General H. Lumsden's

Shermans continue the advance to the Tunisian frontier (US Army Military History Institute).

X Corps, containing 1st Armoured Division (Major-General R. Briggs) and 10th Armoured Division (Major-General A. H. Gatehouse).

The plan for Operation Lightfoot, as the opening phase of the Second Battle of Alamein was known, required XIII Corps to mount holding attacks while XXX Corps delivered the main blow in the north, capturing the minefields and clearing two corridors through which the armoured divisions of X Corps were to pass. The battle began at 21:40 on 23 October with a heavy bombardment by 592 guns, 456 of which had been crammed into XXX Corps' sector, firing concentrations which erupted among the enemy's artillery positions until 21:55. From 22:00 until 22:07 further concentrations were fired against selected targets at the forward edge of the defended area and then the guns reverted to divisional control. Meanwhile, the shadowy figures of the mineclearing parties and the infantry had risen from their trenches and started forward, followed slowly by their supporting Valentines.

Resistance was fierce. Those who fought on that and succeeding nights were left with blurred impressions of bursting shells, drifting dust clouds, congestion in the minefield gaps and darkness suddenly stabbed by the fire of local killing. Progress was slower than had been expected and although gains were made the armoured divisions were unable to debouch from their lanes in the Meteiriya and Kidney Ridge areas.

Stumme succumbed to a heart attack on the 24th and von Thoma, the commander of the DAK, took over the Axis army until Rommel returned the following evening. Rommel appreciated at once that he was enmeshed in a 'battle without hope'. He was shaken by the volume and flexibility of the 'tremendous' artillery fire and depressed by the carefully rehearsed British infantry/tank tactics which were steadily gnawing their way into his positions. 'The storming parties,' he later wrote, 'were accompanied by tanks which acted as mobile artillery, and forced their way into the trenches at the point of the bayonet. Everything went methodically and according to a drill.' It was true that he was inflicting heavy casualties, but his own strength was being whittled away and his losses could not be made good. On 27 October, while counter-attacking Briggs' 1st Armoured Division at Kidney Ridge, he lost a disproportionate number of tanks as a direct result of the remarkable stand of a single motor battalion.

Some two miles west of Kidney Ridge lay the Rahman Track, which ran from north to south and provided the Axis army with its principal means of lateral communication. Briggs was determined to sever this but the ground between the ridge and the track was dangerously open and during the night of 26/27 October two of his motor battalions were detailed to secure intervening localities codenamed Woodcock and Snipe, the intention being that these would serve as a firm base for a further westward thrust by his division.

Snipe was the objective of the 2nd Battalion The Rifle Brigade, commanded by Lieutenant-Colonel Victor Turner, but following a combination of navigational errors in the darkness the battalion actually reached a position half a mile south of its target. This consisted of an oval depression measuring 900 by 400 yards, formerly used as a German engineer stores depot, and since it was suitable for defence Turner ordered its consolidation. He had available 13 6-pounder anti-tank guns of his own, plus a further six belonging to 239 Battery of 76th Anti-Tank Regiment, Royal Artillery. These were dug in around the perimeter and camouflaged with scrub while the battalion's carriers went out to reconnoitre. It was soon apparent that the outpost had been established in close proximity to the tank leaguers of 15th Panzer and the *Littorio* Armoured Division.

Outpost Snipe began killing tanks at dawn and went on killing them until last light. It stood off repeated attacks by tanks and infantry, the riflemen and gunners holding their fire until the last possible minute, and it was shelled constantly until its interior became a shambles of smashed guns, carriers and jeeps, dead and dying. The principal object of the Axis armour, which was joined during the afternoon by 21st Panzer Division, was to counter-attack Briggs' armoured brigades, but in so doing it exposed its vulnerable flanks to fire from Turner's position. Conversely, whenever it turned to attack the outpost it exposed its flanks to the fire of the armoured brigades and thus piled up casualties to no purpose. Dusk found the battered garrison still full of fight but it was now critically short of ammunition and at 23:00 the survivors withdrew with one 6-pounder, having rendered the rest unusable.

The defence of Outpost Snipe became a legend throughout the Eighth Army and a month later a Committee of Investigation visited the now silent hollow to examine the wrecks which still surrounded it and analyse the action. It concluded that 21 German and 11 Italian tanks, plus five assault guns or tank destroyers, had been destroyed outright, and that a further 15, possibly 20, tanks had been knocked out and recovered, although few of the latter can have been repaired by the time the battle ended. Turner, who had been wounded when a shell splinter penetrated his steel helmet, was awarded the Victoria Cross and a high proportion of his officers and men were decorated.

At sea a determined effort was being made to improve Rommel's supply position, but between 26 October and 1 November four ships with thousands of tons of fuel and ammunition aboard were sunk by the RAF, one of them on the point of entering Tobruk harbour. Knowing how slender were his opponent's resources, Montgomery abandoned his thrust in the Kidney Ridge area and embarked on a 'crumbling' battle, switching the emphasis of his attack from one sector to another, so compelling the Axis to burn priceless fuel

as they responded to each new threat.

Morshead's Australians were ordered to advance northwards to the coast, isolating a heavily defended locality known as Thompson's Post. Their attack began during the night of 28/29 October and made slow progress in the face of bitter opposition which inflicted heavy casualties on the assaulting infantry battalions and the supporting Valentines of 46 RTR. Subsequently, Rommel recorded that the British tanks and infantry had succeeded in blowing a gap in his line, cutting off the 2nd Battalion 125th Panzer Grenadier Regiment and a Bersaglieri battalion in Thompson's Post, where they resisted all attempts to dislodge them with a ferocious determination. In addition, the 125th Regiment's 3rd Battalion had been all but wiped out by morning, the battle having raged with tremendous fury for six hours.

The attack was renewed during the night of 30/31 October, the Australian 2nd/32nd Battalion securing a footing north of the railway. From this newly-won ground the 2nd/24th and 2nd/48th Battalions advanced due east across the rear face of Thompson's Post but had to retire by first light to positions close to the 2nd/32nd, having sustained crippling casualties. Nothing deterred, the

Valentine under its dummy lorry canopy and cab, known as a 'sunshade', prior to the Second Battle of Alamein (Australian War Memorial).

2nd/3rd Pioneer Battalion attacked to the north again, cutting the coast road.

Throughout the hours of darkness 40 RTR, commanded by Lieutenant-Colonel J. L. Finigan, had been moving slowly forward up the mine-littered Stake Track, the way being painfully cleared by 295 Company Royal Engineers. The regiment was down to 32 Valentines, although reserve crews were drawing repaired tanks and would be bringing them up during the day. Shortly before first light it reached the railway north-west of Thompson's Post. At this point Finigan's tank was immobilized by mine damage and when he changed tanks the same thing happened. Fully aware of the vital importance of supporting armour to the Australians, he dismounted and led the way on foot through what remained of the minefield until he met Lieutenant-Colonel H. H. Hammar, commanding the 2nd/48th Battalion. Hammar had been wounded in the face and doubted whether more than 60 of his men were still on their feet. Finigan therefore crossed the railway and deployed his regiment facing west to await the inevitable counter-attack.

Rommel, determined at all costs to prevent a breakthrough on the sensitive sector of the coast road, was seriously alarmed to learn that British armour had arrived in the area and promptly moved his field headquarters to the ruined mosque of Sidi Abd el Rahman. At 10:00 he was joined there by von Thoma, who was ordered to mount a counter-attack with 21st Panzer and 90th Light. This began an hour later and made little progress, as did further attacks during the afternoon, all being broken up by 40 RTR, supported by the 6-pounders of 289 Anti-Tank Battery Royal Artillery, field artillery concentrations and bombing. The burden of the action, however, fell on the outgunned Valentines, which were engaged not only by tanks, tank destroyers and anti-tank guns, but also by the enemy's artillery, their rear protected by smoke shells which masked them from the defenders of Thompson's Post. Stubbornly, the Fortieth stuck it out, trading four tanks to the Germans' one, their personal casualties amounting to nine officers and 35 men, a high proportion of the three-man crews. When dusk put an end to the fighting a battered handful rallied, earning a sincere tribute from the Australians' official historian: 'The courage of these men made their action one of the most magnificent of the war.'

Next day the DAK renewed the pressure, pushing the Australians back just sufficiently for the garrison of Thompson's Post to be extracted during the night. The bitter struggle had, nonetheless, succeeded in its object, for once Rommel's attention was firmly concentrated on the coastal sector Montgomery decided to mount a fresh attack further south. Codenamed Supercharge, this would go in just north of Kidney Ridge and consist of three phases:
(a) breaking into the enemy's position
(b) overcoming his anti-tank gun screen
(c) bringing to battle and destroying his armour.
The first phase would be executed by the 2nd New Zealand Division and 23rd Armoured Brigade, the second by 9th Armoured Brigade, and the third by 1st Armoured Division.

Freyberg's division was by now extremely short of men and the assaulting infantry brigades were drawn from 51st and 50th Divisions, deployed with 152 Brigade on the left, supported by 50 RTR, and 151 Brigade on the right, supported by 8 RTR. At 01:05 on 2 November, both brigades crossed their start lines and advanced behind a creeping barrage towards their objectives. The combined infantry/tank tactics went exactly according to plan and by first light the newly won positions were being consolidated.

At 06:15 Brigadier John Currie's 9th Armoured Brigade (3rd Hussars, Royal Wiltshire Yeomanry and Warwickshire Yeomanry) passed through and embarked on its death ride against the enemy's anti-tank

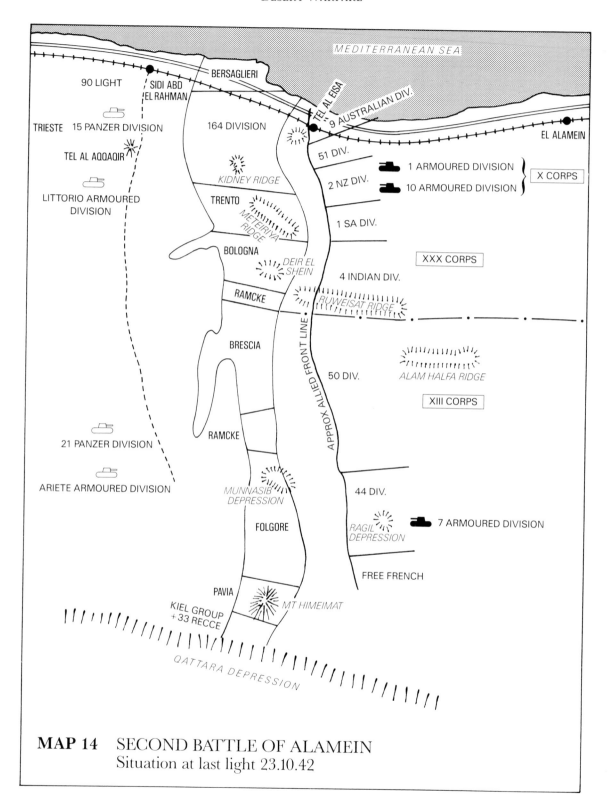

MAP 14 SECOND BATTLE OF ALAMEIN
Situation at last light 23.10.42

gun screen. The growing light behind the British tanks gave the German gunners excellent silhouettes at which to aim while they were themselves able to work in the gloom of the western horizon. Notwithstanding, cavalry dash took the brigade through the screen, crushing the guns and killing their crews, until the Rahman Track was reached. The penetration drew the Axis armour like a magnet and by the time 1st Armoured Division arrived Currie had lost 87 of his 94 tanks; he had been told that, if necessary, he must accept 100 per cent casualties in attaining his object.

The subsequent action, a furious gunnery duel that took its name from the nearby Tel el Aqqaqir, lasted throughout the day and littered the desert with burning tanks. The British sustained the heavier loss, but when it was over the Italians had been written off and the DAK had been reduced to 24 tanks. While the battle was in progress the armoured cars of the Royal Dragoons were able to work their way through its southern fringe and out into the enemy's rear areas, where numerous prompt and willing surrenders by Germans and Italians provided ample evidence that, behind its hard shell, the Axis army had had enough.

Rommel himself recognized that the end had come and, despite frantic urgings from Hitler, decided that he must salvage what he could from the wreck of his army. During the night of 3/4 November probes by the 51st Highland Division, directed on a south-

Axis tanks, self-propelled artillery and tank destroyers captured during Second Alamein (Imperial War Museum).

Sherman of 8th Armoured Brigade passing through Mersa Matruh on 7 November 1942. The pursuit of Rommel's army after Second Alamein was hindered by torrential rain and fuel shortages (Imperial War Museum).

westerly axis from the ground won in Supercharge, revealed that the enemy had gone and the 4th South African Armoured Car Regiment slipped out to the west. As the breakout became general, 7th Armoured Division smashed its way through the remnants of the mechanized Italian XX Corps, thereby outflanking 15th and 21st Panzer Divisions, which were attempting to hold off 1st Armoured Division to the north, and causing them to withdraw. During the latter engagement, von Thoma's tank was knocked out and he was captured by Captain Grant Singer commanding the 10th Hussars' Reconnaissance Troop. Montgomery received the Afrika Korps's commander with professional courtesy and entertained him to dinner. Singer was killed the following day and von Thoma, genuinely sorry that his young captor had died when the worst of the fighting was over, wrote his father a note of condolence.

The Second Battle of Alamein had lasted 13 days, as Montgomery predicted it would. Total Axis casualties amounted to 55,000, including 30,000 prisoners, of whom nearly 11,000 were German. Rommel's material losses included 450 tanks, 1,000 guns and 84 aircraft. His German divisions were reduced to skeletons and most of his Italian divisions, lacking transport, were destroyed where they stood.

The Eighth Army sustained 13,500 casualties (a figure also predicted by Montgomery), including approximately 4,500 dead, the majority incurred by the infantry divisions. 500 tanks had been knocked out, of which all but 150 were repairable. 110 guns were destroyed by shellfire, most of them anti-tank guns. In the air 77 British and 20 American aircraft were lost.

Montgomery has been criticized not only for failing to organize a *Corps de Chasse* which could have been used in the same manner as

Chauvel's Desert Mounted Corps after Megiddo, but also for the tardy manner in which the general pursuit was conducted in the immediate aftermath of the battle, this being aggravated by the demands of too many units for fuel and heavy rain which made the task of supply lorries impossible for a while. In the event, it mattered little, for the victory was so complete that Rommel did not stop until he reached the Mersa Brega bottleneck on 15 November, having abandoned all his gains in Egypt and the whole of Cyrenaica as well. He was now fully aware that the Anglo-American First Army had landed in Morocco and Algeria on 8 November and reflected bitterly on the sudden ability of Hitler

and Mussolini to find the resources with which to hold Tunisia, resources which might have made all the difference to his own campaign had they been made available in July or August.

Despite the effort and ingenuity displayed by the Eighth Army's supply services, which employed every means at their disposal including water transport and the repaired railway, the number of formations which could be supported during the long advance constituted only a fraction of the army's total strength. There was little fighting but for the veterans of earlier battles there were many poignant reminders of the past, none more so than the uncleared battlefield east of Aslagh

Infantrymen of the 51st Highland Division aboard a 23rd Armoured Brigade Valentine during the final stages of the advance on Tripoli (Imperial War Museum).

Ridge, where the British gun crews lay beside their silent 25-pounders and layers still sat staring into infinity.

Montgomery closed up to Mersa Brega with the 7th Armoured, 2nd New Zealand and 51st Highland Divisions. On 13 December the New Zealanders executed a wide turning movement through the desert to the south and this caused Rommel, threatened with encirclement, to withdraw another 200 miles to Buerat. On 14 January 1943 he was similarly levered out of this position and, since Tripoli was indefensible, retired across the Tunisian frontier. During the early hours of 23 January Tripoli was entered unopposed by 11th Hussars, whose armoured cars had fired the first shots of the desert war 31 months previously. A close second in the race was 40 RTR, with C Squadron 50 RTR under command, carrying the 1st Battalion Gordon Highlanders. At noon Montgomery received the formal surrender of the city from the Italian Vice-Governor of Tripolitania.

The war in North Africa would continue until 12 May, but it would be fought among the spring-green hills and farmland of Tunisia, which reminded many of southern Europe. The war in the desert was over; neutral and uncaring, the sands returned to their timeless, shifting silence.

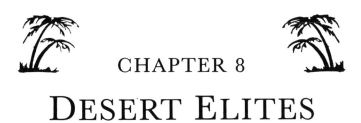

CHAPTER 8

DESERT ELITES

The term elite in itself implies a body of carefully-selected men whose proven ability sets them apart from ordinary soldiers, yet in considering the oldest of desert elites, the French Foreign Legion, one is immediately faced with the fact that, for much of its history, the Legion's recruits have been self-selecting.

Since its formation in 1831, the Legion has served on all of France's battlefields around the world but, thanks largely to the glamorous image cast by Ouida's *Under Two Flags* and P. C. Wren's *Beau Geste*, it is with the deserts of North Africa that it is generally associated in the public mind and, until its depot was moved

A French Foreign Legion patrol sets out from Bir Hacheim, 1942 (Imperial War Museum).

to Aubagne, near Marseilles, during the 1960s, its spiritual home was Sidi-bel-Abbes in Algeria.

Despite the fact that Wren may himself have served in its ranks—his would-be biographers are frustrated by a blank period of five years, the duration of an enlistment—the Legion is far from grateful to him for the portrait which his stories have painted. It has never sought to recruit the scum of society since, by definition, these men lack the basic qualities required in military life. Nor does it promote paranoid sadists, for common sense tell us that NCOs of this type make mortal enemies and quickly become the target of stray rounds in action. What the Legion has always offered is a home for men with nowhere else to turn from their problems, be they domestic, financial or political, plus anonymity and the chance of adventure. Reward was never an incentive, for the Legionnaire received just enough to get himself drunk on pay nights. A reputation for severe discipline and hard training served to discourage the faint-hearted but those who persevered found themselves part of a unique international brotherhood whose motto was *Legio Patria Nostra*—The Legion Is Our Country. Many found that they needed nothing else and re-enlisted time and again.

The Legion has always attracted a high proportion of the best graduates from St Cyr and other French military academies, while serving in its ranks could be found numerous former officers from the armies of Europe. A famous story tells how an inspecting officer once asked a recruit what he had been in civilian life; the man replied that he had been a general! Thus, the standard of personal initiative at all levels remained high and suitable candidates could be rewarded with a commission, provided that they were sufficiently fluent in French. The composition of the Legion has always tended to reflect what was taking place elsewhere in the world. After the First World War, for example, there were so

many members of the minor aristocracies of Central and Eastern Europe serving with one regiment that someone suggested wryly that it should add Royal to its title. When the Russian Civil War ended there was an influx of former Tsarist officers, and the Spanish Civil War produced a flow of Republican recruits. There was always a large German contingent, swelled after the Second World War by former members of the Wehrmacht and Waffen-SS. That so large a percentage of its members had already seen extensive active service was another factor which made the Legion so formidable an opponent.

Curiously, the French attitude to the Legion has always been ambivalent. On the one hand, the average Frenchman is well aware of its reputation and is pleased by the results it produces, often in impossible circumstances; on the other, he considers it slightly disreputable that *La Grande Nation* should employ a mercenary force to fight her battles. Likewise, the relationship between the Legion and the rest of the French Army was equivocal. The sole reason for the Legion's existence was hard soldiering, a philosophy which might be admired but not always followed by its comrades in arms, especially when the nation was afflicted by political crisis. In 1917, for example, when the Army was crippled by mutiny and seemed on the verge of collapse, the Legion remained loyal. Conversely, in 1961 the Legion felt betrayed by de Gaulle on the Algerian question, but its so-called Centurions' Revolt attracted little support. Such differences were echoed at the more personal level by off-duty brawls between French troops and Legionnaires, serving to remind the latter of their isolation and consolidating their *esprit de corps*.

It has sometimes been said that the Legion's collective psyche contains a death-wish and indeed its songs are often sad and funereal. Yet it was inevitable that the Legion would be given the dirtiest and most dangerous jobs to do and if its history does

Often left to fend for itself, the Foreign Legion has a long tradition of self-reliance (Imperial War Museum).

contain countless examples of suicidal heroism by individuals then its heavy emphasis on tradition and sacrifice is in part responsible. However, deliberate, cold-blooded suicide was an element which could never be discounted, particularly in isolated desert outposts where drink, unending monotony, boredom and too much introspection could lead to what the men called *cafard*, recognized today as clinical depression.

For those unwilling to destroy themselves desertion offered an extremely dangerous alternative, usually by way of Spanish Morocco. Some got through, some perished in the desert or were killed by Arabs, and some joined the Legion's Muslim enemies; those who were caught were sentenced to a term in the penal battalion, where the best they could expect was to be fed if they made 1,000 bricks a day. Nevertheless, there were always men willing to risk everything to regain their freedom and at one stage desertion reached such serious proportions that a commander let it be known that he had promised the local tribesmen a certain sum for every deserter captured—and five times that for the man's head!

If, in action, the Legionnaire displayed

some of the characteristics of the Knights Templar, many of his other activities had more in common with those of the Roman Legionary. Like those of every military formation, the Legion's ranks contained men with a wide variety of skills which could be put to good use, and as units were often placed in situations in which their only asset was their own resources, self-help became a way of life; *demerde-toi* was the Legionnaire's phrase. All over French North Africa the Legion built forts, blockhouses, roads, bridges, barracks and even schools which remain as monuments to its presence.

The Legion arrived in North Africa in 1835 and remained until 1962. During that time, as French influence was extended steadily southwards, its units were almost constantly engaged in battles, sieges and ambushes, held lonely outposts and marched to their relief. Latterly, it became adept in counter-insurgency operations during the Algerian War of Independence. It was in Africa that the Legion adopted the distinctive *képi blanc* as its headgear, and it was in Africa that its unique slow step was evolved as the most economic means of traversing soft sand. In fact, the Legion was as renowned for its marching ability as it was for its fighting qualities. 'March or die' was no empty threat; heavily burdened, men marched under the broiling sun for their very survival, knowing that the desert had no pity on stragglers.

The value of mobility in desert warfare was quickly appreciated by the Legion, which formed a small camel unit as early as 1853. The first of the famous Mounted Companies was formed in 1881 and such was its success that others followed. *La Belle France,* however, was a niggardly mistress who demanded of her soldiers a first class job at cut rates, and she was only willing to supply enough mules for half the men. Nothing deterred, the Legionnaires took it in turn to ride or march alongside, covering up to 40 miles a day, each mule carrying its own fodder and 15 days' rations for two men. Water was shared with the animals which, as a last resort, could be eaten. One such Mounted Company survived until 1939 but elsewhere the mule had been replaced by motor transport which, as the years passed, was itself forced to give way to the helicopter and the concept of air mobility. In 1940 the Legion formed a special mechanized company to patrol the vast wasteland of the Sahara. This performed its task so well that three more companies were formed after the Second World War, assuming the traditions of some of the old Mounted Companies. These *Compagnies Sahariennes* were expert in desert navigation and adopted a uniform appropriate to their role, including a voluminous cloak, baggy trousers and sandals. The Legion did not raise its first cavalry regiment until after the First World War, its ranks being quickly filled with former cavalrymen, many of whom had served in the old Imperial Russian and Austro-Hungarian armies. Two squadrons were mechanized for forward reconnaissance in 1929, followed by the rest of the regiment over a 10-year period. A second cavalry regiment, raised in 1939, was mechanized from the outset and, together, these evolved into the Legion's armoured element.

The defeat of France in 1940 produced schisms within the Legion just as it did in every aspect of French life. Legionnaires loyal to de Gaulle, notably the 13th Demi-Brigade, fought in East Africa, Syria and with the British Eighth Army in the Western Desert. Legionnaires loyal to the Vichy government continued to serve in French North Africa, and in Syria the 6th Regiment fought against its former comrades. After Vichy France was occupied by German troops in 1942, the two factions were re-united in the common cause and took part in the Tunisian campaign. A third group consisted of German Legionnaires whose repatriation was demanded by Germany following the French surrender. In total, approximately 2,000 men were released by the

Legion and permitted to 'rehabilitate' themselves by fighting in the Western Desert with the 90th Light Division. As they were being shipped from Italy to Libya they made a scornful if silent statement to the effect that they were the only professional desert warriors in the entire Axis army; it consisted of flinging their newly-issued solar topis into the sea.

For the post-war Legion, which began adding parachute units to its establishment in 1948, the trauma of Indo-China was followed by the trauma of Algeria. Here the war against the nationalist guerrillas, lasting from 1954 until 1962, consisted of two distinct phases. First the insurgents were physically isolated from their support bases in Tunisia and Morocco by barriers of electrified wire, mines and radar sensors, patrolled by mobile units, covered by artillery fire and under constant observation from the air.

Then, their groups operating in the interior, notably in the Aurès and Kabylie mountains, were systematically destroyed in a protracted series of cordon and search operations which employed ground and air mobility, on-call artillery and direct air support to achieve their ends. Once contact with a guerrilla unit was obtained it was relentlessly pursued until its survivors were wiped out. By 1960 the insurgents had been forced to disperse their major units into fugitive bands and, in military terms, France was on her way to winning the war. Unfortunately, the intransigent attitudes of both the French settlers and the nationalists destroyed any chance of an honourable solution. International opinion, coupled with political cynicism and warweariness at home, led de Gaulle to accept the inevitability of Algerian self-determination. The Army was stunned by what seemed a flagrant betrayal, and the Legion in particular felt that it had fought and died for nothing. On 22 April 1961 the Legion's 1st Parachute Regiment, together with other paratroop units, staged what amounted to a mutiny in Algiers, circulating copies of a protest made

by the Roman centurion Marcus Flavinius, who had served in North Africa with II Legion Augusta 2,000 years earlier: 'If we must leave our bones to bleach uselessly on the desert road, then beware the legions' anger!' The coup collapsed through lack of support after several days. De Gaulle threatened to dissolve the entire Legion, but contented himself with disbanding the 1st Parachute Regiment, courtmartialling its officers and dispersing its men. The 'lost paras' had learned the sad lesson of their time, namely that expediency was a more valuable currency than honour. Their fate was preferable to that of their Muslim comrades, who had served with equal loyalty and been promised that France would never abandon them; once the French had withdrawn they were butchered in their thousands by the jubilant nationalists.

After the Algerian war the Legion's strength was drastically reduced, enabling it to pursue a policy of selective recruiting in which only the best of those who offer themselves are accepted; and since it seeks to attract the best the pay and conditions offered are better than at any time in its history. It continues to provide garrisons for France's overseas territories but its primary function is that of an intervention force capable of rapid deployment outside Europe. If it has bade its farewells to its old home in Algeria, it has certainly not seen the last of Africa, nor of desert warfare. Since 1962 it has seen active service in Djibouti on the Gulf of Aden, intervened three times in Chad, which Libya's Colonel Gaddafi has sought to control, rescued hostages from Kolwezi in Zaire and contributed to an international peace-keeping force in Beirut.

The Legion was—and remains—an elite in the classic mould but as the Second World War progressed a second type of elite began to emerge, based on the principle that a small group of highly trained and motivated men can frequently achieve better results than a much larger force, or indeed results which

Chevrolets of the Long Range Desert Group assist each other through a salt marsh (Imperial War Museum).

cannot be obtained by any other means. Of these, the Long Range Desert Group (LRDG) and the Special Air Service Regiment (SAS) were of particular relevance to the fighting in the Western Desert.

Something of Major Ralph Bagnold's desert travels during the inter-war years has already been described in Chapter 5. In 1939 Bagnold began presenting GHQ in Cairo with his ideas for the use of a long range reconnaissance force which was capable of operating deep in the Libyan desert. Wavell was interested but would not sanction potentially provocative operations into neutral territory. These reservations vanished once Italy declared war in June 1940 and a patrol, commanded by one of Bagnold's former companions, was despatched into the enemy's hinterland. The information obtained by this confirmed that the Italians were singularly

lacking in aggressive intent and since Egypt was in no immediate danger of invasion it was possible to re-route a vital convoy carrying three armoured regiments (3rd Hussars, 2nd and 7th Royal Tank Regiments) by the longer but safer Cape route from the United Kingdom to Egypt. The safe arrival of these, and particularly of 7 RTR's Matildas, was a most important element in the success of Operation Compass and its aftermath.

Meanwhile, in October 1940 Major Orde Wingate arrived in Cairo and, prior to his departure for Eritrea, impressed GHQ sufficiently with his own ideas on long range penetration that Bagnold was able to expand his as-yet modest patrol organization into what became the Long Range Desert Group. His long experience in the desert determined the sort of recruit he was looking for; the man would already be a trained soldier, but he would also have some practical knowledge of motor vehicles and, above all, he would possess the qualities of physical fitness, stamina, intelligence, imagination, initiative, self-discipline, iron determination and the ability to function as part of a team regardless of rank. The recruit was selected by interview and if he failed then or on a subsequent patrol he was returned to his unit. Volunteers came from all over the Army, many being willing to accept a drop in rank. There were large contingents from the Royal Tank Regiment and the 2nd New Zealand Divisional Cavalry Regiment; Guardsmen formed G Patrol, Southern Rhodesians S Patrol and Yeomen from the Cavalry Division Y Patrol, while the Indian Long Range Squadron consisted of Indian troopers with British officers and NCOs. Similarly, Bagnold's experience told him that the British vehicles then in service were unsuitable for the LRDG's requirements. Chevrolet 30 cwt trucks were acquired from the Egyptian Army and General Motors, plus some Ford 30 cwt trucks which operated with their radiator grills and bonnets removed, and, fitted with sand channels, radiator condensors and a variety of automatic weapons, these formed the basis of the unit's equipment. In March 1942 the LRDG reached its full establishment of 25 officers and 324 other ranks, manning 110 vehicles.

Training included driving and recovery techniques in all sorts of terrain, desert navigation of the highest standard, long range radio communications using different types of aerial, and survival. The Group's basic unit was the Patrol, which normally operated in two halves, each of five or six vehicles. On operations shaving was abandoned to conserve water and most men sported some sort of beard, adding to the piratical impression conferred by their varied clothing. Elements of uniform were retained, supplemented by clothes suited to the environment such as knitted cap comforters, the Arab burnous, bush shirts, shorts, sandals and goatskin coats—

in fact, whatever the wearer found most comfortable. Back at base, the patrols shaved and smartened up to the standards of their parent regiments. Latterly, the LRDG evolved its own cap badge, a scorpion within a wheel, the designer of which is said to have been stung by one of these venomous creatures, which then itself died!

Bagnold commanded the LRDG until August 1941, by which time the unit was firmly established and was already regarded as an elite. Indeed, Colonel David Stirling, who founded the SAS, was to comment that in his opinion the Group was the finest of all units serving in the desert. Operating from oases far to the south of the main battle area, its patrols used the vast empty spaces with which they were familiar to penetrate far into the enemy's rear, there to carry out reconnaissance of specific objectives, intelligence gathering missions which included surveillance of traffic on the coast road, the insertion or extraction of agents and SAS teams, and occasionally direct action such as harassing attacks, ambushes and minelaying. Missions might include one or all of these elements and the flexibility of the organization enabled patrols to be detailed for additional tasks once they had reached their operational area. The Libyan Arabs, many of whom were Senussi, were fiercely motivated by hatred of the Italians and were of considerable assistance. In Tunisia, however, the local population was greedily impartial and sometimes treacherous. The scale of the Group's efforts can be gauged by the fact that between 26 December 1940 and 10 April 1943 there were only 15 days on which one or more of its patrols was not operating on the enemy's open flank or deep in his rear. During that period the LRDG was controlled at the highest level by the Director of Military Operations at GHQ.

The concept of small raiding teams which would operate against the enemy's airfields, inflicting damage out of all proportion to the numbers of men involved, was devised by Lieutenant David Stirling, a Scots Guards officer serving with a commando unit, while he was recovering in Cairo from injuries sustained during a parachute jump. Recognizing that the military establishment would reject his idea out of hand unless he could personally convince the most senior officers of its validity, he bluffed his way into GHQ and after one unsatisfactory interview wandered into the office of Major General Neil Ritchie, then serving as Auchinleck's Deputy Chief of General Staff. Startled by the subaltern's unheralded entry, Ritchie was nonetheless impressed by what he had to say and brought the proposal to Auchinleck's attention. Auchinleck approved and Stirling, promoted to captain, was

given permission to raise and train a small unit which would be known as L Detachment Special Air Service Brigade, a cover name intended to suggest that a paratroop formation had arrived in the Middle East.

As Stirling had predicted, the establishment did not welcome the creation of a private army commanded by a newly-promoted young captain who chose to work outside the proper channels, and he was given the minimum assistance compatible with orders. Thus, from the outset, the SAS was thrown upon its own resources. Stirling was forced to beg, borrow and literally steal what he needed, as well as develop the explosive incendiary bombs the unit would require for its missions. Training included advanced map-reading,

Lieutenant-Colonel David Stirling, the founder of the Special Air Service Regiment, with one of his jeep patrols. The patrol's arms, equipment and dress are all suited to the environment in which it is to operate (Imperial War Museum).

familiarization with small arms of all kinds, including captured German and Italian weapons, desert marches so severe that even former commandos were stretched to the limit, and parachute jumps. Despite set-backs and active opposition, Stirling never lost faith. When a senior RAF officer derided the whole idea, he led a 40-strong raid on the airfield at Heliopolis. His teams penetrated the base without being detected, stuck labels on every aircraft in sight, and vanished silently whence they had come.

The unit's first mission was to coincide with the start of Operation Crusader. It was detailed to attack airfields in the Gazala–Tmimi area during the night of 17/18 November 1941, having been para-dropped in darkness 24 hours earlier. The intervening period of daylight was to be spent lying up and observing targets. Once the raids had taken place the SAS teams would head for a rendezvous point, where the LRDG would be waiting to transport them to Siwa Oasis. In the event everything went wrong. The drop was made in gale-force winds which scattered the teams and their supply cannisters. The bomb fuses were lost and since nothing could be achieved without them Stirling was reluctantly forced to cancel the operation. Of the 60 men who had set out on the raid, only 22 reached the rendezvous.

Such a disaster would have crushed lesser men, but Stirling persevered. He was greatly impressed by the LRDG's efficiency and recognized that it could provide a more certain means of transporting his teams to within marching distance of their objectives than parachute drops. The LRDG approved of the idea and, as one of its officers commented, 'It was an ideal partnership. We could exploit to the full what was our greatest asset—the ability to deliver a passenger anywhere behind the enemy's lines at any time asked.'

The future of the SAS was now assured. It became the scourge of the Luftwaffe and the Regia Aeronautica, destroying approx-imately 400 of their aircraft on the ground before the desert war ended, plus uncounted tons of aviation fuel, bombs, ammunition and other stores. After Rommel launched his invasion of Egypt in June 1942 it acquired jeeps, which it armed with one Browning and twin Vickers K air-cooled machine-guns. Guided by LRDG navigators, it used the mobility thus conferred not only to maintain attacks on the enemy's airfields but also to disrupt his tenuous supply line and although raids on Benghazi and Tobruk ended badly its overall success was such that in Cairo concern was expressed about possible damage to the railway between Mersa Matruh and Tobruk, which would be needed by the Eighth Army when it advanced. A signal telling the SAS to leave it alone produced an apologetic response to the effect that, unable to resist the temptation, they had just blown it up! In all, the railway was attacked on seven occasions, depriving the Axis of its use for 13 of the crucial 20 days immediately prior to the Second Battle of Alamein.

In October 1942 L Detachment, now numbering 30 officers and 300 other ranks, including a French contingent, became the 1st Special Air Service Regiment. It now had its own navigators and after Alamein established a base at Bir Zalten, some 150 miles south of El Agheila, from which night raids were mounted against the coast road to Tripoli. These were so successful that for a period all movement after dark was suspended; evidently the enemy believed that the risk of being strafed by the RAF in daylight was the lesser of the two evils. By the middle of January 1943 the SAS had shifted operations far to the west and were raiding deep into Tunisia, where, with the end of the campaign in sight, Stirling was captured near Sfax. Quite apart from the physical damage which he and his regiment had inflicted, they had lowered morale in the enemy's rear areas to the point at which no one felt safe, and troops had been diverted from the front to guard airfields and the line of communications. The Wehrmacht needed no furious reminders from Hitler that these men were extremely dangerous and it was already doing everything in its power to hunt them down.

Montgomery, while restoring orthodoxy to the Eighth Army, recognized the professionalism of the LRDG and SAS. Shortly after Stirling's capture he was able to outflank the formidable defences of the Mareth Line by routing the 2nd New Zealand Division through the desert to the south, basing his plan on detailed patrol reports. A few days later he wrote a personal note to Lieutenant Colonel Guy Prendergast, commanding the LRDG.

> I would like you to know how very much I appreciate the excellent work done by your patrols and by the SAS in reconnoitring the country up to the Gabes Gap. Without your careful and reliable reports the launching of the 'left hook' by the New Zealand Division would have been a leap in the dark; with the information they produced the operation could be planned with some certainty and, as you know, went off without a hitch. Please give my thanks to all concerned and best wishes from Eighth Army.

The North African campaign proved the value of special forces beyond any possible doubt. The SAS went on to win fresh laurels in Europe and expanded five-fold. In 1945 the regiment was disbanded, only to be re-formed as a Territorial Army unit two years later. In 1952 a regular SAS regiment was formed in Malaya during the anti-communist emergency and has remained in existence ever since. It prides itself on its ability to operate anywhere in the world, adapting its techniques to the prevailing conditions and has frequently proved its ability to succeed where larger units would fail.

In 1958/59 it was engaged in the northern territories of the Sultanate of Muscat and Oman, lying at the entrance to the Persian Gulf, through which passes much of the world's oil supply. Because of the area's economic and political sensitivity the United Kingdom provided military support for the Sultan, who was in danger of being ousted by dissident factions. The dissidents had established themselves on a large, fertile plateau known as Jebel Akhdar (Green Mountain) which towered 10,000 ft above the surrounding plain. There were comparatively few routes leading up the sheer cliffs of this natural fortress and these were so easily defended that the Jebel had never fallen to direct assault. An early appreciation of the difficulties led to a request for a complete British brigade but the only troops available were an SAS squadron, a troop of Life Guards and some Royal Signals personnel, supported by local units. Guided by a loyal sheikh, two SAS troops made an astonishing climb in total darkness up an untried route considered so difficult by the defenders that their sangars were left unmanned. Although a toe-hold on the summit was obtained and counter-attacks were beaten off, it was clear that the force would be unable to clear the 10 by 20 mile plateau unassisted. A second SAS squadron was flown in from Malaya and a similar series of climbs was made with donkeys carrying heavy weapons and radio equipment. Complete surprise was achieved and the rebels, harried by rocket and cannon firing RAF Venoms and convinced that a parachute supply drop was an airborne landing, fled, leaving most of their weapons behind.

The SAS was also involved in the Aden Emergency, which lasted from 1963 until 1967, patrolling in the Radfhan massif or playing a dangerous game known as Keeni-Meeni among the teeming alleys of Aden itself. This involved plain clothes surveillance by members of the Regiment who could pass for Arabs, and put an end to the careers of a number of Cairo-trained assassins. In this context, however, there could be no final victory, since political expediency inhibited the British reaction in Aden as much as it had that of the French in Algeria. When the last British soldier left without regret on 29 November 1967, Aden declared itself to be the Marxist Republic of South Yemen.

In 1970 an SAS squadron returned to Oman, which the South Yemenis were attempting to destabilize by supporting an insurrection in the southern province of Dhofar. The principal role of the SAS teams was that of training, organizing and leading the *firqas*, which were anti-guerrilla units formed from rebel defectors, a technique which had been used to good effect in Kenya and Malaya. Complete defeat of the rebels and their South Yemeni mentors was not achieved until 1975, but a psychological turning point was reached on 18 July 1972 when the coastal town of Mirbat was attacked at dawn by a 250-strong group of insurgents armed with AK-47 assault rifles, mortars, machine-guns and anti-tank missiles. The town was held by a 10-strong SAS training team under Captain Michael Kealy, 25 men of the Dhofar Gendarmerie, the 30-strong local *firqa*, all armed with modern weapons, and 30 Omani Askaris with vintage bolt-action rifles. The battle raged with the utmost ferocity for three hours, often at close quarters. Kealy had, however, managed to radio for assistance and shortly after 09:00 Strikemasters of the Sultan's Air Force howled in to bomb and strafe the attackers. Simultaneously, 18 more SAS troopers were lifted into the defences by helicopter. The guerrillas fled, leaving many of their casualties behind. Their precise loss is uncertain but in the battle itself and in the violent recriminations which followed the disastrous failure of what had been intended as a showpiece attack it is believed that about half were killed or wounded. The garrison's casualties amounted to four killed, two of them SAS, and three wounded, including one SAS. Kealy, who had been the soul of the defence throughout, was awarded the DSO.

The SAS, born in the desert, has not served in that environment since the Dhofar War. If it is called upon to do so again, its accumulated experience, wisdom and flexible outlook will confirm that it remains an elite.

CHAPTER 9

DESERT WARFARE SINCE 1945

Since 1945 there have been few periods when a desert conflict of one sort or another has not raged in the earth's arid areas. In the main, these have been concentrated in the Middle East, where the departure of the old Imperial powers and the establishment of the state of Israel have unleashed tensions which were hitherto controlled or which lay dormant, aggravated by nationalist fervour and exploited by the Soviet Union in a determined attempt to extend its influence across the oil-rich lands of the area. Most have been of comparatively short duration and tend to emphasize the lessons of what has passed before.

Within Egypt, demands for a British withdrawal from the country grew steadily, often accompanied by widespread unrest. On 22 July 1952 the reign of the portly and pleasure-loving King Farouk was ended by a coup of nationalist army officers under the leadership of General Mohammed Neguib and Egypt was declared a republic. Two years later Neguib was himself ousted by his more radical deputy, Colonel Gamal Abdel Nasser. When, on 13 June 1956, British troops finally ended their long presence, Nasser was already negotiating with the communist bloc for arms and promptly began playing off the United States against the Soviet Union in an attempt to obtain the best possible terms for the financing of his Aswan Dam project. This was accompanied by a barrage of anti-Western propaganda and, predictably, the United

States withdrew its offer of support on 19 July. A week later Nasser nationalized the Suez Canal Company, in which the British government retained a substantial holding. Great Britain and France regarded his action as a threat to world peace and began preparing a military response. In this they were joined by Israel, whose ships were denied passage through the Canal or the Straits of Tiran, the latter being the only entrance to the Gulf of Aqaba, at the head of which lay the Israeli port of Eilat. Furthermore, Nasser was known to be encouraging raids on Israeli settlements and the Israeli cabinet felt that a major reprisal was overdue.

On 21 October a secret meeting took place at Sèvres in France. Those present included the French Prime Minister, Guy Mollet, the British Foreign Secretary, Selwyn Lloyd, the Prime Minister of Israel, David Ben-Gurion, his Defence Minister, Shimon Peres, and General Moshe Dayan, his Chief of Staff. The purpose of the meeting was to co-ordinate their strategy against Egypt and the result was a plan which was to be implemented in two stages. In the first Israel was to invade Sinai, ostensibly in hot pursuit of terrorist groups, and advance towards the Suez Canal. In the second, Great Britain and France would apparently intervene in an effort to end the fighting, effecting an assault landing which would culminate in a protective occupation of the Canal Zone.

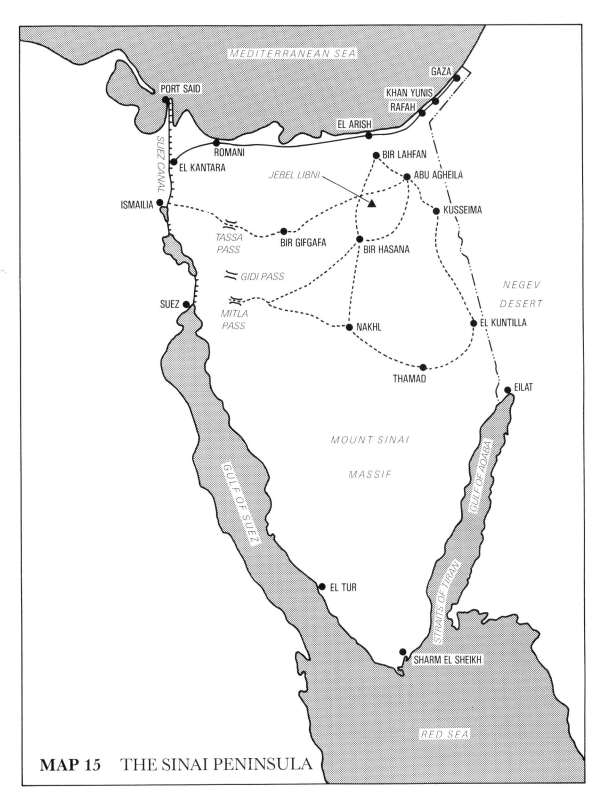

MEDITERRANEAN SEA

GAZA

KHAN YUNIS
RAFAH

EL ARISH

PORT SAID

ROMANI

BIR LAHFAN

EL KANTARA

JEBEL LIBNI

ABU AGHEILA

SUEZ CANAL

ISMAILIA

KUSSEIMA

TASSA
PASS

BIR GIFGAFA

BIR HASANA

GIDI PASS

NEGEV
DESERT

SUEZ

MITLA
PASS

NAKHL

EL KUNTILLA

THAMAD

EILAT

MOUNT SINAI

MASSIF

GULF OF SUEZ

GULF OF AQABA

STRAITS OF TIRAN

EL TUR

SHARM EL SHEIKH

RED SEA

MAP 15 THE SINAI PENINSULA

The terrain in which this and subsequent battles between the Israeli and Egyptian armies were fought is quite distinctive. The Sinai peninsula is separated from Egypt proper by the Suez Canal and the Gulf of Suez. It is triangular in shape, having a maximum width of 130 miles in the north, and is 240 miles long from the Mediterranean coast to Sharm el Sheikh at its southern tip. From the northern shore the ground rises steadily across a sand, gravel and rock plateau to the 8,664 ft Mount Sinai massif, then falls steeply towards the Red Sea. The landscape is hot, parched and sterile, absorbing less than 10 in of seasonal rainfall each year. There are three possible routes across the Sinai from the Israeli frontier to the Canal. Of these the most northerly is the best, following the coast from Gaza through Rafah, El Arish and on to El Kantara. In the centre there is a road from Kusseima through Abu Agheila to Ismailia.

Further south a track leads from El Kuntilla through Thamad to the Mitla Pass, from which the town of Suez can be reached. These routes are connected by a north-south track running from El Arish through Bir Lahfan to Abu Agheila and on past Jebel Libni to Nakhl, with a branch joining Abu Agheila with Bir Gifgafa and the Mitla Pass.

Israel mobilized ten brigades for the operation, which was codenamed Kadesh, some being deployed close to the Jordanian frontier to mislead the Egyptians. These included six infantry brigades, the 202nd Parachute Brigade, the 27th and 37th Mechanized Brigades and 7th Armoured Brigade. At this period in its history the Israeli Armoured Corps (IAC) had yet to prove itself in battle and its equipment consisted of 100 up-gunned Shermans, 100 AMX-13 light tanks, and 42 self-propelled guns of various types. M3 half-track APCs were available for

Up-gunned Israeli Shermans in action in the Gaza Strip, 1956 (Courtesy Eshel Dramit Ltd).

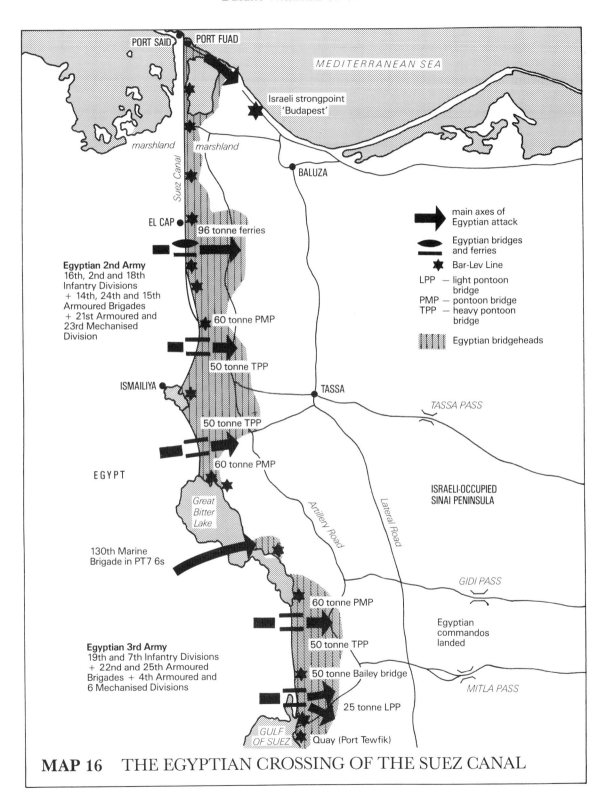

PORT SAID PORT FUAD

MEDITERRANEAN SEA

Israeli strongpoint
'Budapest'

marshland *marshland*

Suez Canal

BALUZA

EL CAP

96 tonne ferries

Egyptian 2nd Army
16th, 2nd and 18th
Infantry Divisions
+ 14th, 24th and 15th
Armoured Brigades
+ 21st Armoured and
23rd Mechanised
Division

60 tonne PMP

50 tonne TPP

ISMAILIYA

TASSA

TASSA PASS

50 tonne TPP

60 tonne PMP

EGYPT

*Great
Bitter
Lake*

ISRAELI-OCCUPIED
SINAI PENINSULA

Artillery Road *Lateral Road*

130th Marine
Brigade in PT7 6s

GIDI PASS

60 tonne PMP

Egyptian
commandos
landed

Egyptian 3rd Army
19th and 7th Infantry Divisions
+ 22nd and 25th Armoured
Brigades + 4 Armoured and
6 Mechanised Divisions

50 tonne TPP

50 tonne Bailey bridge

MITLA PASS

25 tonne LPP

*GULF
OF SUEZ* Quay (Port Tewfik)

→ main axes of
Egyptian attack

Egyptian bridges
and ferries

★ Bar-Lev Line

LPP — light pontoon
bridge
PMP — pontoon bridge
TPP — heavy pontoon
bridge

Egyptian bridgeheads

MAP 16   THE EGYPTIAN CROSSING OF THE SUEZ CANAL

some mechanized infantry units, but others were forced to ride in commandeered civilian lorries and buses. The Israeli Air Force (IAF), flying Mystère IV, Ouragan and Vautour jet fighters, was much smaller than that of Egypt, although it had the advantage of being able to deploy its entire strength over the battlefield.

Operation Kadesh was to begin at 17:00 on 29 October with the seizure of the eastern end of the Mitla Pass by parachute drop, thereby preventing the intervention of Egyptian reinforcements as the battle developed in central Sinai. Some 20 minutes prior to the drop, the Egyptians' command telephone net was to be destroyed by piston-engined P-51 Mustangs flying through the overhead wires. During the next phase the capture of the strong Egyptian position at Abu Agheila, the hub of the Sinai road system, was to be followed by an advance westward. The third phase would consist of the elimination of the Egyptian forces in Gaza and Rafah, followed by a parallel advance along the coast road. Finally, mechanized units would advance south to capture Sharm el Sheikh, reopening the Straits of Tiran to Israeli shipping.

The Egyptian Army was by far the stronger and could muster 40 Centurions, 150 T-34/85s, 50 IS-III heavy tanks, 40 AMX-13 light tanks, 200 Archer and 100 SU-100 tank destroyers, and 200 BTR-152 APCs. Much of this strength, however, was retained in Egypt to counter the Anglo-French invasion, which Nasser now regarded as inevitable, and the same was true of the Vampire and MiG-15 jets flown by the Egyptian Air Force. The Egyptian deployment in Sinai was, in fact, purely defensive in character, despite the bellicose threats broadcast by Nasser through the medium of Radio Cairo. The 3rd Infantry and 8th (Palestinian) Infantry Divisions, both supported by tank and tank destroyer battalions, were concentrated respectively in the areas El Arish/Abu Agheila and Gaza/Rafah, while the 1st Armoured Brigade, equipped with

T-34/85s and SU-100 tank destroyers, lay further back at Bir Gifgafa. An independent infantry brigade, stationed west of the Mitla Pass, covered the town of Suez, but elsewhere in Sinai there were only light mechanized units.

Only one battalion of Colonel Ariel Sharon's 202nd Parachute Brigade was detailed for the drop at the Mitla Pass and this, commanded by Lieutenant-Colonel Raphael Eitan, secured its objectives at the eastern exit after a brief skirmish and dug in to await the rest of the brigade, which, supported by a squadron of AMX-13s and an artillery battalion equipped with 25-pounders, had already commenced an overland advance from the frontier. At El Kuntilla, Sharon circled the defences and attacked from the west, using the setting sun to blind the garrison. The post soon surrendered and Sharon pressed on through the night. At dawn on the 30th he used the rising sun to similar effect against the defenders of the fortified village of Nakhl, but the garrison fled before an assault could be launched, leaving behind a number of APCs in running order. The acquisition of these was providential, as the column's civilian vehicles were labouring in the heavy going and, their radiators boiling as the sun climbed, were beginning to fall behind. By 22:30, however, the brigade's leading elements had reached Eitan's isolated battalion, having been on the move for 28 hours since leaving their concentration area on the Jordanian frontier, 190 miles distant.

Sharon, a first class soldier, had fulfilled his mission, but he now demonstrated the less attractive aspects of his personality, namely that he was an ambitious and ungovernable subordinate. He obtained Dayan's permission to send a patrol into the pass, this being granted by the latter in the belief that Sharon was seeking to improve his defences and on the understanding that it was not to become involved in combat. Sharon's real intention was the capture of the pass, an action which the General Staff had never considered to be necessary or desirable. A major attack was launched, and although the pass was taken during the evening of 31 October 202 Brigade lost 38 dead and 120 wounded in the process. The Israeli Army could not afford such needless casualties and Sharon was subjected to severe criticism which he managed to survive, partly because of his record and partly because of his political influence.

The importance of Abu Agheila was appreciated by both sides. It had been extensively fortified by the Egyptians and was held by two brigades, supported by an artillery regiment and 23 Archer tank destroyers. The Israeli battlegroup detailed to capture the position was designated Task Force 38, consisting of the 7th Armoured, 4th and 10th Infantry Brigades joined later by part of the 37th Mechanized Brigade, under the overall command of Colonel Yehuda Wallach. At dawn on 30 October the Egyptian outpost at Kusseima was stormed by the 4th Infantry Brigade. Colonel Uri Ben-Ari's 7th Armoured Brigade probed the eastern and southern faces of the Abu Agheila perimeter but when its attacks ran into fierce opposition its reconnaissance element was ordered to search for a way round. The Wadi Daika, lying some way to the south, was found to be clear, its defenders having joined the crowd of fugitives from Kusseima, and after Israeli engineers had improved the route somewhat, a Sherman battalion and some mechanized infantry units, commanded by Lieutenant-Colonel Avraham Adan, was pushed along it and by 05:00 on 31 October had isolated the enemy complex from the west. Ninety minutes later Abu Agheila village was captured and the outer shell of the defences had been broken open.

Adan was preparing to attack the positions surrounding the El Ruafa Dam, inside the perimeter, when he was counter-attacked by a battalion of T-34/85s, approaching from the direction of El Arish. Long range gunnery

halted the Egyptian advance, which was then dispersed by air strikes. Adan resumed his own attack and by evening had taken El Ruafa despite fierce resistance which knocked out several tanks, damaged every one of the remainder and inflicted 80 casualties. His battlegroup had hardly finished its replenishment when the Egyptians mounted a determined counter-attack which failed with the loss of four Archers destroyed and 37 killed. The following day the last remaining Egyptian positions at Um-Shihan and Um-Katef were unsuccessfully assaulted by elements of the 10th Infantry and 37th Mechanized Brigades. During the night of 1 November, however, the Egyptians were ordered to break out in small groups and make for El Arish. They had fought hard and well and deserved better than to die in the desert from thirst or heat exhaustion, this being the fate of many; the luckier ones were picked up by the Israelis.

Meanwhile, leaving Adan's battered force at Abu Agheila, Ben-Ari had concentrated the remainder of 7th Armoured Brigade and was moving westwards to intercept the Egyptian 1st Armoured Brigade, consisting of two T-34/85 battalions, an APC battalion and an SU-100 company, which was understood to have left Bir Gifgafa with the intention of intervening in the battle. To Ben-Ari's bewilderment, the desert was all but bare of Egyptian armour. He therefore decided to press on across central Sinai and did not halt until he had reached a point some 10 miles short of Ismailia, this being the Israeli stopline agreed with the British and French. His action was widely regarded as being highhanded and risky, but he was defended by Dayan.

Elsewhere, Rafah was attacked at midnight on 31 October by 1st Infantry Brigade and Colonel Chaim Bar-Lev's 27th Mechanized Brigade. Minefields delayed the assault for a while but at length the Palestinian positions were taken in bitter hand-to-hand fighting and Bar-Lev's brigade broke out towards El Arish along the coast road. The advance was temporarily halted by the defenders of the Jiradi Defile, where the road passes through an area of deep dunes some miles east of El Arish. Bar-Lev called down an air strike and under cover of this moved an AMX-13 battalion and mechanized infantry into the dunes, levering the Egyptians out of their positions. El Arish was entered on the morning of 2 November, hard on the heels of its evacuation not only by the remnants of 3rd Infantry Division, but also by the 1st Mechanized Division. The latter had been committed to the Sinai front on the outbreak of hostilities and had just arrived after a difficult journey during which it had been strafed by the IAF. Bar-Lev followed up and by evening had reached Romani and established contact with Ben-Ari on his left.

The reason for the sudden Egyptian collapse in central and northern Sinai was that British and French aircraft had begun bombing air bases in Egypt on the evening of 31 October. In Cairo the high command correctly interpreted this as being the prelude to the invasion and decided to withdraw as many formations as possible, including the 1st Mechanized Division and the 1st Armoured Brigade, for the defence of Egypt. The Egyptian Air Force was also concentrated, leaving the skies above Sinai the undisputed property of the IAF.

Gaza was attacked at 02:00 on 2 November by the 11th Infantry Brigade and part of 37th Mechanized Brigade, the Egyptian governor surrendering the town after the notorious Ali el Muntar ridge had fallen. While the fighting was in progress, Colonel Avraham Yoffe's 9th Infantry Brigade had been driving steadily down the east coast of Sinai towards Sharm el Sheikh. Simultaneously, Sharon's 202 Parachute Brigade was redeployed from the Mitla Pass and drove down the west coast, having dropped an advance guard at El Tur. Yoffe's men won the race and by 09:00 on 5 November had cap-

tured the position after overcoming half-hearted resistance.

Israel's losses in the brief campaign amounted to 181 killed, 25 tanks and 11 aircraft. About 2,000 Egyptians were killed and 6,000 taken prisoner, equipment losses including 100 tanks and tank destroyers, numerous artillery weapons and APCs, nine aircraft and one destroyer, the *Ibrahim Awal*, captured off Haifa.

Operation Musketeer, the Anglo-French invasion of Egypt, commenced on 5 November with parachute drops on Port Said and Port Fuad at the northern end of the Canal. Seaborne landings followed the next day and while fighting continued in Port Said an exploitation force broke out and headed south. No opposition was encountered and it had almost reached El Kantara when the United Kingdom and France, menaced by crippling American economic pressures, agreed to accept the United Nations' demand for a ceasefire to be effective from midnight. Given the nature of the operation, casualties were remarkably light, but the diplomatic humiliation destroyed British and French prestige for a generation.

Thus, despite his decisive defeat in Sinai, Nasser emerged the political victor and was able to claim that the Israeli success would have been impossible without British and French support. He became the hero of a major part of the Arab world, established closer links with Syria and, with Soviet assistance, made Egypt a major military power. The more conservative elements, however, were not inclined to pursue his fervent brand of Arab nationalism. In 1962, for example, he sent troops to fight on the republican side during the Yemeni Civil War, but the opposing monarchist faction was openly supported by Saudi Arabia. The Egyptian contingent grew to a strength of 35,000, becoming bogged down in an anti-guerrilla campaign which was expensive both in terms of casualties and lost equipment. It was withdrawn in 1965 having achieved little save to harden the resolve of the royalists. Nevertheless, Nasser's implacable determination that Israel was to be destroyed guaranteed immense support throughout the Middle East. By May 1967 he had 100,000 well-equipped troops deployed in Sinai and war was again inevitable.

Curiously, although Radio Cairo's daily broadcasts promised the dismemberment of Israel among the victorious Arabs, the dispositions of the Egyptian Army in Sinai were again purely defensive in their nature. Its Commander-in-Chief, General Abdul Mortagy, was a keen student of the Montgomery set piece battle and an admirer of the Soviet Army's concept of a defence in depth designed to erode an attacker's strength, followed by a strong armoured counter-stroke that would inflict a decisive defeat. Mortagy was correct in his appreciation that the Israelis would attack first and, given that his own army's command, control and communication apparatus was less efficient, his strategy seemed sensible. On the other hand, his deployment was simply a scaled-up version of that which had been found wanting in 1956, and although it did contain echoes of Alam Halfa, its emphasis on holding large stretches of open desert for their own sake was dubious in the extreme and sharply reminiscent of the Italian dispositions at Sidi Barrani in 1940. Mortagy was probably aware that it made better sense to establish his defended zone in western Sinai, but that would mean abandoning large areas of Egyptian territory without firing a shot, and that was politically unacceptable.

On 4 June 1967 he had the equivalent of seven divisions in position on or close to the Israeli frontier. The 20th (Palestinian) Infantry Division, with 50 Shermans, was stationed in the Gaza Strip; the 7th Infantry Division, with 100 T-34/85s and IS-IIIs, was responsible for the defence of Rafah, the Jiradi Defile and El Arish; the Abu Agheila complex was held by the 2nd Infantry Division with the 3rd Infantry Division deployed in depth

to the west at Jebel Libni, each with 100 T-34/85s and T-54s. The 6th Mechanized Division, again with 100 T-34/85s and T-54s, blocked the axis El Kuntilla–Nakhl, along which Sharon's brigade had advanced to the Mitla Pass. At Bir Gifgafa and ready to deliver the Egyptian counter-stroke was Major General Sidki el Ghoul's 4th Armoured Division, with 200 T-55s, while between Kusseima and El Kuntilla was a second armoured formation, designated Task Force Shazli after its commander, Major General Saad el Din Shazli, equipped with 150 T-55s, which was to drive into the Negev and isolate the port of Eilat. Altogether, there were 800 tanks and tank destroyers immediately available, plus a further 150 in reserve, but their value was somewhat reduced by the fact that of these only 350 were serving in armoured formation, the remainder being subordinate to local infantry commanders with many dug in as part of static defence systems. With so many divisions in the field and numerous precedents which confirmed the importance of the operative level of command in desert warfare, Mortagy was also at fault in not establishing intermediate corps headquarters. But perhaps his greatest error was to regard his opponents as a conventional army with adequate reserves. The Israeli Army, always conscious of its casualties, could not afford to be drawn into an attritional war of position and this in itself indicated that while it possessed the initiative it would impose its own conditions on the battle.

Israel was fully aware of the threat from her neighbours and had begun mobilizing her reserves on 20 May. The mission of the Southern Command, under Major General Yeshayahu Gavish, entailed nothing less than the destruction of the Egyptian army in Sinai and an advance to the Suez Canal, which was to become a natural military frontier. Since 1956 the armoured corps had been regarded as the weapon of decision. Under Ben-Ari, followed by Bar-Lev, the IAC had been expanded and equipped with Centurions and M48 Pattons, both up-gunned with the excellent British 105 mm tank gun. In 1964 Brigadier Israel Tal took over the corps and set about raising the standard of its gunnery, honing this to perfection the following year during the so-called Water War on the upper Jordan, in which a series of successful long range shoots eliminated Syrian armour in emplacements on the Golani foothills.

The major formation of the IAC was now the armoured division, organized on the flexible American system, enabling all-arms battlegroups to be detached quickly for specific missions. Gavish had three armoured divisions at his disposal. One, under the newly-promoted Major General Tal, was deployed opposite the Gaza Strip and Rafah, with the regular 7th Armoured Brigade under command and a tank strength of 250, including Centurions, M48s, Shermans and AMX-13s. The second, commanded by Major General Ariel Sharon, was positioned opposite Abu Agheila with 150 tanks, including Centurions, Shermans and AMX-13s. In reserve and lying between Tal and Sharon was Major General Avraham Yoffe's division with 200 Centurions, its task during the break-in phase of the battle being to prevent intervention by the Egyptian 4th Armoured Division or Task Force Shazli. There were also two independent armoured brigades, Colonel Amnon Reshef's with 30 AMX-13s near Gaza, and Colonel Albert Mandler's with 50 Shermans in the southern Negev. Southern Command's total tank strength amounted to 680 with 70 in immediate reserve, but it will be seen from the above that the great majority of these were serving with armoured formations.

The Israeli offensive in Sinai, Operation Red Sheet, was to begin at 08:15 on 5 June, hard on the heels of a pre-emptive strike by the Israeli Air Force against Egyptian air bases throughout Sinai and Egypt. This operation, codenamed Focus, was planned by Major General Motti Hod and was timed to start at

07:45 in the interval between the return of the enemy's dawn patrols and the departure of senior Egyptian Air Force officers for their offices through the dense Cairo traffic. Through incessant practice, Hod's ground crews had reduced the turn-round time of their Mystères and Mirages to a mere 7½ minutes, a fraction of that required by their opponents. During the first hours of Focus the Egyptians lost 300 of their MiGs, Sukhois, Ilyushins and Tupolevs, most of them destroyed in their parking areas. The Israelis next turned their attention to airfields in Syria, Jordan and Iraq. By late afternoon the Arab air forces had ceased to be a major factor in the war and Hod was able to divert squadrons to support the ground fighting.

At zero hour a paratroop brigade commanded by Colonel Raphael Eitan, supported by Reshef's AMX-13s, broke into the Gaza Strip and immediately became involved in savage fighting with the Palestinians. To their left Tal's armoured division, spearheaded by Colonel Schmuel Gonen's 7th Armoured Brigade, also cut its way into the Strip. Gonen's task was to break out along the El Arish road and, leaving the paratroopers to fight their bloody way into Gaza, he smashed through Khan Yunis with his Centurions and M48s, regardless of casualties. At Rafah, however, he was counter-attacked by the 7th Infantry Division's armoured element, led by its IS-IIIs. These were well armed and heavily armoured but they had not been designed for the sort of fast-moving battle that was taking place. Checking them from the front with his Centurions, Gonen used an area of sand dunes to swing his M48s unexpectedly on to their flank and by noon all that remained were burning wrecks and smashed anti-tank guns.

The tempo of the operation now accelerated dramatically. With the Centurion battalion leading, the brigade roared along the coast road. The defenders of the Jiradi Defile, taken completely by surprise, were pinned down by high explosive and machine gun fire and the Centurions swept through. By the time the M48s arrived, however, the Egyptians had recovered and were manning their weapons. With difficulty, the Pattons fought their way through, but several were lost and the remainder all bore scars from the encounter; casualties included the battalion commander killed, and three of his company commanders wounded. Gonen's third battalion, equipped with Shermans and AMX-13s, wisely did not make the attempt. Some light tanks and a battalion of mechanized infantry moved into the dunes to the south but were immobilized by soft sand. At midnight, following artillery preparation, a second mechanized infantry battalion and a reserve Centurion company mounted a frontal attack. It took four hours of hard fighting before the position was finally cleared and the remainder of Tal's division began moving through the defile. By then, Gonen's two leading battalions had long since reached El Arish, which was taken so far ahead of schedule that a parachute drop and an amphibious landing designed to assist Tal in his capture of the town had to be cancelled at the last minute.

Meanwhile, Sharon's division had assaulted the Abu Agheila complex, the defences of which were even stronger than they had been in 1956. Two of his armoured battalions succeeded in cutting the tracks to El Arish and Kusseima while the third engaged the eastern perimeter, against which the main assault was to be delivered that night by three infantry battalions. At 22:30 the heaviest artillery programme yet fired by the Israeli Army, involving two 25-pounder battalions, one 155 mm howitzer battalion, one 160 mm mortar battalion and two 120 mm mortar battalions, began erupting in the enemy positions. As the Egyptian artillery began to reply, Israeli helicopters flew in and deposited a paratroop battalion just behind the gun lines. These were quickly stormed and as the opposing gunfire died away the Israeli infantry, equipped with coloured flares to mark their progress, began advancing from the east with Sherman support. Concurrently, a Centurion battlegroup broke in from the west and joined the paratroopers. After fierce close-quarter fighting the two groups met in the centre of the complex and the surviving Egyptians melted into the darkness.

Simultaneously, Yoffe's division had been advancing westwards from the frontier, its Centurions traversing an area of dunes which the Egyptians believed to be tank-proof. By evening the leading elements were through and had taken up ambush positions covering a track junction at Bir Lahfan, it having been correctly anticipated that the Egyptian 4th Armoured Division would use this route as it advanced from its base at Bir Gifgafa to counter-attack Tal at El Arish. Ghoul, the Egyptian commander, had been as shaken as any of his colleagues by the whirlwind Israeli offensive and it had taken him most of the day to plan and prepare his counter-stroke. The troops involved consisted of a T-55 brigade and a mechanized infantry brigade, and while it was perfectly sensible that he should use a night approach march that would enable him to attack at first light, it was far from sensible that his vehicles should advance into the unknown with their headlights on. The Israelis watched them coming, set their sights and opened up in a blaze of gunfire at 23:00. Lights were quickly extinguished as the column scattered, but it was too late. Fourteen T-55s and a number of fuel and ammunition trucks were already illuminating the battlefield with their flames, while the only indication of the Israeli presence was the livid flash of their guns in the distant darkness. Ironically, although the T-55s were equipped for night fighting the only Centurion to sustain damage was one which used its own light projector. As the sporadic, long-range fire fight continued, Tal despatched Gonen's 7th Armoured Brigade down the track from El Arish and by dawn this was in action against the Egyptians' left flank. By 10:00 the 4th Armoured had clearly had enough and was involved in a rapid and disorderly retreat towards Jebel Libni, pursued by the Israeli armour as far as the latter's parlous fuel state would permit, and harried on its way by the IAF.

As his tanks replenished their fuel and ammunition during the morning, Gavish met his three divisional commanders and issued orders for the next phase of the fighting. The essence of these was that Tal and Yoffe would advance *through* the retreating enemy and seize the three passes leading from the Sinai plateau to the Suez Canal: the Mitla in the south and the smaller Giddi and Tassa further north. After Sharon had completed mopping up in the Abu Agheila area, he would drive the remaining Egyptians towards them, so placing the enemy between the hammer and the anvil. The very intensity of the previous day's activity ensured that 6 June would be comparatively quiet, but on the coast road a battlegroup commanded by Colonel Israel Granit advanced 40 miles without meeting serious opposition and at Jebel Libni the 3rd Infantry Division withdrew from its now exposed position, harassed by Tal and Yoffe.

On 7 June, the rested and replenished Israelis renewed their ferocious offensive. Mortagy did what he could to prevent the complete collapse of his army, deploying reinforcement armour on the northern sector. These fresh units were encountered by Granit's battlegroup between Romani and El Kantara and a gunnery duel ensued. Granit, however, had been joined by some of Eitan's paratroopers, who had driven west at top speed as soon as they had secured Gaza, and as the battle raged they used their half-tracks and jeep-mounted recoilless rifles to deliver a wide hook on to the enemy's flank. Caught between two fires, the Egyptian tanks were destroyed and Granit resumed his advance, becoming the first Israeli commander to reach the Suez Canal.

Spearheaded by Gonen's 7th Armoured Brigade, Tal's division advanced on Bir Gifgafa, where the 4th Armoured Division had rallied. The Centurions and Pattons savaged the Egyptian armour in a two-hour contest, but that night an AMX-13 unit, occupying a blocking position some miles to the west, came under simultaneous pressure from fugitive tanks attempting to escape from Sinai and reinforcements trying to enter it, losing several vehicles before a company each of Centurions and Shermans arrived to disperse its attackers. By the morning of 8 June, Tal was aware that he faced only broken remnants and pushed through the Tassa Pass to the Canal, where contact was established with Granit's battlegroup.

Yoffe's division took a south-westerly axis from Jebel Libni through Bir Hasana and Bir Tamada to the Mitla pass. Speed was essential and his advance guard, commanded by Colonel Yiska Shadmi and consisting of two Centurion battalions and a mechanized infantry battalion, frequently caught up with retreating columns and ploughed through them with guns blazing. The IAF was also strafing the route ahead regularly, this being something of a mixed blessing as Shadmi's tanks were compelled to force their way through a tangle of wrecked and burning vehicles. Many of the Egyptians who fled across the sand, abandoning their equipment, also rid themselves of their boots. Nevertheless, hard usage and shortage of fuel was taking its toll of the Israeli vehicles and when Shadmi established his road-block at the eastern end of the pass his battlegroup had been reduced to nine Centurions, several of which were on tow, two infantry platoons and three 120 mm mortar half-tracks. With this little force he stood off repeated attacks by the Egyptians converging on the pass, each attack adding to the wreckage which inhibited the success of the next. As more troops arrived, their vehicles contributed to the three-mile jam tailing back along the road, subjected by the IAF to continuous bomb, cannon and rocket attacks. By the time the rest of Yoffe's division broke through to Shadmi at first light on the 8th the latter's four remaining Centurions were down to their last few rounds, but the epic stand had achieved its object. Mortagy had directed those of his formations that could to retire through the pass with the result that disorganized elements of Task Force Shazli, 4th Armoured, 3rd Infantry and 6th Mechanized Divisions were trapped between Yoffe and Sharon, who was closing in rapidly from the east.

Sharon's division had driven south from Abu Agheila on 7 June and was joined next day by Mandler's armoured brigade, which had crossed the frontier at El Kuntilla. The 6th Mechanized Division's rearguard, consisting of one armoured and one infantry brigade, was overwhelmed near Nakhl with the loss of 60 tanks, 100 guns and 300 vehicles. An iron ring had closed round the survivors of Mortagy's army and those who were unable to escape as individuals or in small groups were forced to surrender. All of Sinai was now lost to Egypt, for on 7 June Israeli patrol craft reported that the fortifications at Sharm el Sheikh had been abandoned.

The Israeli victory in the Sinai campaign of 1967 was as complete as any in the history of desert warfare. In four days an army of seven divisions had been utterly destroyed, the Israelis estimating the Egyptian casualties at 15,000. Eighty per cent of the Egyptian Army's entire equipment stock was lost in Sinai, including 800 tanks (300 of which were captured intact), 450 artillery weapons and 10,000 vehicles of various types. The Israelis sustained the loss of 275 killed and 800 wounded, but were able to repair most of their battle-damaged tanks.

In Cairo the media had unwisely proclaimed Egyptian victories during the first two days of the fighting, the result being that defeat came as a stunning psychological shock. The average Egyptian soldier had fought well,

earning the respect of his opponents, but the same was not always true of his officers. A number of senior commanders known to have deserted their men and sought safety in flight were court-martialled and severely punished. Field Marshal Abdel Amer, the Army's Commander-in-Chief, who at one stage had lost his head and begun issuing orders direct to formations in Sinai without consulting Mortagy, the field commander, committed suicide rather than face trial. Nasser himself offered to resign but remained in office at the overwhelming request of a public which refused to believe that he bore any responsibility for the disaster.

Elsewhere, the small Royal Jordanian Army, which maintained the high standard of discipline, training and battlecraft instilled into the Arab Legion by its former British officers, came close to inflicting a defeat on the Israelis before it was compelled to abandon Jerusalem and retire behind the Jordan. However, the Soviet trained and equipped Syrian Army was bundled off the apparently impregnable Golan Heights with 2,500 killed, 5,000 wounded, and the loss of approximately 100 tanks and 200 artillery weapons. Israel agreed to a ceasefire during the evening of 10 June, six days after the fighting began, having acquired militarily-defensible frontiers. During the recriminations which followed, the Egyptians and Syrians blamed the catastrophe on inferior equipment, training and tactical concepts. This represented a serious blow to Soviet prestige throughout the Arab world and the Kremlin agreed to make good the lost equipment immediately.

If the Israelis hoped that the results of the Six Day War would bring the Arabs to the negotiating table, they were to be sadly disillusioned. At the Khartoum Summit Conference of Arab States held in September 1967, a resolution was passed declaring that there would be no recognition of Israel, no negotiations with Israel and no peace with Israel. Nasser was aware that the bulk of Israel's armed forces consisted of recalled reservists, and that their mobilization could not be maintained for long without inflicting serious damage on the national economy. Likewise, her small regular army was vulnerable to a contest of attrition and it was such a contest that he intended imposing, divided into three phases. The first, called Defensive Rehabilitation, was designed to restore Egyptian strength, confidence and morale. This was to be followed by Offensive Defence, in which the Israeli troops in Sinai would be harried on their own ground. The final or Liberation phase would consist of the recovery of Sinai. His attempts to implement this policy, commencing in the autumn of 1967 and continued sporadically until 1970, are now known collectively as the War of Attrition.

In many ways, the policy was counterproductive. The Defensive Rehabilitation phase involved heavy artillery exchanges across the Canal. During these the towns of El Kantara, Ismailia and Suez were so badly damaged that 750,000 refugees fled into Egypt and the important oil refineries at Suez were wrecked by Israeli shellfire, burning for several days. The cost of continued mobilization, the collapse of the tourist industry and the loss of revenue from the closed Canal meant that only massive injections of Soviet and Arab money prevented Egypt from tottering over the brink of insolvency.

Despite this, by September 1968 there were 150,000 fully-equipped Egyptian troops deployed along the Canal and Russian MiG-21 fighters, anti-aircraft weapon systems and T-55 tanks were pouring into the country, together with thousands of Soviet advisers who reorganized and trained the armed services. Nasser, satisfied that he had achieved

A dead Egyptian soldier and a knocked-out Egyptian tank make a macabre tableau in the wake of the war in the Sinai desert (Associated Press Ltd).

Defensive Rehabilitation, decided that the Offensive Defence phase should begin. This took the form of even heavier artillery exchanges and commando raids across the Canal. The Israelis struck back on 31 October with a helicopter commando raid deep into Egypt, destroying Nile bridges some 300 miles south of Cairo, and a period of comparative calm ensued along the front.

The Israelis had indeed sustained serious casualties and they were worried as to how best the Canal might be defended. In the end full forward deployment was abandoned in favour of a chain of fortified observation posts and a mobile response to any Egyptian crossing, and to this end two lateral tracks were constructed a few miles east of the Canal. The shell-proof observation posts, originally 30 in number, were built from concrete and their head-cover was reinforced with rails lifted from the old Trans-Sinai railway. Although they were known as the Bar-Lev line, after the Israeli Chief of Staff, Lieutenant General Chaim Bar-Lev, they actually possessed little capacity for sustained defence and were normally manned by a 15-strong infantry squad armed with nothing heavier than light machine-guns and mortars. Further defensive measures taken by the Israelis included the bulldozing of high sand ramparts on the eastern bank of the Canal, providing not only an obstacle but also cover from view and some protection against direct gunfire.

When fighting was renewed in March 1969 the Egyptian Chief of Staff, General Abdel Muneim Riadh, was killed by artillery fire, as were several members of his staff. On 1 May Nasser announced that the Liberation phase had begun, and although this apparently differed little from what had gone before, it continued for the next 16 months and reached new levels of intensity.

The Israelis responded with a series of dramatic commando raids. On 9 September tank landing craft crossed the Gulf of Suez and disembarked four T-55 tanks and three BTR-50 APCs which had been captured during the Six Day War. The battlegroup was ashore for eight hours, during which it destroyed radar installations at Ras Abu-Daraj and Ras Za'afrana, beat up outposts and camps and inflicted several hundred casualties which included several senior officers and their Soviet advisers. The familiar vehicles had aroused no suspicions until they actually opened fire and by the time the Egyptians had co-ordinated their reaction they had re-embarked and were on their way home. As a direct result of this raid, the Egyptian Chief of Staff, the Commander-in-Chief of the Egyptian Navy and the commander of the Red Sea sector were all dismissed and Nasser sustained a heart attack from which he never fully recovered. In another raid, executed in December, recently arrived surface-to-air missile (SAM) control and target acquisition radar sets were lifted by helicopter from their complex at Ras Ghareb and flown back to Sinai.

In July 1969 the Israeli General Staff took the decision to employ the IAF, now equipped with F-4 Phantoms, as a counter to the marked artillery superiority possessed by the Egyptians. During the next six months the IAF secured complete air superiority, shooting down 48 aircraft for the loss of five of its own, and went on to strafe gun positions and anti-aircraft defences along the Canal, eliminating the Soviet-supplied SAM-2 missile screen without undue difficulty. In January 1970 the IAF extended its raid beyond the Canal, bombing targets close to Cairo. In response to Nasser's desperate plea for help, the Soviet Union shipped in a complete air defence division, armed with more sophisticated SAM-3 missiles which were manned by Russian personnel. On 24 March many of the newly-installed missiles were temporarily put out of action by a heavy air attack. The Russians revised their strategy and instead of siting the missiles in individual batteries along the Canal they concentrated them in mutually

supporting clusters deployed in a single belt 12 miles to the west, low level defence being supplied by radar controlled ZSU-23-4 self-propelled anti-aircraft guns and large numbers of SAM-7 shoulder-launched air defence missiles. By July these measures were beginning to take effect and after several aircraft had been lost, Israel was forced to ask the United States to supply electronic counter-measures (ECM) equipment. July also witnessed a clash between Israeli Mirages and Russian-manned MiG-21Js, five of the latter being destroyed in exchange for one Israeli aircraft damaged.

On 8 August both sides accepted a ceasefire based on a plan prepared by William Rogers, the American Secretary of State. The Egyptians had incurred 10,000 casualties in 1970 alone and were no nearer to liberating Sinai. The Israelis had also sustained what was for them serious loss, and although they emerged the tactical victors the installation of the Egyptian air defence cordon meant that they were in a less favourable strategic situation at the end.

Nasser died on 28 November 1970. He was succeeded as President by Anwar el Sadat, who was equally determined to restore Arab

Left *A Centurion tows part of the Israeli bridging train towards the Suez Canal during the critical phase of the Yom Kippur War, 1973. Overhead, an IAF Phantom provides air cover for the operation* (Courtesy Eshel Dramit Ltd).

Below *An Israeli Patton battalion and M113 APCs in a area of soft going, Sinai, 1973* (Courtesy Eshel Dramit Ltd).

The Centurion served the Israelis well in both the Six Day and Yom Kippur Wars (Courtesy Eshel Dramit Ltd).

honour and recover the territories lost in 1967, but was more pragmatic in his approach. Thus, while he was reconciled to further conflict, he recognized that it was not in his country's best interests to remain an armed camp and was privately prepared to accept the existence of Israel as a fact of life once some tangible military success had been achieved. Equally, he was not prepared to allow Egypt to become a Soviet fief by default and in July 1972 20,000 Russian military advisers were asked to leave the country, despite the fact that the Soviet Union continued to supply large quantities of arms.

Israeli raid on an Egyptial radar station. Captured vehicles were used in this incident during the War of Attrition (Courtesy Eshel Dramit Ltd).

Bar-Lev Line observation post. The headcover incorporates rails lifted from the Trans-Sinai Railway (Courtesy Eshel Dramit Ltd).

Sadat's strategy involved a major crossing of the Canal, followed by consolidation of defences along its east bank. A break-out into Sinai would not be attempted since it would expose the Army to the sort of mobile battle in which the Israelis were clearly the masters. The crossing would be timed to coincide with a Syrian assault on the Golan Heights. The detailed operational planning of the crossing was the responsibility of General Saad el Din Shazli, the Army's Chief of Staff, a popular officer who had led most of his men to safety during the 1967 débâcle in Sinai. Shazli's problems fell under three major headings: the need to achieve complete surprise and secure his objectives before Israel's reserves could be mobilized; the crossing itself; and the defeat of Israel counter-attacks.

The first he solved by choosing 6 October 1973 as the date for the crossing, this being Yom Kippur, the Day of Atonement, the holiest day in the Jewish calendar, during which neither public transport nor broadcasting operated. To Arab eyes, this represented adequate repayment for the pre-emptive strike with which the IAF had begun the Six Day War.

For much of its length the Canal is only 200 yards wide and in terms of major military engineering is not a difficult obstacle to cross. Again, the Egyptian Army had received large quantities of bridging and amphibious warfare equipment from the Warsaw Pact and with this it endlessly rehearsed its assault crossing techniques. Even so, the sand ramparts raised by the Israelis on the east bank were impassable to vehicles, but an ingenious solution to this problem was found by using high-pressure water hoses to blast gaps in them.

Shazli knew that the crossing would at-

Israeli self-propelled artillery in action during the Yom Kippur War (Courtesy Eshel Dramit Ltd).

tract immediate counter-attacks by Israeli aircraft and armour. Under cover of the ceasefire which followed the War of Attrition he moved forward the air defence cordon, augmented by the latest SAM-6 missiles, until its protective umbrella extended some distance beyond the Canal. The question of anti-tank defence, however, presented serious difficulties, for Shazli rightly believed that his own tanks and anti-tank guns would not be available in adequate numbers for many hours after the infantry had secured their bridgeheads. His answer to this was to equip each infantry division with 314 RPG-7 close-range anti-tank rocket launchers and 48 portable AT-3 Sagger wire-guided anti-tank missiles.

Altogether, the Egyptian Army deployed 285,000 men and 2,000 tanks for the assault. Its soldiers were highly trained, knew exactly what they had to do and were motivated as they had never been before. Every contingency

had been allowed for in Shazli's meticulous planning and this generated a self-confidence which had been absent in previous Egyptian operations.

Supported by intense artillery fire and air strikes, the crossing commenced at 14:00 on 6 October. It succeeded beyond anyone's wildest dreams. The Egyptian leadership had steeled itself for a bloodbath and was prepared to accept up to 30,000 casualties, of whom one third would be killed; in the event, the crossing cost 208 lives. Only 16 of the Bar-Lev observation posts were fully manned and although some continued to offer resistance, the majority had been captured. Local counter-attacks had been defeated with serious loss and the IAF was unable to influence the battle. When dusk descended Major General Abdel Muneim Wassel's Third Army had secured bridgeheads from the Gulf of Suez to the Great Bitter Lake, and Major General Saad Mamoun's Second Army had been equally successful along the rest of the Canal. Bridgeheads were joined, expanded to a depth of three miles, and consolidated. Engineers worked frantically to put in their bridges and as soon as these had been completed armour began to roll across. By the evening of 7 October the five infantry divisions on the east bank had been joined by 1,000 tanks, ensuring that a major Israeli counter-attack would smash itself against a fully-integrated anti-tank defence.

The only aspect of the operation which yielded less than satisfactory results was the insertion of commando units by helicopter into the area of the Mitla and Gidi passes. Fourteen of the helicopters were shot down by the IAF and those commandos who did succeed in landing were eliminated before they could close the passes to Israeli reinforcements approaching the front from the east. The Egyptian 130th Marine Brigade, equipped with amphibious PT-76 light tanks and BTR-50 APCs, crossed the Great Bitter Lake in the hope of reaching the commandos but its thin-

Above *Once Israeli armour had crossed the Suez Canal, its primary task was the destruction of Egyptian SAM sites. Yom Kippur War, 1973* (Courtesy Eshel Dramit Ltd).

Below *Tank battle in Sinai* (Courtesy Eshel Dramit Ltd).

Above *Israeli paratroopers demonstrate the air mobility technique employed to capture Abu Agheila during the Six Day War* (Camera Press).

Below *Egyptian PT-76 amphibious light tanks and Marine infantry training for the Suez Canal crossing prior to the Yom Kippur War* (Camera Press).

skinned vehicles were no match for the Israeli armour and the operation was cancelled.

Despite this local success, there could be no denying the fact that the Israelis were in disarray. They were unquestionably guilty of under-estimating their opponents and many had doubted whether the Egyptian Army was capable of such an operation. Southern Command was now the responsibility of Major General Shmuel Gonen, the former commander of 7th Armoured Brigade, and his major reaction force was Major General Albert Mandler's 252nd Armoured Division, a regular formation. Mandler's division possessed 280 tanks, but of these 100 were dispersed along the Canal, the intention being that they were available to defeat purely local attacks on the Bar-Lev observation posts, and the remainder were concentrated 65 miles east of the front. In the Israeli Army it was a tradition that no call for assistance went unanswered. When the Egyptian crossing took place, therefore, the nearest tank crews felt honour bound to respond to the desperate pleas of the Bar-Lev garrisons for help. They advanced into a hail of fire in which the impact of the Sagger was as devastating as it was unexpected. On the northern sector more tanks were lost as they floundered into the marshland bordering the Canal. As the rest of the division arrived it too was committed to piecemeal attacks, with the result that by the evening of the 7th the Israelis had sustained the loss of 170 tanks, destroyed or out of action and in need of heavy repairs. All that had been achieved was the rescue of one or two garrisons while a few others managed to break out with their wounded.

However, two reserve armoured divisions, the 143rd under Sharon and the 162nd under Adan, were entering Sinai and during the night of 7/8 October Gonen held a conference to plan a major counter-stroke, attended by the three divisional commanders and General David Elazar, the Chief of Staff. The Israelis were seriously shaken and although

there was a measure of agreement that the correct medium term response was to carry the war to the west bank of the Canal, using the Egyptians' own bridges, it was felt that in the present circumstances such a course of action was premature. Instead, the conference made the fundamental error of assuming that the Egyptians would break out of their bridgeheads into Sinai, as the Israelis themselves would have done. It was therefore decided that on the northern sector Adan's division would drive into the flank of the breakout on a north-south axis. On the southern sector Sharon would come to Adan's assistance if he got into difficulties, but if not he would mount a similar drive of his own to the south.

In fact, beyond making local improvements to their positions, neither Egyptian army had any intention of breaking out, and had not Adan's reconnaissance unit been detached in pursuit of enemy commandos he would have learned of the true situation. Instead, when his advance commenced at 08:00 on 8 October, it did so in a fog of war made the denser by Egyptian jamming of his radio communications. No opposition was encountered and at 10:30 Gonen, with Elazar's approval, ordered Sharon to move southwards. Meanwhile, Adan had realized that he was running parallel to the Egyptian positions and swung his brigades hard right to engage in a furious and inconclusive fire fight which cost his division 70 tanks, of which 20 were recovered after dusk. Gonen, suddenly grasping the enormity of the mistakes which had been made, recalled Sharon, but the latter was now far distant and it was not until after 17:00 that his leading units began entering the southern edge of the battle. Adan, barely able to contain local counter-attacks, was grateful for the gathering darkness which enabled him to disengage.

The Egyptians had fought well and their jubilation at having stood off the attack was entirely justified. In the Israeli camp,

Above *Loading a Snapper anti-tank guided missile on to an Egyptian quadruple launcher. The Snapper was used by the Egyptians in the Six Day War* (Camera Press).

Left *Egyptian transport begins moving through a gap in the sand rampart constructed by the Israelis on the east bank of the Canal; gaps such as this were made with high-pressure water hoses* (Camera Press).

Below *Jubilant Egyptian second echelon troops are ferried across the Canal* (Camera Press).

Above *Egyptian T-55 formation breaking leaguer in Sinai* (Camera Press).

Below *This pair of Israeli M60A1 Pattons were knocked out during attempts to relieve Bar Lev Line garrisons trapped during the early days of the Yom Kippur War* (Camera Press).

recriminations were rife. Adan felt that he had been let down, and neither he nor Sharon had any great regard for Gonen, who was technically their junior and somewhat ill at ease at having them under his command. Not all of the criticism levelled at Gonen was justified, but his operational planning had been based on a faulty premise and his handling of the battle had been uncertain. Elazar felt that he had no alternative other than to appoint General Chaim Bar-Lev to the command of the Sinai front and Gonen, putting his personal feelings aside, loyally agreed to remain as the latter's deputy. Bar-Lev was in no mood to stand any nonsense and when Sharon mounted an attack of his own on 9 October, contrary to orders, he recommended that he be dismissed. General Moshe Dayan, the Minister of Defence, refused on the grounds that it would be contrary to the public interest at a time of national crisis.

In addition to their command difficulties, the Israelis were also troubled by the failure of their armour. After the campaigns of 1956 and 1967 they had placed too much faith in the tank alone and reduced the proportion of artillery and mechanized infantry in their armoured divisions. Since it was now apparent that the enemy's dismounted Sagger operators could be unsettled by sustained automatic and artillery fire, the appropriate balance was restored as quickly as possible, ensuring that the events of the war's early days would not be repeated. Simultaneously, the IAF was painfully learning to cope with the Egyptian air defence cordon, using a combination of decoy flares and chaff, steep diving attacks and ECM.

During Sharon's unauthorized action on the 9th, his reconnaissance unit had discovered the vulnerable boundary between the Egyptian Second and Third Armies and it was decided that when the time came it would be on this, the Deversoir sector, that the Israelis would launch their own crossing of the Canal. Meanwhile, Egyptian armoured and mechanized formations continued crossing to the east bank, and Bar-Lev's divisions continued to absorb reinforcements.

On 10 October a tank battalion from the Egyptian 1st Mechanized Brigade probed south down the coast of the Gulf of Suez to Ras Sudar, where it was halted by an armoured battlegroup under the control of General Yeshayahu Gavish, commanding southern Sinai. As the engagement took place beyond the range of the SAM cordon, the IAF was able to intervene and the Egyptian force was wiped out. This small success was balanced on the 13th when Mandler unwisely transmitted the location of his divisional command post in clear; minutes later he was killed by accurate Egyptian artillery fire. Command of his division passed to Brigadier General Kalman Magen.

How long the stalemate in Sinai might have lasted is open to debate, had not events elsewhere influenced the course of the campaign. During the desperate fighting on the Golan Heights the Syrians had come close to breaking through into Galilee, but at the critical moment their advance had wavered. In the nick of time Israeli reserve armoured formations had arrived to restore the situation, inflicting a major defeat on the Syrians and pursuing them across the frontier. Now, Damascus was broadcasting frantic appeals for help and Sadat could only comply or risk losing face before the entire Arab world.

Neither Shazli nor the Egyptian Minister of War, General Ahmed Ismail Ali, wished to commit their troops to a war of movement and the action at Ras Sudar confirmed their worst fears concerning operations conducted beyond the range of their air defence umbrella. Nevertheless, the political situation made it imperative that the Egyptian Army should mount a fresh offensive and with extreme reluctance they produced a plan which required the Third Army to seize the Mitla and Gidi passes while the Second Army took Tassa. During the second stage both armies

Above *Part of the Israeli 7th Armoured Brigade making its epic stand on the Golan Heights, October 1973* (Werner Braun, Camera Press).

Below *An Israeli Centurion advances into Syrian territory, October 1973* (Werner Braun, Camera Press).

Above *During the Yom Kippur War the Israelis restored the balance between tanks and mechanized infantry in their armoured formations. This open leaguer in Syria contains Patton tanks and elderly but still serviceable M3 half-tracks* (Neil Libbert, Camera Press).

Below *Up-gunned Israeli Sherman with consolidation stores aboard, Syria 1973* (David Newell-Smith, Camera Press).

Above *Gunners prepare to ram home a shell into the chamber of an Israeli 155 mm self-propelled howitzer, which is based on the Sherman tank chassis* (Camera Press).

Below *SAM-3 missile site captured intact, Egypt 1973* (Camera Press).

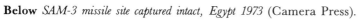

would wheel inwards and capture Bir Gifgafa, where the Israelis had established their major base in Sinai, so compelling Bar-Lev's divisions to withdraw or be destroyed. Shazli also included a third thrust line, the objective of which was the Baluza road junction at the northern end of the front, where the coast road joined the principal lateral track running behind the Israeli positions. Since no other lateral route existed between Baluza and El Arish the loss of the junction would have serious consequences for the Israelis' as the Egyptians could either advance south into their rear areas, or east to El Arish, or both, forcing Bar-Lev to strip the front of troops to contain the threat. This imaginative element of Shazli's plan earned the Israeli's sincere admiration when its details became known, but in its final form it was so diluted as to represent a mere shadow of the original concept.

Ironically, it was on the Baluza sector that the Israeli defences were at their weakest.

Bar-Lev was aware of the Egyptian preparations and such was the measure of restored Israeli confidence that he decided to postpone his own crossing of the Canal until Shazli's offensive had been blunted and his armour written down. Approximately 1,500 Egyptian and 500 Israeli tanks were now facing each other along a 100-mile front and the scene was set for the largest tank battle since the Second World War.

The Egyptian attack began at 06:30 on 14 October. South of the Great Bitter Lake the Third Army's advance, led by the 4th Armoured, 6th Mechanized, 7th and 19th Infantry Divisions, was blocked by Magen's division. To the north of the lake the Second Army, spearheaded by the 21st Armoured, 23rd Mechanized, 2nd and 16th Infantry

Once the Egyptian SAM cordon had been eliminated on the southern sector of the Sinai front, IAF Phantoms were able to intervene decisively in the ground fighting, Egypt, 1973 (Werner Braun, Camera Press).

Centurions belonging to one of Major General Adan's armoured brigades, taking up positions to confront the Egyptian attack (Courtesy Eshel Dramit Ltd).

Divisions, was halted by Sharon and Adan. A furious gunnery duel erupted along the front, each side supported by its artillery. From the outset the Israelis had the best of the exchange, the design of their Centurions, M60 and M48 Pattons enabling them to fight better hull-down than the Egyptian T-55s and T-62s; significantly, the only Israeli formation to sustain serious casualties was a brigade equipped with captured T-55s. The Sagger teams, pinned down by artillery and machine-gun fire, played little part in the battle. At Baluza, held by a mechanized infantry brigade and its organic Sherman battalion, the Egyptians mounted a slow-moving set-piece assault with the 18th Infantry Division, supported by part of the 15th Armoured Brigade. The Shermans held their fire until the range had closed to within 1,000 yards, destroying 34 of the opposing 60 T-62s, and the attack was abandoned.

By early afternoon the offensive had clearly failed and the Egyptians were withdrawing into their own lines, the day's fighting having cost them 264 tanks, a large number of APCs and 1,000 casualties. Shazli, sensing that an Israeli riposte would quickly follow, recommended that the two armoured divisions should be withdrawn to the west bank but was overruled by Sadat after a sharp exchange of views.

Given the intensity of the fighting on the 14th, the Israelis had sustained incredibly low casualties, some sources suggesting that only ten tanks were lost. Whatever the figure, Bar-Lev's plan for crossing the Canal, codenamed Gazelle, was activated immediately. At dawn on 15 October, Sharon's division advanced towards the shore of the Great Bitter Lake and then swung north into the flank of the Egyptian Second Army, striking the congested assembly area into which the 21st Armoured and 16th Infantry Divisions had withdrawn after their defeat the previous day. After a savage and protracted struggle a corridor to the Canal was secured, and although this remained under fire a paratroop brigade under Colonel Danny Matt began crossing at 01:35 on 16 October. By 05:00 the brigade's crossing was complete and the paratroopers had consolidated a bridgehead three miles wide, including crossings over the Sweet Water Canal. At 06:43 the first of 28 tanks from Colonel Chaim Erez's armoured brigade was landed on the west bank from unifloat rafts. During the morning, 21 of these broke

Right *'Rush hour' on Akavish (Spider) axis to the canal, jammed by supply columns of a two-division task force* (Courtesy Eshel Dramit Ltd).

Below *Patton tanks rushing to the Suez Canal during the counter attack* (Courtesy Eshel Dramit Ltd).

Above *Regular Patton tank unit in Sinai* (Courtesy Eshel Dramit Ltd).

Below *IDF MII3 APC and infantry in dismounted attack* (Courtesy Eshel Dramit Ltd).

out and eliminated the nearest SAM sites.

The war in Sinai now hung upon the point of balance. With difficulty, Sharon resisted attempts by the 21st Armoured Division and 14th Armoured Brigade to close the corridor while the bridging trains were slowly and laboriously brought forward along prepared routes. These were so often cut that Adan's division, which was scheduled to cross into Matt's bridgehead, was forced to mount a series of local counter-attacks to clear them. By evening it was apparent that the bridges would not go in that night, nor possibly the next. Dayan, visiting Southern Command Headquarters, expressed serious reservations about the wisdom of continuing with Gazelle, but Bar-Lev, supported by Gonen, insisted that it must be seen through.

Once Shazli was convinced that Matt's bridgehead was of more than local significance, he proposed that it should be destroyed by Third Army, using the 4th Armoured Division and 25th Armoured Brigade, which would be withdrawn to the west bank for the purpose. Ismail rejected the idea, insisting that the following day the Israeli corridor would be severed by the converging attacks of 21st Armoured Division from the north and 25th Armoured Brigade from the south. Wassel, the Third Army's commander, believed that the latter would be cut to pieces long before it entered the fray, but complied with his orders.

It was a gloomy but accurate prediction. On the 18th Adan reacted quickly to reports that the brigade was moving north along the eastern shore of the Great Bitter Lake, disengaging his armour and redeploying it in ambush on the flank of the enemy advance. The Egyptians drove into a ring of fire from which there was no escape, losing 86 of their 96 T-62s, all their APCs and their transport echelon. Elsewhere during the day Matt and Erez had defeated determined attempts by Egyptian commandos and the 23rd Armoured Brigade to overrun their bridgehead, and

Sharon had fought 21st Armoured Division to a standstill, albeit at the cost of a quarter of his tanks, enabling the first of the Israeli bridges to be launched.

Adan replenished his division and began crossing the Canal that night. On the morning of the 18th he broke out of the bridgehead and drove south on a two-brigade frontage to secure the Geneifa Hills, destroying SAM sites as he went. Sharon, meanwhile, had finally captured Chinese Farm and the bloody three-day struggle for the corridor was over. That night a second bridge was launched, followed by a third.

Bar-Lev promptly accelerated the tempo of the battle. On the 19th, Magen's division crossed the Canal and, echeloned back to the west of Adan's troops, joined the drive south into the Third Army's rear areas. Those elements of Sharon's division not involved in cleaning up the area around the corridor also crossed and swung north to reach the outskirts of Ismailia, so providing a hard shoulder on both banks which would permit operations in the south to continue unhindered.

The awful truth now dawned on the Egyptian High Command. The Third Army was in real danger of being encircled, the Second Army seemed to be similarly threatened; and an Israeli drive on Cairo was a possibility that could not be ignored. The greater part of the Army was tied down on the east bank of the Canal and the residue was obviously unable to counter all the options. Shazli had done his best and earned a respected place in the annals of desert warfare, but he had been opposed too often by Sadat and Ismail, who were concerned with political as well as purely military considerations. He collapsed with nervous exhaustion and was replaced by General Abdel Ghani Gamasy. Sadat, anxious to contain the damage as far as possible, requested Soviet Prime Minister Alexei Kosygin to arrange a ceasefire through the medium of the United Nations.

The Iranian 'revolutionary guards' learning the tricks of the trade from a former army instructor, who now wears the traditional turban. The Mullah forces showed surprising skill in built-up area fighting (Courtesy Eshel Dramit Ltd).

Adan and Magen, aware of this, continued their advance to the south, intending to trap Third Army before negotiations could be concluded. Too late, Wassel was given permission to transfer the 4th Armoured and 6th Mechanized Divisions to the west bank. The Egyptians threw everything they had into the battle but were unable to stem the tide of tanks, APCs and self-propelled artillery, for the elimination of the SAM sites meant that the IAF was able to intervene in strength. Shortly after noon on 22 October Wassel informed Ismail that his army had been cut off.

The Second Army accepted the terms of the UN ceasefire that night, but when Wassel's troops persevered in their attempts to break out Adan and Magen resumed their advance, reaching the Gulf of Suez late on the 23rd. Next day, although Adan's attack on the town of Suez was repulsed with serious loss, Wassel narrowly escaped capture when his headquarters on the west bank was overrun, and the IAF completed the destruction of the bridges linking the two portions of his command. Those elements of the Third Army isolated on the east bank faced a slow death

from the oldest desert enemy of all, thirst, before pressure from the United States and the Soviet Union imposed a second and lasting ceasefire.

For both sides, the Yom Kippur War had involved heavy loss of life and the quantity of equipment destroyed was immense. The Israelis had been driven to the brink of defeat but had returned to win a spectacular victory which left them in possession of 1,000 square miles of Egyptian territory on the west bank of the Canal. Conversely, the Egyptians felt that they had restored their military honour on 6 October and their Second Army still retained the gains which it had made during the first days of the war. There was, therefore, a basis for the honourable peace which was subsequently negotiated, under the terms of which Israel relinquished the Sinai but obtained Egyptian recognition and a secure southern frontier.

The Arab-Israeli wars were short, violent, attracted world-wide attention and confirmed the lessons of earlier desert conflicts. The longest war to have been fought in a desert environment since 1945 is that between Iran and Iraq, which began in 1980 and, at the time of writing, is still raging. Initially, the Iranian order of battle included three armoured divisions and an independent armoured brigade, equipped with a total of 875 Chieftains, 400 M48 Pattons and 460 M60A1s. The Iraqis deployed four armoured divisions, two mechanized divisions and an independent mechanized brigade equipped with some 2,000 tanks, of which approximately 100 were T-72s and the remainder T-54/55s and T-62s. The form the war has taken is one of periodic local offensives by one side or the other, which either run down of their own accord or are contained and driven back by a counter-offensive. Neither army is strong enough to inflict a decisive defeat on the other, and neither seems capable of securing an objective which will cause the other to sue for peace. To date, the war has claimed over one

An Iraqi T-62 entering Qasr-el-Shirin, one of the first cities captured during the war in 1980 (Courtesy Eshel Dramit Ltd).

million lives and the wholesale destruction of equipment. Attempts to break the stalemate have included the use of chemical weapons by the Iraqis, while the Iranians have exploited political and religious fervour among their larger population by mounting horrific 'human wave' attacks; predictably, these have made little headway in the teeth of concentrated machine gun and artillery fire. Such elements have added a nightmare quality to the fighting. Recently a ceasefire has been concluded which leaves the contestants in approximately the same positions they held at the start of the conflict.

However, some indications as to the form future desert wars might take were revealed by the briefly reported and soon forgotten Ogaden War of 1977/78. The Ogaden region, much of which consists of desert, was claimed by Ethiopia and Somalia. In June 1977 the Somalis occupied the territory and advanced as far as the Ahmar Mountains, besieging the local Ethiopian garrison in the town of Harar. Both countries were clients of the Soviet Union, which attempted to exert a moderating influence, but that November the Somalis broke the connection and expelled their Russian advisers.

The Kremlin decided that such intransigence must be punished and threw its weight behind Ethiopia, despatching General Vasili Petrov, then First Deputy Commander of Ground Forces, to plan and co-ordinate a

Iraqi BDRM-2 fitted with an MG turret, leading a convoy of vehicles over the Karun River (Courtesy Eshel Dramit Ltd).

Above *Iraqi tanks in position on the Khorramshahr dock. Although only a few miles from Iraq, it took over six weeks to capture this town, defended in the main by ill-equipped Iranian militias* (Courtesy Eshel Dramit Ltd).

Below *What look like Iraqi MiGs swing into the attack near Ahwaz so the Iranian NCO takes no chances as he directs his men to find cover. However, it is actually an Iranian Phantom about to dive on to the nearby Iraqis!* (Courtesy Eshel Dramit Ltd).

counter-offensive. Large quantities of arms were supplied, including several hundred T-54/55 tanks, modern APCs, air-portable ASU-57 assault guns, artillery, jet aircraft and helicopters. Given that the enemy was a small, under-equipped Third World nation, such force might be viewed as excessive, but the Soviet Union was still extremely sensitive regarding the defeat of the Arab armies it had trained and equipped and was determined to restore its prestige with a quick, easy victory, even if it involved an element of overkill. As further proof of this, it was resolved that rather than rely on the native Ethiopians, 11,000 Cuban troops would be used to spearhead the counter-offensive. The Cuban contingent, which included a parachute regiment, was unfamiliar with the BMP and BMD APCs and a slight delay followed while they were trained in their use by East Germans.

Despite this, Petrov was able to commence operations on 6 February 1978, a frontal assault in the mountains being accompanied by a wide left hook around the northern end of the Ahmar massif. The Somalis, shaken by constant air strikes and heavy artillery fire, abandoned the siege of Harar and retired to prepared positions at the Kara Marda Pass and Jigjiga, where they continued to offer determined resistance for the rest of the month. The Somali units holding the northern end of the line, however, had been defeated by a series of parachute and air-landing operations involving 20 Mil-8 and ten Mil-6 helicopters flown by Russian pilots and Petrov decided to employ his air-mobile assets against Jigjiga. On 5 March a landing zone was secured at Genasene, 17 miles north of the town, and 70 ASU-57 assault guns were lifted in. These vehicles had long since been classed as obsolete, but in the prevailing circumstances they were adequate for the task they had been set. Driving south, they attacked the defences from the rear while a frontal assault was in progress. Resistance collapsed with heavy loss of life and three days later

An Iraqi T-62 crosses the Karun River on a barge. On top of the rise is camouflaged command vehicle, probably directing crossing operations. On the left a bulldozer clears the banks (Courtesy Eshel Dramit Ltd).

Somalia agreed to withdraw from the Ogaden.

The Arabs and Israelis had both employed the helicopter in the tactical context, but what made Petrov's application of air mobility so interesting was that it was made at the operative level, which, as we have seen, is critical in desert warfare. It remains for future commanders to exploit fully the potential revealed, representing as it does a great leap forward.

BIBLIOGRAPHY

Adan, Avraham, *On the Banks of the Suez*, Arms and Armour Press

Barker, A. J., *Townshend of Kut*, Cassell

Braddon, Russell, *The Siege*, Mayflower

Buchan, John, *A History of the Great War*, Nelson

Burman, Edward, *The Templars*, Crucible

Callwell, Colonel C. E., *Small Wars*, Purnell

Carver, Michael, *Dilemmas of the Desert War*, Batsford

Carver, Michael, *El Alamein*, Fontana

Carver, Michael, *Tobruk*, Pan

Churchill, Winston, *The River War*, Four Square

Falls, Cyril, *Armageddon 1918*, Weidenfeld and Nicolson

Fisher, David, *The War Magician*, Corgi

Fraser, David, *And We Shall Shock Them—The British Army in the Second World War*, Hodder and Stoughton

Geraghty, Tony, *March or Die—France and the Foreign Legion*, Grafton

Geraghty, Tony, *Who Dares Wins*, Fontana

Heckmann, Wolf, *Rommel's War in Africa*, Granada

Herzog, Chaim, *The Arab-Israeli Wars*, Arms and Armour Press

Holmes, Richard, *Bir Hacheim*, Pan/ Ballantine

Lucas Phillips, C. E., *Alamein*, Pan

Macksey, Kenneth, *Beda Fomm*, Pan/ Ballantine

Messenger, Charles, *The Unknown Alamein*, Ian Allan

O'Ballance, E., *The Story of the French Foreign Legion*, Faber and Faber

Perrett, Bryan, *A History of Blitzkreig*, Robert Hale

Perrett, Bryan, *Knights of the Black Cross—Hitler's Panzerwaffe and its Leaders*, Robert Hale

Perret, Bryan, *Soviet Armour Since 1945*, Blandford

Perrett, Bryan, *Wavell's Offensive*, Ian Allan

Playfair, I. S. O. and Molony, C. J. C., *History of the Second World War—The Mediterranean and Middle East.*

Roberts, Major General G. P. B., *From the Desert to the Baltic*, Wm Kimber

Schmidt, Dana Adams, *Yemen—The Unknown War*, Bodley Head

Swinson, Arthur, *The Raiders*, Purnell

Warner, Philip, *Dervish*, Macdonald

Warner, Philip, *The SAS*, Sphere

Wise, T., *The Knights of Christ*, Osprey

Ziegler, Philip, *Omdurman*, Collins

INDEX